NEW

These Are Our People

By

Sister M. Celine, O.S.F.

and

Mary Synon, LL.D.

IN ACCORDANCE WITH THE EDUCATIONAL PLAN OF
RT. REV. MSGR. GEORGE JOHNSON, PH.D.
THE CATHOLIC UNIVERSITY OF AMERICA

Ginn and Company

BOSTON · NEW YORK · CHICAGO · ATLANTA · DALLAS
PALO ALTO · TORONTO

Acknowledgments

For kind permission to reprint copyrighted material, acknowledgment is made to the following:

Brandt & Brandt for "Travel," from *Second April*, published by Harper & Brothers, copyright, 1921, by EDNA ST. VINCENT MILLAY; CARL CARMER for "The Cathedral of St. Louis," from *Frenchtown*; *Child Life Magazine* for "Neighborly," copyright, 1926, by VIOLET ALLEYN STOREY; ANN NOLAN CLARK and the Bureau of Indian Affairs for "Sheep Corral"; Doubleday & Company, Inc., for "Trees," from *Trees and Other Poems*, by JOYCE KILMER, copyright 1914, by Doubleday & Company, Inc.; Exposition Press, Inc., for "Luck," by WILFRED GIBSON, "Church Lets Out," by JEANNETTE V. MILLER, and "Sight," by CORA BELL MOTEN, all from *Anthology of Contemporary Verse*; Ginn and Company for "Fisherman's Song," by BLANCHE JENNINGS THOMPSON; Harcourt, Brace and Company, Inc., for "Wheels and Wings," from *Magpie Lane*, by NANCY BYRD TURNER, copyright, 1927, by Harcourt, Brace and Company, Inc.; Harper & Brothers for "Trains," from *I Go A-Traveling*, by JAMES TIPPETT, copyright, 1929, by Harper & Brothers; Henry Holt and Company, Inc., for "Psalm of Those Who Go Forth Before Daylight," from *Cornhuskers*, by CARL SANDBURG, copyright, 1918, by Henry Holt and Company, Inc., copyright, 1944, by Carl Sandburg, and "The Pasture," by ROBERT FROST, from *Complete Poems of Robert Frost, 1949*, copyright, 1930, 1949, by Henry Holt and Company, Inc., both by permission of the publishers; Houghton Mifflin Company for "Roads Go Ever Ever On," from *The Hobbit*, by J. R. R. TOLKIEN; Laidlaw Brothers, Inc., for "A Song of Praise," by LOUISE ABNEY, from *The World Around Us*; Little, Brown & Company for "The Mermaidens," from *Tirra-Lirra*, by LAURA E. RICHARDS; Isabel Garland Lord for "Do You Fear the Wind?", by HAMLIN GARLAND; The Macmillan Company for "The Shopper," from *Selected Poems*, by SISTER M. MADELEVA, "Four-Leaf Clover," from *When the Birds Go North*, by ELLA HIGGINSON, and "Snow in the City," from *Branches Green*, by RACHEL FIELD; George A. Pflaum, Publisher, for "May Altars," by SISTER MARYANNA, O. P., reproduced from *The Young Catholic Messenger*, by courtesy of George A. Pflaum, Publisher, Inc., Dayton, Ohio; NANCY BYRD TURNER for "First Christmas Night of All"; The Viking Press, Inc., for "Shells in Rock," from *Under the Tree*, by ELIZABETH MADOX ROBERTS, copyright, 1922, by B. W. Huebsch, Inc., 1950, by Irov S. Roberts, reprinted by permission of The Viking Press, Inc., New York; Blake L. Woodson for "The Workers," by MARY BLAKE WOODSON; Yale University Press for "A Comparison," from *Songs for Parents*, by JOHN FARRAR. Verses not otherwise credited were written for this reader by MARY SYNON.

Faith and Freedom

Nibil Obstat:

HENRY J. BROWNE, PH.D., *Censor Deputatus*

Imprimatur:

✝ PATRICK A. O'BOYLE, D.D., *Archbishop of Washington*

WASHINGTON, NOVEMBER 1, 1955

COMMISSION

ON

AMERICAN

CITIZENSHIP

THE

CATHOLIC

UNIVERSITY

OF AMERICA

RT. REV. MSGR. WILLIAM J. McDONALD

PRESIDENT OF THE COMMISSION

RT. REV. MSGR. JOSEPH A. GORHAM

DIRECTOR

MARY SYNON, LL.D.	**SISTER MARY LENORE, O.P.**
EDITORIAL CONSULTANT	CURRICULUM CONSULTANT

PUBLISHED FOR THE CATHOLIC UNIVERSITY OF AMERICA PRESS

WASHINGTON, D. C.

Contents

4

III · Wind, Sea, and Sky

IV · The Sower and the Seed

V · The House by the River

VI · On a Thousand Hills

VII · Treasures of the Earth

VIII · From Dawn to Dusk

IX · For God and Country

Glossary

I

The Kingdom of God

"See how the lilies grow; they neither toil nor spin, yet I say to you that not even Solomon in all his glory was arrayed like one of these. But if God so clothes the grass which today is alive in the field and tomorrow is thrown into the oven, how much more you, O you of little faith!

"And as for you, do not seek what you shall eat, or what you shall drink; and do not exalt yourselves (for after all these things the nations of the world seek); but your Father knows that you need these things. But seek the kingdom of God, and all these things shall be given you besides."

LUKE 12, 27–31

9

Our Country

I love the high stars of the West,
I love the deeps of Northern mines,
I love the harbors of the East,
I love the smell of Southern pines.
No matter if I never see
The pines, the mountains, or the shore,
I know they are my native land
And I shall love them evermore.

The man who labors in the mine,
The man within the factory,
The girl who works within the shop,
Are all Americans like me.
We lift our eyes up to the flag
That floats above our nation free,
We love our country and our God
Who made our country strong and free.

10

Rich and poor, black, white and yellow,
the boys of his neighborhood were all the same
to Eddie Patterson. He did not know
that he was a true Christian, but he did
know that he must stay loyal to

Eddie Patterson's Friends

I. *Plans for a Party*

Mrs. Patterson and her two daughters, Lucy and Katy, were getting supper in the large, cheerful kitchen of the Patterson house. As they worked, they were talking about Eddie, the youngest of the family.

"Saturday will be his birthday," said Mrs. Patterson, taking a golden-brown apple pie from the stove.

"Just the same, you'll be sorry if you give him a party," Katy told her. "You know, Mother, that something always goes wrong at Eddie's parties. Don't you remember when he turned the hose on the other children and spoiled their best clothes?"

"He didn't know they were going to move in front of the hose," her mother said.

"Don't you remember when he shot off all the firecrackers at once?" asked Katy.

"That wasn't his birthday. It was one Fourth of July." Mrs. Patterson smiled as she remembered the excitement of that day.

"Don't you remember when—" started Katy, but her mother stopped her.

11

"I remember it all, Katy," she said, "but Eddie is the only one of the family who is still in grade school. The rest of you are all growing up. He will be grown, too, in a little while. I want him to have all the fun he can while he is still a child."

Lucy stopped peeling potatoes. "We'll have the party," she said. "When Mother talks like that, Katy, she has already decided the kind of cake she'll bake."

"It will be devil's food," said Mrs. Patterson.

"Then devil's food it will be," Katy laughed. "Shall I make light or dark frosting?"

"Chocolate," said Lucy. "That is the kind Eddie likes best."

"Where is Eddie now?" their mother asked.

"Down at the streetcar corner," Lucy said, "waiting for Father and Mary."

All three of them laughed then. They did not need to look out of the kitchen window to know that Eddie was waiting for the streetcars that would bring home their father and their oldest sister.

"It's a habit," Lucy said.

"It is not a bad one," said Mrs. Patterson.

Habit it certainly was. Six days a week, in rain or snow, in sunshine or in twilight, Eddie Patterson sat on a packing box in front of Gannon's grocery. A group of boys and girls always stood around him.

"Eddie whistles the birds out of the trees to come to him," Mr. Gannon said, as the crowd gathered.

12

Boys and girls of the neighborhood came. Children came from the other side of St. Martin's parish. Children came from the public schools. Children of many races and religions gathered around Eddie.

He never seemed to say much. He listened more often than he spoke; but he gave everyone who spoke to him a wide smile. He never shouted with joy at anyone's coming, but he gave each child who came a smile of welcome. He never led any games, but he never said no when the others asked him to join them.

"Eddie's a good scout," the boys of the neighborhood said. The smiling Yim Kee, whose father ran the Chinese laundry, said nothing; but he stood for hours watching Eddie. So did Frank Bell, the boy whose father had been arrested by the police. So did eager little George Washington Lee whose father worked as porter on a train.

13

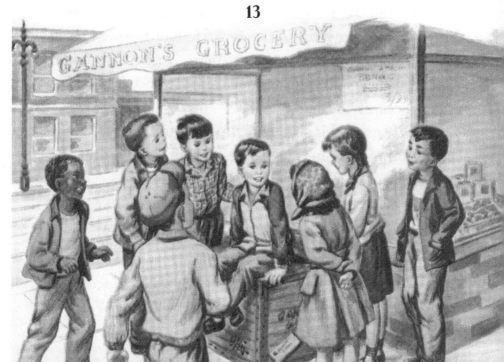

Older people spoke to Eddie, too, men and women and boys and girls coming home from work. "Hello, Eddie," they all said. "Waiting for someone?"

"Waiting for Mary," he would say until his sister Mary had come and gone. Then, "Waiting for Dad," he would tell them, until his father came down the street.

His father worked in the car shops, the only big industry of the town. The Pattersons lived in a house that did not look big, but which somehow seemed to have room for them all—for their father and mother and Dan and John and Mary and William and Lucy and James and Katy and Eddie.

Dan once told Eddie that their house had rubber walls, but Eddie knew that his big brother was teasing. Eddie knew that the walls were not made of rubber, but of wood and plaster.

Dan and John worked in the car shops with their father. William went to college. He had to ride nearly thirty miles every day to get there. Lucy and James and Katy went to high school. Mary worked in one of the offices at the car factory.

"It's a good thing you earn plenty of money," Lucy sometimes told her. "Eddie certainly couldn't do without it."

"He never spends it on himself," said Mary. "He always gives it to people who need it more than we do."

14

"He finds odd people," Katy sighed.

"He finds people whom other people don't notice," said her older sister.

"But they're odd," said Katy.

"What if they are?" asked Mary.

"That's all right for you to say," Katy told her. "You're not here when he brings them around. It embarrasses me when all the other girls in the block laugh at Eddie's crowd. They'll laugh if we let Eddie ask anyone he wants to the party."

"Let them laugh," Mary said.

Katy could not throw off her worry so easily. She was sure that Eddie would invite odd children to his birthday party, children who would not know one another, children whom the neighbors' children did not know and would be embarrassed to know.

"We must do something about this," she said to Lucy.

"Why don't we ask Mother to give Eddie a surprise party? Then we could do the inviting. We could ask the neighbors' children, some of the boys and girls in Eddie's room at school, and the younger brothers and sisters of our friends."

"That's a good suggestion," said Katy.

When the girls asked their mother if they might give a surprise party, Mrs. Patterson agreed. She did not know why the girls were so eager to do the inviting. A surprise party, she thought, would please Eddie.

15

II. *The Uninvited Guests*

Not one of the Pattersons told Eddie about the party, although each one did something special for his birthday. Dan and John and their father and mother put money together to buy a bicycle. William bought the portable radio that Eddie had been longing for.

Mary gave Lucy and Katy money for all the party trimmings—games and paper caps and candies and flowers. Everyone helped; but Lucy and Katy sent out the invitations. They asked only the children they knew.

"It will be a very exclusive party," Katy told her mother.

"I hope Eddie will like it," Mrs. Patterson said.

"Don't tell him anything about it, Mother," begged Katy. "We want it to be a real surprise."

Mrs. Patterson did not tell Eddie. Mary did not tell him. The children Lucy and Katy had asked did not tell him. Someone did, though.

On Friday Mrs. Patterson went to Mr. Gannon's grocery. "We are having a party for Eddie," she said, as she ordered supplies for the refreshments.

Early Saturday morning she started to work with Katy and Lucy. They made cakes. They ordered ice cream. They counted candles. They set out candies. They put fresh flowers in bowls and vases. They began to make chicken salad and olive sandwiches.

16

"It is going to be a lovely party, really exclusive," said Katy. "We will have everything ready at three o'clock. Then the children will begin to come. At half-past three we will send James down to Gannon's to get Eddie. Won't he be surprised!"

Then the telephone rang. A mother was calling. "I am sorry," she told Katy, "that Fred cannot come to the party for Eddie. He has the measles."

"Oh!" said Katy, "I'm so sorry."

The telephone rang again. Another mother was calling. "I am sorry," she informed Mrs. Patterson, "that Billy cannot come to Eddie's party. Billy has the measles."

"Oh, I am sorry," said Mrs. Patterson regretfully.

The phone kept ringing all morning. Every time it rang it gave notice that another child had measles.

"What shall we do?" Katy moaned.

"Just go on with the few who will come," said her mother. She looked at the sandwiches and the cakes and the ice cream and the candies. "There is enough here to feed all the children in St. Martin's School. Do you suppose," she worried, "that Eddie is getting the measles, too? Where is he now?"

"Where is he always when he is not in school?" laughed Katy. "In front of Gannon's."

Eddie was sitting on the packing box near the store. Yim Kee and Frank Bell and George Washington Lee and four other small boys were with him. Some of them were talking about marbles and tops and trades, but Eddie was not listening.

He was thinking of what Mr. Gannon had just said to him. "Happy birthday, Eddie! That's quite a party you're going to have at your house, isn't it?"

"I don't know," Eddie had replied.

"Your mother said she expects the children at three o'clock. You'd better be getting dressed, hadn't you?"

"I'll be dressed," Eddie said.

He was not thinking of dressing as he sat on the box. He was wondering if there would be enough food for Yim Kee and Frank Bell and George Washington Lee and the others if he took them home with him. Not for a moment did he think that Katy and Lucy had not sent them invitations because they had not wanted them. It was, he thought, because they did not know these boys who were his friends.

18

"Have they a lot of food over at our house?" he called in to Mr. Gannon.

"Plenty," said the grocer. "Your mother bought enough food to feed a lot of guests."

Eddie looked at the clock on the grocery wall. It was three o'clock. "Come on, fellows," he said, "I am having a party."

III. Happy Birthday

The seven boys went up the street with Eddie. As they went, other children joined them. "Eddie Patterson is having a party," was the cry that drew them.

"Come on to the party," Eddie called.

At ten minutes past three, twenty-four children followed Eddie in through the front door of the Patterson house.

"Where did you get them?" gasped Lucy.

"They are my friends," Eddie said. "Isn't this my party, Mother?"

"It is your party," his mother said, "and your friends are welcome, Eddie."

"It's a surprise party, isn't it?" George Washington Lee asked.

"It is certainly a surprise party," Mrs. Patterson said, "but I think the surprise is not on Eddie."

She and Katy started the children playing "Going to Jerusalem" with the dining-room chairs. Then after a

while she called them to the table for the salad and olive sandwiches, ice cream, and cake. They were all on second and third helpings when Mr. Patterson and Mary came home from work.

"Happy birthday!" they called to Eddie.

"It is, thank you," he said.

"I think," Eddie's mother said, as they followed her back to the kitchen, "that this is the happiest birthday Eddie has ever had."

"Of course it is," said Mary. "He is making other people happy."

"That is like Eddie," said his father.

"But, Mother," said Katy, "he is so weird, liking all these odd children."

"He isn't weird, Katy," her father said. He smiled at his wife. "Remember little Jerry Donovan?" he asked her.

"No one who knew him could ever forget him," his wife replied.

"Who was he?" Lucy asked.

"He was a boy who lived near us when we lived in a town in Pennsylvania," her father explained. "Like Eddie, he used to make friends with all the children who didn't have other friends. I suppose that, even when he was a little boy, he had the true missionary spirit. For he grew up to become Father Gerard Donovan, the devoted missionary who went to China—"

"—and became a martyr," said Mrs. Patterson.

"For our Faith," said Mary.

"Do you think that maybe Eddie—" Katy began.

"We don't know," her father said. "I only know that I'm proud to have a son who doesn't judge his friends by what they can do for him, but by what he can do for them."

"I see," Katy said slowly.

"So do I," said Lucy. "We had a lesson in citizenship yesterday at school. Father Patrick said just about what Father has said. I suppose," she went on, "that Eddie is the best citizen of us all."

"He's a pretty good one," said his father.

At the moment the good citizen was staring, a little wildly, at the flowers and the candles, at the scraps of cake, at the melting ice cream, at the candies scattered on the disordered table. Around him shone wide-eyed, happy faces, white and yellow and black.

Somehow he knew that he should be happy. So much had been given him—many different gifts, even a portable radio, and a party for twenty-four of his friends. He had been happy, but now his head and his eyes ached. He didn't know what was the matter with him, but something was wrong.

"Happy birthday to you," someone shouted again.

The children took up the song. All the Pattersons came back to the dining room and joined the children.

"Happy birthday to you,
Happy birthday to you,
Happy birthday, dear Eddie,
Happy birthday to you."

"Thank you, everybody," he said and began to cry.

Yim Kee stared at him.

Frank Bell stared at him.

George Washington Lee stared at him.

All the other children stared at him.

Mary and Lucy and Katy stared at him.

His dad stared at him.

His mother gave him one long look. "You poor child!" she sighed. She moved beside him and put her arm on his shaking shoulder.

"The celebration is over," she informed everyone as she lifted Eddie from the chair and led him toward the door. At the doorway she turned back. She gave the Pattersons and the guests a look that told them almost as much as her one word. "Measles," she said.

22

Discuss the following questions. Be sure that you know the reasons for your opinions. You do not have to agree, but be sure that you can show good reasons for your thinking. Express any difference of opinion with courtesy and good nature.

1. Eddie was a quiet boy. He did not seem to like exciting things or adventure. But many children of different races and religions were loyal to him. Should you have liked him? Why or why not?

2. Do you think that God was pleased with the way the boys and girls in this story lived and played together? Were they putting into practice the real "spirit of America"?

3. Would you call Eddie a "good scout"? If you would or would not, be ready to prove your opinion.

4. Would you have done what Eddie did with the money given to him? Or would you have spent most of it for yourself? Which one of Eddie's friends should you have enjoyed helping the most?

5. Why did Katy and Eddie disagree in their ideas as to who were their friends? Do you agree with Katy or with Eddie?

6. Would you call Eddie a good citizen? Why?

7. Does Eddie remind you of anyone you know? Is it someone in this room, in this school, in your neighborhood, or perhaps in your own family?

23

Neighborly

My mother sends our neighbors things
  On fancy little plates.
One day she sent them custard pie
  And they sent back stuffed dates.

And once she sent them angel food
  And they returned ice cream;
Another time for purple plums
  They gave us devil's dream.

She always keeps enough for us
   No matter what she sends.
Our goodies seem much better
   When we share them with our friends.

And even if they didn't, why,
   It's surely lots of fun,
'Cause that way we get two desserts
   Instead of only one!

One for brother, one for sister,
   Two for mother more,
Six for father, hot and tired,
   Knocking at the door.

VIOLET ALLEYN STOREY

Many great Americans have helped
boys to become good citizens,
but no one has done more than

Father Flanagan of Boys Town

With five homeless boys and ninety borrowed dollars a young priest started one of the most unusual homes in the United States.

Father Flanagan found two of the boys living on the streets, three of them arrested by the police. The place was Omaha, Nebraska. The time was twelve days before Christmas in the war year of 1917. The priest was Father Flanagan, and the home was the beginning of Boys Town.

Father Flanagan, born in Ireland, was the assistant pastor of St. Patrick's Church in Omaha at a time when baking, hot winds destroyed the crops in that part of the country. There was no work for farm laborers, and thousands of these men came into the city, begging food and shelter.

Father Flanagan opened what he called a workingman's hotel. Those who could pay a dime for a meal and a bed paid it, but no one was turned away because he could not pay. Through four years the hotel cared for tens of thousands of men, sometimes as many as five hundred in one night. To care for them, Father Flanagan begged from the people of Omaha.

Through those years Father Flanagan thought a lot about the men who came to his hotel. He asked them

26

questions about their homes and their families, and he found that nearly all of them had been homeless boys with no one to love and care for them. He decided that he should work, as he said, "Not with the twisted oak, but with the young sapling." He would start a home for homeless boys, giving them not only food and shelter, but an education to make them better men.

The home opened on a feast day of Our Blessed Mother. By Christmas it held fifty boys. Their Christmas dinner was bits of chopped beef, potatoes, milk, bread without butter, and—sauerkraut.

It was no holiday feast, but the spirit of the home was already showing. Father Flanagan found one of the boys carrying upstairs another boy almost his own size. "He's too heavy for you," he told the young lad.

"He's not heavy," the boy said. "He's my brother."

By spring so many boys flocked to the new home that Father Flanagan had to move to a larger building. There he could care for one hundred and seventy-five; but soon that also proved to be too small. He decided then to move to the country, and bought—on borrowed money—a farm of one hundred and sixty acres, ten miles west of the city.

Before his death in 1948 Father Flanagan was caring for a thousand boys. People all over the world knew about Boys Town. It now covered nearly a thousand acres and held a farm, dairy, laundry, school buildings, store, bank, field house, post office, swimming pool, cottages, and a church. Special doctors cared for the health of the boys.

In Boys Town the priest set up a plan so that the boys could govern themselves. A boy mayor and other officers, chosen by the boys themselves, managed the work and the play of the home. This plan still works today.

Boys Town now has a grade school, a high school, and a trade school. Boys of all colors and religions are taken into the town. There are two classes in religion, one for Catholics and another for those who are not Catholics. All of the boys are taught that religion is the base of good citizenship.

"I believe that every boy is created by God to become a good citizen," Father Flanagan once said. "The homeless boy with his dirty face, his frightened look, and his ragged clothes, is precious to the Sacred Heart. For he too is one of God's own."

Father Flanagan died several years ago. He is buried in the chapel of Boys Town under a marble stone which reads, "Father Flanagan, Founder of Boys Town, Lover of Christ and Man. July 13, 1886— May 15, 1948." Another great priest carries on his work; and the spirit of Father Flanagan lives in the home on the Nebraska highway, a home that has shown the world the meaning of service for God to the least of God's children.

PROVING WHAT YOU SAY

Number your paper from 1 to 6. Read the following statements. Write *Yes* for the sentences that are true and *No* for those that are false. When you have finished, find the sentence in the story which will prove that you have answered correctly.

1. Boys Town was started shortly before Christmas.
2. Father Flanagan was born in America.
3. Anyone who wanted to sleep in the workingman's hotel had to pay ten cents.
4. Father Flanagan felt that he could do more good by helping young boys rather than men.
5. The home opened on a feast day of Our Blessed Mother.
6. Money had to be borrowed in order to build a larger home.

Do You Fear the Wind?

Do you fear the force of the wind,
The slash of the rain?
Go face them and fight them,
Be savage again.
Go hungry and cold like the wolf,
Go wade like the crane:
The palms of your hands will thicken,
The skin of your cheek will tan,
You'll grow ragged and weary and swarthy,
But you'll walk like a man!

HAMLIN GARLAND

All kinds of people make up the world,
and every one of them has
something to give, even in a

Festival Dance

I. *Plans for the Dance*

The Woodland Park group won the silver cup for the best performance at the Harvest Festival in Greenfield. Everyone who saw the dance given by the group said they certainly deserved to win the prize. But few people knew how much of the praise belonged to Carl Stiller or how much Sally Wilson had done to make that praise possible.

If you know Greenfield, you know Sally Wilson. She is the youngest of the Wilson children, who live with their father and mother in the big white house near the college. She is the girl with the bright eyes and the sunny smile who is the friend of everyone she knows. And she knows nearly everyone in the town.

Her best friends are her neighbors, the children who live in Woodland Park. Some of them go with Sally to St. Michael's School, others go to the public school. They go to different churches, but when school is out and on holidays they have many good times together. They go together to flag-raisings and Fourth of July celebrations and harvest festivals. They all cheer for the Greenfield team at baseball and football and basketball games.

31

Ruth Golden is Sally's dearest friend. She is a quiet girl who follows Sally's lead, but she is usually the one who gives Sally ideas for parties and games.

Ruth is the one who thought of the festival dance for the big harvest celebration which Greenfield has every year. She told Sally, and Sally told her father. Mr. Wilson told the committee who were making plans for the harvest festival, and they thought it was a fine idea.

Each neighborhood in the town was to send a group of dancers to the festival. Sally was chosen leader of the group from Woodland Park.

"What are we to do?" she asked when her mother told her of the plans.

"Dance," her mother said. "And you had better choose a dance which all of you know."

That afternoon Sally went to talk over the problem with Ruth.

"We can learn a dance," Ruth said.

"How?"

"We will all get together and practice," replied Ruth firmly.

Sally called the children of the neighborhood into the big living room of the Wilson house. She told them of the festival and of the part they had been given in it. They all wanted to do everything they could to make the festival a success, but they did not know how to begin.

"We will have to do something," Sally said. "You can dance very well, Ruth. Why don't you show us?"

"It is not so easy as that," Ruth said. She stood up before them to explain the different steps. "I could show you better with music," she declared.

"Joan can play the piano," said Sally.

Joan was willing to try, but she could not play well enough to set the dancers moving. Neither could anyone else. They tried hard, but the dance dragged badly.

"I don't believe we shall ever be able to get up on a platform and dance before people," Sally told her mother one evening.

The Woodland Park group was not doing well in its practice for the Greenfield festival. Then, one afternoon, without any thought of the festival, Sally brought Carl Stiller home from school with her.

II. *The Boy Who Liked Wood*

Carl Stiller was a quiet, dark boy who sat across from her in the room at St. Michael's. He had been in the school only a little while, and the children felt that they did not know him. He had come to Greenfield with his father from Germany. His mother was dead, and he and his father lived alone. His father worked in one of the furniture factories.

Mr. Stiller was a tired-looking man with drooping shoulders who prayed in church with so much feeling that Sally sometimes thought he must really be seeing God as he talked to Him. Carl prayed like his father when he joined the children in school.

Carl spoke English so badly that he was hard to understand. The children all looked at him bashfully as he went among them. Finally Sister Helen saw how lonely he was, and she spoke to Sally.

"Will you be kind to Carl?" she asked her. "He is a stranger among us, and I think he needs a friend. He seems so lonely and unhappy."

"I don't know how to make friends with him," Sally said, but because she made friends with everyone she found a way. She had in her desk a big book of drawings of different kinds of woods. Once she had seen Carl watching her as she read it. Now she drew it out and handed it to him.

"Would you like to look at this?" she asked him.

"Thank you," Carl said. "Thank you very much." He studied the pictures carefully before he returned the book. "I like wood," he told her.

"Why?" she asked him. In his work at the college her father handled and studied wood, but it seemed strange for a boy to like it.

"I have always liked wood," Carl said. "In my village, the village where I lived in the old country, wood was the heart of our lives, just as the Play was the soul."

"Say that again," said Sally, and Carl repeated it. Then he explained what he meant.

"I lived in a little town in Germany," he said. "It is one of the great Catholic towns of the world. Once every ten years, when there was no war in Germany, the people of my village used to put on a play about the life of Christ. They called it the Passion Play."

"I have heard of it," said Sally.

"People used to come from all over the world to see it," Carl went on. "The people of the village always played the parts of Christ, of His Holy Mother, of His apostles and disciples, of Pilate, of the High Priest, of many of the people of Jerusalem. For years and years they studied their parts. If we had stayed in our village in Germany, I should be studying a part now. Perhaps, if I were very, very good, I might be allowed to study the part of Saint John, the dearly loved disciple of Our Lord."

"Why didn't you stay there?" Sally asked. "It sounds as if it were a lovely place."

"It is a lovely place," Carl said sadly, "but our country went into a great war. We could no longer give the Passion Play. Then my father brought me here to America. Now he works in the furniture factory where he carves wood."

"What does he carve?" Sally wanted to know.

"Chairs, tables, chests of drawers. He makes beautiful carvings, but they are not the statues he used to make, statues of Our Lord and Our Lady. In the evenings he teaches me to make these statues. That is why I like wood so well. I know that out of wood one may make prayers." The boy held up a tiny statue that he had carved. "Look!" he told Sally.

"It is beautiful," she said.

36

"If I had the wood, I would make one for you," Carl said bashfully.

"Come home with me after school, and I will get you the wood," Sally said.

"Thank you," said Carl.

As they walked toward Woodland Park he told her, as well as he could, of his life in Germany. It had been a happy life. All the people of the village had served God by their daily work and by their plans for the great Passion Plays. They would have been glad to live always in the peace of their mountain valley; but peace went from the valley and, in time, some of the people left their native land.

"It is hard to leave your own country," Carl said, "but sometimes it is harder to stay there."

"It is fine to be an American," Sally said.

"It is more than fine," Carl told her. "It is—what do you say?—heavenly. Freedom is a gift of God."

When they came to the big white house near the college no one was at home. Ruth Golden was waiting on the porch for Sally.

"This is Carl Stiller," Sally told her. "He has come home with me to carve something in wood. He can carve wood beautifully. He comes from Germany."

She went into the house and came back with a piece of smooth, dark wood.

"This is beautiful," Carl said. His fingers stroked it gently. "From this I shall make a statue for you."

37

He arose to go, and suddenly Sally felt that he did not want to leave. He was going, she thought, to an empty house where he would be alone until his father came home from the factory. "Wouldn't you like to stay?" she asked him. "We are going to practice for a festival dance in a little while."

"That is kind of you," said Carl Stiller. "I shall be glad to stay. Is there anything I may do to help you?"

"Oh, no," Sally started to say, but Ruth spoke. "Can you play the piano?" she asked.

"A little," he said.

"I think," Ruth said, "that you may be able to do a great deal for us. Joan broke her wrist this morning."

III. *How Carl Helped*

Carl Stiller did more than a little for the dancers who came to Sally's house. He saw that the steps they were trying to do had no plan, no beauty. They were just hops, skips, and jumps.

"I know a dance," Carl said bashfully, "that we used to do in the old country."

"Will you teach it to us?" Sally asked.

"Of course," said Carl, "I shall be glad to."

Carl could play the piano better than any boy or girl whom they had ever heard. He played so well that even clumsy feet fell into the rhythm of the dance. From the piano stool he directed the dancers.

"One-two-three. Left foot up. One-two-three. Turn and swing. One-two-three. Right foot up. One-two-three. Turn and swing."

Day after day Carl came home from school with Sally. Day after day he put the children through practice which tired them, but left them cheering.

"That boy is a wonder," Sally's mother told Mr. Wilson. "He is training them as if they were real dancers. He must be a born dancing master."

"I don't believe he is," Mr. Wilson said. "Have you noticed his fingers? He is a born artist, a carver. Perhaps he is a great enough artist to have more than one way of expressing himself. And he is trying to express something."

"What do you suppose it is?" Mrs. Wilson asked.

"I imagine it is thankfulness," Mr. Wilson said, "thankfulness to Sally for making him a friend, to all the children for taking him into their group, to our land for welcoming him."

"Perhaps it is," Mrs. Wilson said.

Whatever was his reason, Carl worked at the job Sally and Ruth had given him. Nothing but a perfect performance would satisfy him. He kept the girls whirling until they were dizzy. He made the boys bend until they were weary. He played softly, and he played loudly. He got up from the piano stool and showed the group how a step should be taken. He led and he inspired them.

Finally, the day before the Harvest Festival, he spoke one word of praise, his first to them. "Good!" he said. When they clapped their hands, he held up his own. "You must do just as well tomorrow," he told them. "It is for the honor of this group."

They did as well the next day.

The Woodland Park group was the best trained, the best directed, the most perfect in every way, of all the groups at the festival. The dance they gave was so festive, so happy, so joyful that everyone who saw it cheered. They cheered again when the chairman of the festival called Sally Wilson to receive the silver cup as the prize for the best of the festival groups.

For a moment Sally stood in front of the hundreds of people who had come to see the festival. The chairman handed her the gleaming cup.

"I don't deserve this," she said. "It belongs to Carl —to Carl Stiller." She held it out toward him, but Carl shook his head.

The cup stands on a table in the Wilson living room. The children of Woodland Park voted that this was the place for it, since the room was their neighborhood gathering place. Everyone who sees the gleaming cup admires it, but Sally has another treasure that is more precious.

It stands on a little table in her own room. Before it there is always a vase of flowers. It is a statue in dark, smooth, brown wood, a statue of Our Blessed

Mother. It is the statue which Carl Stiller carved for Sally. It is a little statue of great beauty, but Mr. Wilson says that its greatest beauty lies in the souls of the boy who made it and the girl for whom it was made.

"They are the spirit of America," he tells Sally's mother, "the girl who holds out the hand of welcome and the boy who gives his best in return."

"All of them welcomed Carl," says Mrs. Wilson.

"I know," says Sally's father, "but my daughter was the first to welcome him."

Sometimes Mr. Wilson comes up to stand before the little shrine in Sally's room and to admire the statue. He likes it better, he says, than the silver cup down in the living room.

"The cup is a prize," he tells Sally, "but the statue is an offering. It is an offering of the one thing in all

the world that makes life noble, our faith in one another because of our faith in God."

"It is an offering to Our Lady," Sally tells him.

"To Our Lady," her father repeats, "Our Lady of
Freedom."

CAN YOU RETELL A STORY?

How well can you tell a story that you have read?
There are several ways to help you to remember what
you have read. You might write a short summary of
the story or you might make a list of the important
events in the story. Which way do you think will best
help you to remember the story?

1. If you decide to write a short summary of the story,
read the story carefully once. It is divided into three parts.
Write a summary of each part. Be sure that you make the
summary include only the most important ideas in the story.
With the help of these major ideas you will be able to remember the important parts of the story. The summary will
also aid you in telling the story in the order in which the
events happened.

2. If you decide to make a list of the important events to
help you to remember the story, you must first read the story
carefully. Then read it again, listing only the most important events. Your list of events in the story should be in
the exact order in which they happened. Before you tell
the story to the class see how well you can recall it from
your list.

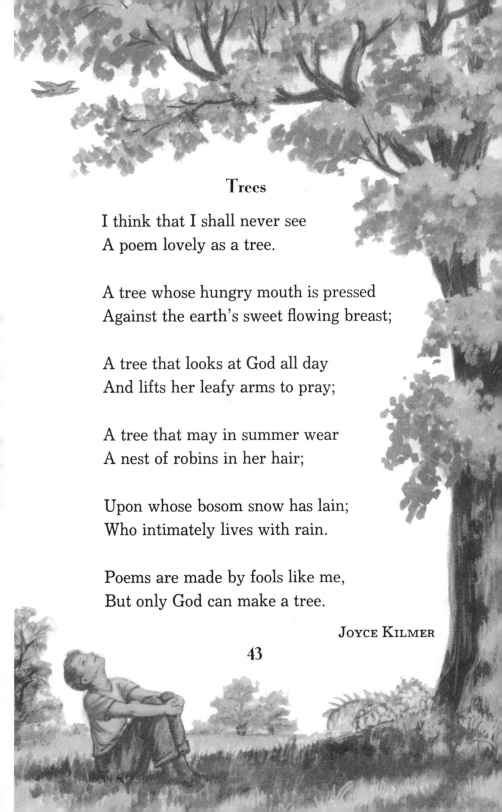

Trees

I think that I shall never see
A poem lovely as a tree.

A tree whose hungry mouth is pressed
Against the earth's sweet flowing breast;

A tree that looks at God all day
And lifts her leafy arms to pray;

A tree that may in summer wear
A nest of robins in her hair;

Upon whose bosom snow has lain;
Who intimately lives with rain.

Poems are made by fools like me,
But only God can make a tree.

JOYCE KILMER

43

We Build America

A long time ago men and women from many countries came to our land. They came to Florida, to Massachusetts, to Virginia, to Maryland, to New York, to Pennsylvania.

They built homes and schools and built churches. They were looking for a way of living that was better than the ways they had known in the Old World. It was a way toward freedom—freedom to earn their living, to speak, to write, to meet, to worship God in the way they wished.

Other men and women followed them across the sea. Together they won their freedom from the Old World nations which had ruled them. Together they founded a new nation, the one which is now the United

States of America. Together they fought the forests, the mountains, and the deserts to make our nation wide and strong.

We Americans are still building our nation in great cities, little villages, and fishing towns.

We are building it on the farms of East and West and North and South, of wheat belt and corn belt and cotton belt.

We are building it in orchards, on the ranches, in the mines, in the forests.

We are building it in the steel mills, in the automobile plants, in the airplane factories.

We are building America in the great shipyards.

God has a great plan for our country. He planned a nation where men would be free, a country where they would use the wealth He set for them in prairies and rivers and mountains.

We Americans have tried to carry out this plan. We have known that the greatness of our land was not in its riches and wealth alone, but in our use of those riches. We have known that we must always share with others what God has set before us.

The builders of our nation have all known this truth. They made America great, and we shall keep our country great by remembering what they knew.

With faith and courage we are living as did those brave people who came from many lands to our great and blessed country.

Can you fill in this outline?

Copy the form of the outline as it is given below. The *major* topics, or most important details, have been stated for you. Find in the story the words or ideas that complete the *minor* topics, or less important details. Notice the use of Roman numerals in the major topics.

We Build America

I. Places settled by early Americans

  A. Florida

  B.

  C.

  D.

  E.

  F.

II. Kinds of freedom they wished to find

  A. Freedom to earn their living

  B.

  C.

  D.

  E.

III. Some ways in which we are still building America

  A.

  B.

  C.

  D.

  E.

God's Promises[1]

God hath not promised
Skies always blue,
Flower-strewn pathways
All our lives through;
God hath not promised
Sun without rain,
Joy without sorrow,
Peace without pain.

But God hath promised
Strength for the day,
Rest for the labor,
Light for the way,
Grace for the trials,
Help from above,
Unfailing sympathy,
Undying love.

ANNIE JOHNSON FLINT

47

II

Highways and Hedges

"A certain man gave a great supper, and he invited many. And he sent his servant at supper time to tell those invited to come, for everything is now ready. And they all with one accord began to excuse themselves. . . .

"And the servant returned, and reported these things to his master. Then the master of the house was angry and said to his servant, 'Go out quickly into the streets and lanes of the city, and bring in here the poor, and the crippled, and the blind, and the lame.' And the servant said, 'Sir, thy order has been carried out, and still there is room.' Then the master said to the servant, 'Go out into the highways and hedges, and make them come in, so that my house may be filled.'"

Luke 14, 16–23

A Song of Praise

God of the great outdoors,
To Thee we give our praise;
To Thee, the Lord of earth and sky,
Our songs of joy we raise.

For grasses softly bending,
Our thanks to Thee we're sending;
For quiet waters flowing,
For soft winds gently blowing,
For smiling skies above us,
For friendly hearts that love us,
For hands that work and souls that sing
Our gratitude to Thee we bring.

God of the city streets,
God of the woodland ways,
God of the hills and vales,
To Thee, our song of praise!

LOUISE ABNEY

50

Hate the sin, but love the sinner
is an old teaching of the Church.
It was a lesson the younger Winter
children learned when they met

The Tall-Tale Boy

1. *Off in the "Ark"*

There was a song festival that year at Altmont, and all the children of St. David's School planned to go to it. On Saturday morning, an hour earlier than usual, they would meet at the school and pile into the big school bus. For days the children could talk of nothing else but this happy trip.

No one talked about it more than did the children in the Winters family. Marie and Ann planned what clothes they would wear. Tom and Chris planned the food they would take. All four of them wondered about the shows they would see, the songs they would hear the big crowd sing.

"Are you sure the bus is to take you to Altmont?" their father asked them on Thursday night.

"Oh, yes," Tom told him. "We'll get there. Everything's set."

"I'm glad of that," he said, "because I have to use the big car on Saturday and so I can't drive you to Altmont."

Everything came apart, however, when, on Friday night, Sister Mary Teresa telephoned to Mr. Winter.

51

"The bus has broken down," she said. "We must find another way to get the children to Altmont. Can you take your own children?"

He started to say that he could not, but the sight of the children's eager faces held him back. "I'll see that they get there, Sister," he promised. He turned away from the telephone. "Where is James?" he asked.

"James!" Four Winters shouted in one voice for their oldest brother. "Oh, James!"

"Here," said a quiet voice as James, a book in his hand, came from the kitchen.

"Will the *Ark* run?" his father asked him. The Winters always called the old car the *Ark* because it had once gone through a valley flood.

"Maybe," James said slowly. "It snorts like a steam engine and it acts like a stubborn mule on the hills."

"Can you get to Altmont in it?" their father asked.

"Altmont?" His oldest son looked worried. "Not by the old road. Maybe on the turnpike. That means more miles."

"Will you try the turnpike?" his father asked.

"All alone?" James looked surprised.

"Your brothers and sisters will be with you."

"Whew!" James whistled. "A lot of help they'll be if the *Ark* breaks down."

"Keep it afloat, son," his father said.

"All right, sir. What time do we go? Seven o'clock? I'll be ready." James started back toward the kitchen, his favorite reading place, but turned at the door to look back at the younger children. "Tell them I'm the boss, Father," he said. "If I'm going to be the captain of the *Ark*, they'll have to do as I say."

"Oh, we will," the four shouted.

The next morning they set off merrily. They shouted and they sang, and they waved to children in other cars. "See you at Altmont," they called. Tom and Chris, beside James in the front seat of the old car, tried to tell their brother how to drive it. "Pipe down," he said. "I've been running this old car long enough to know it."

There were many cars on the turnpike, all of them going faster than the *Ark*. "Can't you step on it just a little?" Tom pleaded as other cars passed them.

"We'll be there in plenty of time," said James.

Ann began to sing "Merrily we roll along," and all

53

but James joined her. They sang all the verses, then sang them over again.

"Nobody is having a better time than we are," Tom said.

Then, suddenly, they all seemed to realize that something was going wrong with the *Ark*. It sputtered and stuttered along the turnpike. It stopped as if it were a stubborn mule.

"What's the matter with it?" Tom cried.

"I don't know yet," said James.

Each one of them had a different guess. "The radiator is leaking," said Chris.

"It's the spark plug," said Tom.

"It's one of the tires," said Ann and Marie.

James found out what it was. It was not a leak in the radiator. It was not the spark plug. It was not the tires. They had run out of gas.

"How much money do you have?" he asked. "We've got to go off the turnpike as soon as we see a gas station on a side road. We'll be lucky if we get that far."

They counted their money slowly, but they gave him what he said would be enough to pay for the gas. Luckily they saw a filling station on a road to the right, and they circled off the turnpike to reach it.

"Going far?" the man at the gas station asked them. "Altmont? Hope you make it." He looked queerly at the *Ark*. "Good luck, kids!"

That was when the Winters noticed the boy who was standing near the gas pump. He was a tall, thin boy, perhaps no older than Tom. He was staring at them as if he wanted to ask them something. His clothes were so worn and shabby that Ann felt sorry for him at one moment, but his eyes were so angry that she disliked him the next moment.

"Some orange crate," the boy said to James.

"It runs," said James, "most of the time, anyhow."

"Going to Altmont?" the stranger asked.

"Sure."

"Give me a lift?" the boy asked.

"Oh, no," Ann wanted to cry. Her father had often spoken of the danger of picking up strangers on the road. But James was saying, "Move into the back with the girls, Chris, and let this fellow sit next to me."

"You'll be sorry," Ann said, but James seemed not to hear her.

II. *Travel Tales*

The shabby boy took the place between James and Tom. He settled himself back on his spine. "Where do you live?" he asked.

"Back on the highway a bit," James said. "Where do you live?"

"Well, most of the time I live in New York City, but I happen to be staying just now back there near the gas station. Ever been to New York City?" No one answered him, and he went on, "Some place, New York City. Biggest city in the United States."

"James has been to Philadelphia," Ann said.

"Oh, Philadelphia," said the boy. "Nice city, but it's not like New York. Chicago's all right, too. So is Los Angeles."

"You've been to all of them?" Tom asked wide-eyed.

"All of them, and a lot more. New Orleans, and San Francisco, and all the places in between."

"How did you go?" Chris called from the back seat.

"Oh, trains, sometimes, airplanes, sometimes. Mostly by automobile, though."

"Hitchhiking?" Tom put in.

"Sometimes, but most of the time I travel in my father's car. He's got a Washington car."

"What kind is that?" James asked politely.

"You mean you don't know a Washington?" The boy looked surprised. "It's a big, long car, and it goes like the wind. Didn't you ever see one?"

"No," said James.

"Did you ever see San Francisco?"

"No." James kept his eyes on the road, but Ann had the feeling that he was staring right through the boy. "Been there often?"

"Oh, yes. We stay at a big hotel out there. We stay at hotels everywhere we go." He began a detailed description of the fine hotels he had visited. Then he began to tell about the cities he had seen. New Orleans was hot, he said. Los Angeles had a lot of flowers. There were many ships at Seattle.

"Did you ever go to Alaska?" James asked.

For the first time the boy hesitated. "Not exactly," he said. "I mean, my father went, but I waited for him."

"So?" James said. That was what he always said, Ann remembered, when he thought that any of them was not telling the truth. This meant that he knew the boy was lying. Of course he was lying, Ann thought. He probably had never been to any of these places. His father did not own a Washington, whatever kind of car it was.

She grew nervous as the boy went on with his tall tales. He had met adventure everywhere. He had ridden with cowboys. He had talked with air pilots.

He had saved children from burning buildings. He never stopped talking until they drove into Altmont.

"Where do you go from here?" James asked him as he jumped from the *Ark*.

"Oh, west," he mumbled. "My father is going to meet me in St. Louis."

"That's a very long way," said Ann.

"He'll send me money to get there," the boy waved his hand grandly.

"Whew!" Tom whistled as the boy left them. "He's been around plenty, hasn't he?"

"So he says," James said.

"You don't believe him, do you?" Ann asked him.

"Sure, I don't," her older brother answered. "Now, listen, all of you. It's wrong to lie. It's a sin, and we all know we shouldn't do it. That boy is the worst liar I ever heard. He's a tall-tale boy, but somehow I'm sorry for him."

"Sorry? Why?" Tom asked.

"Because he's lying to make us think he's somebody he isn't. He isn't fooling us, but he thinks he is. He must be unhappy." James shook his head sadly.

"Well, I'm glad he's gone," said Ann.

The song festival had started when the Winters reached the big stadium where hundreds of children were already singing in chorus. They found the other children from their school and joined with them in "America the Beautiful." When the singing was over, they found a place where they could eat the lunch they had brought from home. Then they wandered around again until another chorus started. They joined in that. When it was over, James said that it was time to start home.

Once, during the singing in the stadium, Ann thought she saw the shabby boy, but he did not come near them. But when they came to the place where James had parked the car, the boy was standing near it. "Going back on the turnpike?" he asked.

"Sure," James said.

"Mind if I go along?"

"I thought you were going to St. Louis to meet your father," Ann said sharply.

"He sent me a message to wait a little while."

"You're telling lies," Ann said angrily. "You told us lies all the way you came with us."

"They are not lies," the boy cried. "I've been everywhere, and I've done everything, and my father has a Washington car, and I am, too, going to meet him in St. Louis."

"Get in," said James.

The boy climbed into the seat beside him. James started the *Ark* with the usual difficulty. No one said anything as they spun back along the turnpike. The shabby boy did not speak until they came to the side road where they had picked him up. "Can you let me off here?" he asked.

III. *A Lesson Learned*

James turned the car off the pike and came up to the filling station. "Here you are," he said.

"Thanks," mumbled the boy, but he did not linger. As fast as his feet would carry him, he ran down the road.

The man at the filling station looked after him. "He's an awful liar," he said, "but somehow I'm sorry for him."

"Why?" James asked.

"The poor kid hasn't anything—or anybody. His father ran off and left him and his mother. She died a couple of years ago. The kid lives at the Grant farm. He does chores for the old man and all he gets is his keep."

"Has he been away often?" asked Tom.

"Away?" The man laughed. "The only place he's ever been is Altmont, and he only goes there when he can sneak off from the farm and someone like you gives him a lift."

"I told you he was a liar," Ann told James as they started back to the turnpike.

"I knew he was," James said.

"Then why did you help him?"

"Maybe it's like this," James said. "I guess the Lord wants all of us to be honest and good, but some of us aren't. And the Lord wants us to help one another. Maybe He wants us to help the liars as much as He wants us to help the honest ones. He helped sinners, didn't He?"

"I guess He did," said Ann.

James did not take his gaze from the road, but he spoke to them all. "We know what that boy is," he said, "and we don't like him for it. But maybe we could help him so that he'll stop being such a liar. Maybe if he knew he had friends, he wouldn't always try to pretend he's so big in everything."

"But how can we do anything for him?" Ann asked.

"We can take him out sometimes in the *Ark*. We may laugh at him when he lies; but we can show him that even if we hate lying, we don't hate him if he tries to overcome it."

"Maybe Father could get old man Grant to send him to school," said Chris.

They were all singing "America the Beautiful" as James turned the car off the turnpike and into their own road.

"Do you think there is a car like the Washington?" Tom asked his big brother.

"I don't know," James said, "but I never heard of it."

"Well, anyhow," said Tom, "I prefer having the *Ark*, even if he did call it an orange crate."

"It gets us around," said James. "Three cheers for the *Ark*!"

"Three cheers for the *Ark*!" shouted the other Winters. And, at that very moment, the *Ark* sputtered and stopped, never to go again. Wearily the youngsters walked down the road toward home. "Well, anyhow," said Ann, "it was a lovely day."

HOW WELL DO YOU UNDERSTAND WHAT YOU READ?

The following exercise will show how well you understand the story you have just read. Number your paper from 1 to 10. After each number write the word or words (chosen from those in parentheses) that will make each statement true.

1. Tall tale means a (long story, made-up story, an impossible story).

2. A festival is a (circus, journey, celebration).

3. A turnpike is a (road, building, post).

4. In this story the *Ark* was a (boat, car, train).

5. The biggest city in the United States is (Philadelphia, Seattle, New York.)

6. Hitchhiking means (getting a ride, getting money, getting food).

7. Singing in chorus is singing (alone, in a group, aloud).

8. The boy hesitated means that he (stopped entirely, went on, stopped for a moment).

9. Spun along the turnpike means that the *Ark* moved (swiftly, in circles, up and down).

10. The boy did not linger means that he did not (wait, answer, read).

Travel

The railroad track is miles away,
    And the day is loud with voices speaking,
Yet there isn't a train goes by all day
    But I hear its whistle shrieking.

All night there isn't a train goes by,
    Though the night is still for sleep and dreaming,
But I see its cinders red on the sky,
    And hear its engine steaming.

My heart is warm with the friends I make,
    And better friends I'll not be knowing,
Yet there isn't a train I wouldn't take,
    No matter where it's going.

EDNA ST. VINCENT MILLAY

He Set America Singing

From the Atlantic Ocean to the Pacific, from the time of Columbus to our own day, America has moved westward. Men, women, and children have walked, ridden horseback, driven covered wagons, steered cars, and piloted planes across the country.

The greatest move to the West took place about a hundred years ago. Eastern farms began to crowd one another. Every year thousands of people were coming to America from Europe. There was land in the West, cheap land a man could buy and farm. The pioneers set out to win it; and as they went westward, on roads and trails, over plains and deserts and mountains, they sang. From every covered wagon, beside every camp-fire, rose the words

> "Oh, Susanna! do not cry for me,
> I come from Alabama
> With my banjo on my knee."

This song had been written by a young man, Stephen Foster. He had been born in a little town in Pennsylvania. When he wrote many of his songs, he had never traveled farther than Kentucky; but his songs were heard on every road across the wide land.

From the time he was a little boy, Stephen had

64

loved music. He liked to wander through the woods near his home, making up tunes and words to fit them. His father sent him to college when he was fifteen, but within a month he returned home. He was too much interested in music to continue his studies at college.

A few years later Stephen went to work for one of his brothers. In his free time he wrote more songs, words as well as music. Soon Stephen Foster and his songs became famous. People all over the country were singing and whistling his tunes.

One day he asked his brother, "What is a good name for a Southern river? I want to use it in a song."

His brother mentioned several, but none of them seemed to fit the song Stephen was writing. Then they looked at a map of the United States.

"Swanee," Stephen exclaimed. "That's it! Way down upon the Swanee River," he hummed.

His brother looked at the map. "But it is spelled S-u-w-a-n-n-e-e," he said.

But Stephen wrote it *Swanee*, and since that day almost everyone has called the river "Swanee," just as they have called the song "Swanee River," although Foster named it "Old Folks at Home."

Although he was born and lived in the North, Stephen Foster wrote many Southern songs. "Nelly was a Lady," "My Old Kentucky Home," and "Old Black Joe" are the best known today. Two of his other

songs, "Jeanie with the Light Brown Hair" and "Come Where My Love Lies Dreaming," are even better known today than they were while Foster lived. There is hardly a week when they are not sung over the radio.

For more than a hundred years the name of Stephen Foster has headed the list of American song writers. But the young musician won little but fame from his work. He did not receive much money for the songs that have given the world so much pleasure, and he died, lonely and penniless, while the soldiers of both the North and the South sang his songs beside their campfires behind the battlefronts of the War between the States.

Today his songs are sung and loved by people all over the world. The young man who loved music is remembered as the man who set America singing.

In order to write his songs Stephen Foster first had to have some pictures in his mind. Do you think you could make a drawing of what you see *in your mind* when you hear one of his songs?

For instance, ask yourself about Swanee River. Think of the land through which it flowed. What would be growing in the fields near it? Who were the people that lived near by? What could they be doing?

Perhaps you would like to illustrate "Oh! Susanna." What group of people sang the song very often when it was first written? How were they traveling? Where were they going?

Do not put too many things into your picture, but try to let your imagination guide you to do your work as neatly as possible.

THINKING ABOUT THE STORY

Think about these questions. Be ready to give good reasons for your answers.

1. Did Stephen Foster do a worth-while thing by writing his songs?

2. Why should the boys and girls of our country be especially grateful to this musician?

3. Why do you think that Stephen Foster's songs are still popular?

Saint Christopher

My father says Saint Christopher,
   Who bore Christ on his shoulder,
Will help me learn to drive the car
   When I'm a little older.

Because, he says, Saint Christopher
   Is used to helping others;
So too we all should learn to help
   Our sisters and our brothers.

He helps the driver on his truck;
   He helps us when we're driving.
He helps the one who's starting out;
   He helps the one arriving.

He keeps us safe from every harm
   That threatens to oppress us;
That's why we ask Saint Christopher
   To guard, and help, and bless us.

I'd like Saint Christopher to know
   That, if these cares beset him,
I'd like to help him as he helped
   The Christ Child when he met Him.

Their father's work took the Morgans South.
They could not take with them the cold
winters and their old friends, but they
found new friends through the sound of

Sleigh Bells in August

I. *What Shall We Take?*

The Morgans were moving South. The shoe factory
where their father worked had already moved from
the little New England town. Mr. Morgan had been
among the first of the factory workers to go, but Mrs.
Morgan and the children waited until the school year
was over.

Sometimes Mrs. Morgan wondered how much of
their lessons the children were learning. For Susan
and Peter, Ellen and David talked of nothing but their
future home and what they were going to take into it.

"I want to take everything I have here," David said.

"So do I, so do I," echoed Susan and Peter and
Ellen.

"We cannot take everything," their mother said.
"We have been piling up things for years and years.
Now we must get rid of some of them."

"Not my toboggan," said Peter.

"Not my sled," said David.

"Not my skates," said Susan.

"Not my sleigh bells," said Ellen.

"Now, children," their mother said, "it would be

silly to take those things down to a place where they do not have snow or ice."

"No snow or ice?" The Morgan children cried out against a climate so terrible. What on earth could children do in winter in a land without sledding and skating?

"We must be sensible," Mrs. Morgan said. "Your father and I decided what we could send by truck. If we tried to take everything we have gathered here, we would need two more trucks. We cannot afford them. Now let us start clearing out the things we will not need."

"But, Mother—" the four Morgans began. Their mother's lifted hand stopped them. Very slowly they began to gather their possessions.

"I can't give up my books," said Susan.

"You won't need to give them up," Mrs. Morgan said. "We can send them in the truck."

"I can't give up the dog house I made for Skippy," Peter declared.

"Skippy died three years ago," his mother remembered. "You said you never wanted another dog."

"Well, we might get one down in Carolina," said Peter.

"I can't give up my rabbit boxes," said David.

"You haven't had a rabbit since you were six years old," his mother reminded him.

"I want to keep my dolls," said Susan.

"Even the broken ones?" her mother asked.

"Yes, even the broken ones," Susan declared.

"You may keep your special ones," Mrs. Morgan decided.

"I'll need my sleigh bells," said Ellen.

"You will not," said Peter. "If I can't take my toboggan, you can't take sleigh bells."

"And if I can't have my sled," David began.

Their mother stopped them. "I have told you what you cannot take," she said firmly.

Mrs. Morgan packed swiftly, but the children helped her slowly. Susan grieved over the broken dolls with which she had not played in years. David brought the sled up from the basement and stared at it day after day. Peter sold the toboggan to Michael Wilson, who had wanted it last winter. Ellen went around the house carrying the sleigh bells and jingling them until her mother told her to stop.

"They don't take up much room, Mother," Ellen said. "Can't I take them if I can carry them in my little bag?"

"All right," Mrs. Morgan said wearily.

"Hurrah, hurrah!" Ellen cried. "And I'll take them out the first time it snows in Carolina."

"But maybe it will not snow in Carolina," her mother said.

"It will snow," declared Ellen firmly.

II. *Journey to Carolina*

By the time the Morgans were ready to leave the New England house, Ellen had packed her little bag so full that she could not squeeze the sleigh bells into it.

"I'll repack it on the train," she told her mother and draped the bells over her shoulders. And so, as the Morgans moved South on a hot July morning, they went to the sound of jingling sleigh bells.

"Jingle, bells, jingle, bells," Susan sang.

The bells jingled again as the Morgan family crossed Boston from the North Station to the South Station. They jingled as they changed trains in Washington, and they kept on jingling on the train to Carolina because Ellen could not get them into her little bag and had to hang them on a hook above her seat. Other train passengers heard them and laughed. Other children came to talk to the Morgans.

"Where are you coming from?" they asked. "And where are you going?"

The bells gave out happy, friendly sounds and brought friendly smiles to the faces of those who heard them. Other women helped Mrs. Morgan. Peter made a speedy friendship with a boy from Florida who was going home after a visit to his grandmother in Philadelphia. Susan talked to a girl from New Orleans.

Even during the night, as the lights were lowered and the train rushed on through the darkness, the sleigh bells jingled. But no one complained. It was as if the bells sang a lullaby to weary travelers.

People smiled and waved to the Morgans as they left the train to change for the one which would take them to their new home. To their delight they found their father waiting for them.

"Will you look at this?" he cried as Ellen rushed at him. "You sound like a fire engine coming."

The ride was short on the smaller train, but it gave the Morgans a chance to look at the country where they would live.

"Why, there are lots of pines," Peter said. "There must be plenty of snow here," he told his mother.

"There isn't," said his father. "It doesn't snow here in a blue moon."

"What is a blue moon?" Ellen asked.

"That's just a saying," said her father. "It means that it snows very seldom."

"But it will snow," she insisted.

"Even if it doesn't, you'll like it here," said her father.

Mr. and Mrs. Morgan liked their new home, but the other Morgans did not. There were other youngsters living near them, but somehow there seemed to be a great wall between them.

"They don't make friends with me," Peter grumbled.

"Wait till school starts," said his mother.

"I can't find anything to do," said David.

"Those girls don't even smile at me," said Susan.

"Perhaps you don't smile at them," her mother said.

"They should smile first. They were here before we came," said Susan.

There was a girl next door whom Ellen watched wistfully. She was about Ellen's age. She was a Catholic, for Ellen saw her at Mass. She looked friendly, but she did not speak, and Ellen hesitated to speak to her. "But I wish I knew her," she thought. "I know we could have a good time together."

Luckily there were many chores to be done in the new house, and Mrs. Morgan kept them all busy. But finally the chores were done, and still the youngsters had made no new friends.

"I don't know why they don't," Mrs. Morgan told her husband.

"Neither do I," he said. "The men at the factory are all very friendly."

"The neighbors have been kind to me," said his wife.

"We'll just have to wait," sighed Mr. Morgan. "I want the children to be happy in our new home."

III. How Ellen Used the Sleigh Bells

August was hot and dry. The pines seemed to droop a little in the heat. Then, for days, a storm threatened.

"We'll have a heavy rain," people said.

"Do you think it will snow?" Ellen asked David.

"Don't be silly," David told her. "Even at home it doesn't snow in August."

But by one of those odd freaks of nature that sometimes happen, the snow came from the mountains. It was not a heavy snow, but it was enough to cover the streets and to lie for a few hours on the pine trees.

"Look at it, Mother!" the Morgans cried.

"I could have brought the toboggan," said Peter.

"I wish I had my sled," said David.

"May I go out?" asked Ellen.

She put on a coat over her lightweight summer dress and hung the sleigh bells over her shoulders. They jingled happily as she danced down the street.

76

The girl next door came out when she heard the happy sound. "What are they?" she asked Ellen.

"Sleigh bells," said Ellen. "Didn't you ever hear them?"

"No," the girl said, "we have just moved here from Florida. I've never seen snow before."

"You haven't?" Ellen cried in surprise. She moved across the yard to tell her neighbor about New England snows and toboggans and sleds.

"Do you think you'll like it here?" the girl next door asked.

"I think I will—if you'll be my friend," said Ellen.

"Why, I'm glad to be." The girl gave a shy smile. "I was afraid to talk to you. There are so many of you, and I have no brothers or sisters. I wish I had."

"They're nice," said Ellen. "I'll be seeing you," she called as the girl's mother came to the door.

A little group of children were standing at the corner as Ellen passed. "Come on," she cried to them. They smiled at her and fell in behind her. "Jingle, bells," they sang after her. Other children laughed at them and joined them. Soon Ellen was leading a little procession through the snow-covered streets.

Men and women smiled to see the happy children rejoicing. "It's worth the snow," they said as the bells jingled merrily.

Mrs. Morgan was standing at the gate as her younger daughter led her followers toward it. "Wait a minute," she said. They waited as she went into the house and came back with cookies for them all. "You must come to see us again," she said.

"We will, we will," cried the children.

The snow was melting as they ran off. "We'll be seeing you," they called to Ellen.

"They are my friends," said Ellen. "The snow brought them, Mother."

"I think it was the sleigh bells," smiled her mother.

"They brought me a friend. Oh, Mother, I'm so glad!" cried Ellen.

"It's going to be all right now," Mrs. Morgan said.

She was right. It was a long time before another snow came to the town, but the friendships started that day grew as the days went on. Even before the Morgan youngsters went to school they had found friends in their new neighborhood. They learned to laugh about the sleigh bells that hung on a hook in the hall but they all felt, as Ellen did, that the bells had rung in their friendships with their neighbors.

"I like this place," Peter said.

"So do I," said David and Susan.

"Even if it doesn't snow as often as we'd like," said Ellen.

WORDS THAT HELP YOU TO UNDERSTAND THE STORY

Arrange your paper as your teacher directs. In each blank write the word or words that best fit into that sentence.

1. The children felt __?__ about moving to a new home.

2. Mrs. Morgan said that they would have to be __?__ about which things they would take with them.

3. Susan __?__ over her broken dolls.

4. Mother let Ellen take the sleigh bells because they __?__.

5. When the other passengers heard the bells they __?__.

6. A blue moon means __?__.

7. At first the children found it __?__ to make friends.

8. It was the __?__ that finally made it easy for the children to feel at home.

9. The children were happy even though it didn't __?__ very often.

10. This story shows us that we should try to make __?__ wherever we live.

Trains

Over the mountains, over the plains,
Over the rivers here come the trains,
Carrying passengers, carrying mail,
Bringing their precious loads in without fail.

Thousands of freight cars hurrying on,
Thro' day and darkness, through dusk and dawn,
Over the mountains, over the plains,
Over the rivers here come the trains.

JAMES TIPPETT

America moved westward on foot,
on horseback, and by covered wagon;
but our nation moved faster with

The Iron Horse

A little more than a hundred years ago a crowd of people gathered in great excitement. They had come to watch the running of the first railroad in our nation. They came on foot or in carriages or in cars which horses were drawing up and down the tracks.

That day they saw a tiny, puffing steam engine. It burned wood, and it smoked like a baby volcano. It had a tall, upright boiler that threw out clouds of smoke and cinders. People laughed and called the engine the "Teakettle." Others called it the "Tom Thumb" because it was so small.

Peter Cooper, who had made the engine, did not mind the jokes. His little engine had already pulled a boxcar at a speed better than ten miles an hour. Now he was ready to try the "Tom Thumb" in a race against a horse.

The engine rocked and snorted, but it held its own against the horse until the engine belt slipped off. Then the horse won. People laughed more than ever, but Peter Cooper did not laugh. "We will prove yet that we are right," he said.

And Peter Cooper did just that. Other men, making improvements on his engine, continued to prove it. Year after year, American railroads grew in size and

importance. In time, great railroad lines crossed the entire country. Men kept on building westward, northward, southward. In building the railroads, they built America.

The railroads on which our great-grandparents traveled were very different from those we use today. They rode in hot, stuffy coaches with windows that would not open or close. The trains jerked and jolted along and sometimes jumped the track. Today we can travel in streamlined, air-conditioned coaches which move smoothly over the tracks with great speed.

There are three reasons for this increased speed—the Diesel engine, stainless steel, and streamlined cars. The engine and cars, made of stainless steel, are light in weight. The Diesel engine burns oil instead of wood or coal. On some of the trains today the engine travels eighty or ninety miles an hour. The first interest of the railroad, however, is not speed but safety. Improvements in the trains have made it possible to join speed with safety.

Railroads have many other comforts for their passengers. Radios tell what is going on in the world. Meals are served in dining cars or at the passenger's seat. Many cars now have separate small rooms that can be changed into bedrooms at night. Trained nurses take care of babies and those who are sick or old. Porters help the passengers in many ways.

Freight trains, as well as passenger trains, have been greatly improved. Steel and wooden boxcars carry such freight as furniture and clothing. Open flatcars are used for shipping heavy machinery. Tank cars carry gasoline and oil. Refrigerator cars are traveling iceboxes which keep meat, fruits, and vegetables cold.

The speed of freight trains has been increased so that it is possible to carry goods across the country in half the time it once took. Because of these improvements people can buy better foods more cheaply than they once could. Our grandfathers and grandmothers can remember the time when bananas and oranges

83

were scarce in nearly all the United States and when grapefruit was eaten only in Florida.

A mighty army of men makes possible the great American railways. First come the thousands of men who lay the tracks and take care of them. Then come the men who build engines and railway cars. There are, too, the caretakers and the repairmen who keep engines and cars in good condition. There are also great numbers of men who work in the stations, selling tickets, making reports, and helping passengers.

There are tens of thousands of men who work on the trains. They have been trained to be good and faithful workers. They watch over the property and lives in their care. They obey faithfully all the orders they receive. These men work for their living; but in their work they remember the comfort and the safety of a great many people.

MATCHING TITLES WITH PARAGRAPHS

Do you recall that every paragraph has one main topic? These titles fit some of the paragraphs in the story, "The Iron Horse." Copy the titles and number them in the order in which the paragraphs which they tell about take place in the story.

Early Travel	The Teakettle, or Tom Thumb
Railroad Workers	Improvements in Passenger Trains
Peter Cooper	Reasons for Increased Speed
The Race	Improvements in Freight Trains

84

The Flower-Fed Buffaloes[1]

The flower-fed buffaloes of the spring
In the days of long ago,
Ranged where the locomotives sing
And the prairie flowers lie low:—
The tossing, blooming, perfumed grass
Is swept away by the wheat,
Wheels and wheels and wheels spin by
In the spring that still is sweet.
But the flower-fed buffaloes of the spring
Left us, long ago.
They gore no more, they bellow no more,
They trundle around the hills no more:—
With the Blackfeet, lying low,
With the Pawnees, lying low,
Lying low.

VACHEL LINDSAY

[1]From *Going to the Stars*, by Vachel Lindsay. Copyright, 1920, D. Appleton & Company. Reprinted by permission of the publishers Appleton-Century-Crofts, Inc.

Wind, Sea, and Sky

"Again, the kingdom of heaven is like a net cast into the sea and gathering in fish of every kind. When it was filled, they hauled it out, and sitting down on the beach, they gathered the good fish into vessels, but threw away the bad. So will it be at the end of the world. The angels will go out and separate the wicked from among the just."

MATTHEW 13, 47–49

Hail, Star of Ocean

Hail, O Star of ocean,
   God's own Mother blest,
Ever sinless Virgin,
   Gate of heaven's rest.

Show thyself a mother;
   May the Word Divine,
Born for us thine Infant,
   Hear our prayers through thine.

Keep our life all spotless,
   Make our way secure,
Till we find in Jesus
   Joys that shall endure.

Praise to God the Father,
   Honor to the Son,
To the Holy Spirit,
   Be the glory one.

OLD HYMN

Good deeds sometimes win rewards
on earth as well as in heaven.
One good deed won

Sails for Manoel

I. *The Blessing of the Fleet*

Manoel met old Mrs. Kelty as he went down the hill
that Sunday afternoon to see the Blessing of the Fleet.
He was in a hurry, for he wanted to miss nothing of
the service; but Mrs. Kelty looked so old and poor and
lonely that he took off his cap and stopped to speak
to her.

"Are you coming to the Blessing?" he asked her,
although he was sure that everyone in the fishing town
was going down to the dock.

"I am not," said Mrs. Kelty. She was a tall woman
who always wore gloomy black. Today Manoel thought
that her face too looked gloomy as she looked at him
and asked, "Why should I be going?"

"It's the Blessing," Manoel told her. "It is beautiful. Didn't you ever see it?"

"I've seen it," she said and pushed past him up the
hill.

"That's odd," the boy thought. Then he remembered
that people said that old Mrs. Kelty was odd.

Mrs. Kelty lived alone in a gray house set apart
from its neighbors. She visited no one, and no one
called on her. Manoel never saw anyone with the old

89

woman when he went to sell her the fish he had caught from the pier. She had a dog that barked wildly at Manoel whenever he came through the gate.

"That's too much," Mrs. Kelty always said when Manoel told her the price; but when he said, "I have only one price," she took out a long, thin billfold from her pocket and counted the money, usually in pennies.

"You're all robbers," she grumbled, but Manoel was sure she did not mean that, and he only smiled at her.

"I have to sell my fish," he said.

He remembered all this for a moment, then forgot it in his excitement at seeing what lay below him. All the fishing boats were coming into the harbor for the Blessing of the Fleet.

White sails looked like great birds as the boats skimmed over the water toward the docks. Even the smokestacks of the boats driven by steam shone brighter than on other days. On the decks of all the boats the fishermen were standing at the rails. There was beauty in the scene. There was a tang in the sharp salt air.

"Oh, boy!" Manoel sighed in delight.

The boy raced down the street, jumping and leaping with joy. It was grand, he thought, to be the son of a fisherman. It was grand to go to school and study so well that his father and mother were proud of him. It was grand to see the harbor and the fishing fleet at work. It was grand to go with his sister Maria and his little brother Philip to Children's Mass in the Church of Our Lady of Good Voyage.

Grandest of all were the Blessing of the Fleet and the celebration that welcomed the fleet home after its work far out on the ocean. The celebration was yet to come, but the Blessing was now, in this hour, and Manoel raced to take part in it.

Down the hill, on another of the steep streets, came the procession—women, children, old men no longer able to go to sea. They moved slowly, reverently, behind the cross-bearer and the altar boys.

"Next year," Manoel promised himself as he watched them, "I shall be one of those boys. I shall do as well as John and Joseph. Then some day I shall be the cross-bearer. I shall hold the cross as high and as straight as Martin does now."

John and Joseph and Martin paid no attention to him as they passed him, but he thought that Father Gama gave him a little smile. Father Gama was wearing vestments of white and gold. The gold gleamed as the priest walked slowly down the hill. The cross shone, too, brighter than the sunshine on the blue waters of the harbor, Manoel thought, as he followed the procession toward the wharves.

The procession spread out as it came to the long pier and made a place for Father Gama. The priest stood at the edge of the platform and raised his right hand. Then he began to pray.

He prayed for the fishermen, that they might win the catch which they would seek. He prayed for their families. He prayed that the men of the fleet might come safely home. As he prayed there was no sound but the sound of his voice and no motion but the movement of the harbor waters.

Then, slowly, the boats began to move past Father Gama. On every boat the priest sprinkled holy water as he said, "In the name of the Father, and of the Son, and of the Holy Spirit."

The fishermen bent their heads reverently as the boats passed the priest. Manoel saw his father in his white-sailed boat and knew that he was praying.

"May the blessing of God be on you," Father Gama said. "The blessing of God," Manoel kept repeating after him until the last boat had gone after the others, out into the open sea. The white sail of his father's boat was the last one the boy saw as the fleet went around Eastern Point.

Manoel knew that his mother and Maria and little Philip must be somewhere in the crowd, but his eyes looked for Captain Peter, his best friend among the many men he had met on the wharves. He found the captain near the door of the sailmaker's workroom.

"Run along with you now," the captain said. "Don't you bother me enough on Saturday mornings?"

"You sound like old Mrs. Kelty," Manoel remarked.

"Joanna Kelty?" Captain Peter's voice grew sharp. "How do you know her?"

"She is a friend of mine," said Manoel.

"You're the only one who could say that for more than thirty years," said the captain. "Well, I'll see you on Saturday."

"Captain Peter, do you think that maybe—on Saturday—you could let me sail your boat for a little while?" asked the boy.

"I do not."

"Well, maybe, some other Saturday—"

"I've told you that I'd let you sail her when you're old enough," explained the captain.

"But I'm—" insisted Manoel.

"I'll tell you when I think you are ready."

"Aye, aye, sir."

II. *The Two Friends*

On Saturday Manoel went down to the wharf. There was no one in the sailmaker's workroom, and so he sat on the pier to wait for Captain Peter. After a while he saw him coming down the hill.

Captain Peter was close to eighty. He was a big man with a white beard and a tanned face and eyes as blue as the skies above the waters. He walked quickly, with his head thrown back as if he were a ship sailing out into the ocean.

"Ahoy!" he called to Manoel.

"Ahoy, Captain!" Manoel called back with a broad smile on his face and followed him up the narrow stairs.

Captain Peter did not even pretend to work there. He sat down in a big chair near a window and looked out at the harbor. "I first saw this place on Saint Martin's Day sixty-two years ago," he told Manoel. "That's a long time in any man's life."

"Were you born here?" Manoel asked him.

"I was not. I was born in Ireland in a fishing town. I was sailing there when I was your age."

"Were you always a fisherman, Captain Peter?"

"What else would I be? Isn't fishing a fine trade for any man? Wasn't Our Lord always a friend of the fishermen? Didn't my own father and mother—God rest their souls!—name me for Peter, the fisherman? Didn't Our Lord Himself call Peter the rock on which

94

He built His Church? Didn't the fishermen go out to preach the Gospel of Christ?"

"Teaching all nations," Manoel added.

"Hasn't it always been the fishermen who've made the world wider? How would men have learned to sail if they hadn't gone out to fish? How would they have found new lands if they hadn't known how to sail?" Captain Peter pointed to the map that hung above Manoel on the wall. "How else would Columbus have discovered America? Where should we all be if it weren't for sailors and fishers?"

"My father wants me to go to work in an office," Manoel said, "but I want to be a fisherman when I grow up. I want to go out with the fleet."

"Do you know how cold it sometimes gets out on the ocean?" asked the old captain.

"I know. My father almost lost his right foot out there last winter by having it frozen."

"Do you know how long the fleet can be out?"

"I know. Sometimes my mother and the other women go every night for weeks to the church to pray for the safe return of the men."

Captain Peter gazed out over the waters of the harbor. "Haven't you seen the people here throwing flowers on the waves on the first Sunday in August? Haven't you seen the flags at half-mast on the ships as they round the Point there? Don't you know what that means? That one man, maybe the captain, maybe one of the fishermen, will never come home?"

"I know," replied the boy sadly.

"You can't know all of it yet, laddie. Only those who have lost someone they loved can know the whole of that sorrow. There's one of them—" he stopped suddenly, then went on, "How's your friend, Joanna Kelty?"

"Old Mrs. Kelty? She's all right. I saw her last night when I took up the fish."

"Did she pay you?"

"She always pays me, but sometimes I'm afraid she can't afford it."

"You're afraid she can't afford it?" Captain Peter puffed out his cheeks. "Well, don't let her go hungry," he said.

"I won't, Captain," Manoel promised.

III. *The Feast Day*

Manoel recalled his promise to the Captain on the day the fleet was due to come back to the fishing town. The radio had given the happy news to the town, and everyone was joyful, Manoel most of all. For Manoel had earned the dollar which had paid for his ticket to the great celebration in the big hall.

Tomorrow night the show would go on. He would be there with the big boys and the big girls to see the dancing and hear the music.

After the little feast at home, when they would welcome his father's return with fried chicken and egg pudding, they would end the meal with a prayer of thanksgiving for all God's blessings. Then Manoel would run down the hill and come to the brightly lighted hall.

He was still thinking about it when he came to Mrs. Kelty's house. The dog barked at him, but Mrs. Kelty said nothing when she opened the door.

"Don't you want any fish?" he inquired.

"I don't know why I bother buying any," she said, "with only myself to cook for."

"I know," Manoel said, "I think maybe it's hard for you to be all alone."

"What do you know about it?" she asked.

"I don't know very much," he said, "but I know how I feel when my mother is away when I go home."

Mrs. Kelty looked at him strangely, and then, suddenly, a great thought came to him. Mrs. Kelty was alone, and she was lonely. She could go nowhere because she had no money. Now if Mrs. Kelty could only go to the celebration—but she couldn't go, of course, because she couldn't afford a ticket. If only—

For an instant he stood beside the door of Mrs. Kelty's house, pondering over the biggest question that had ever come into his mind. In his pocket he could feel the ticket for the celebration which would mark the return of the fleet. He had paid for it with money he had earned. He wanted to use it; but he drew the ticket from his pocket and pushed it at Mrs. Kelty.

"That's for you," he said. "I got it for myself, but I want you to have it."

"I can't take this," she said, but Manoel had already turned away.

"Just see that you go," he shouted back from the gate, as the dog barked at him.

He went to the sailmaker's workroom on the next Saturday morning. Captain Peter was already there, sitting in the big chair near the window, looking out over the sea.

"I didn't see you at the celebration last night," he told Manoel.

"I didn't go."

"I thought you had a ticket. Did you lose it?"

"No, sir."

"What happened to it?"

"I gave it away."

"You gave it away? To whom did you give it?"

"I gave it to a lady who has no money to pay for a ticket."

"You mean Joanna Kelty?"

"Yes, sir."

"Well, I declare!" Captain Peter leaned himself forward in the big chair and gazed at the boy. "I met her there. She talked with me for a long time. It was the first time in years she had talked as long to anyone. All that time she had been blaming me and every other sailor who had been on the *Mary Ann* when her husband was lost from the boat. We couldn't save him, God knows, but she wouldn't believe that."

"Was that why she has always stayed alone?"

"That was why. She is sorry now that she has

lived that way. She told me last night that she'd been wrong in blaming anyone for John Kelty's death from the *Mary Ann*. She'd grown into a lonely old woman who hadn't a friend on earth. She said she was turning a new leaf in her old age. I wondered how the grace of God had come to her after all these years. So it was you!"

"I didn't do anything," Manoel said.

"She said that someone had made her see that there was kindness in the town. You are the only one who has called her a friend in all that time. You are the only one who has ever made a sacrifice for her."

"But she is poor."

"Not in the way you mean, Manoel, but in another way. Well, glory be to God, you have done what no one else in this town ever did. You have brought Joanna Kelty back to her own people. I saw her at Mass this morning, on a Saturday, at that." The old man reached into his pocket, took out his purse, looked at Manoel, then put the purse away. "Do you still want to sail my boat?" he inquired.

"Oh, Captain Peter!"

"If you do, and your father and your mother give you permission, I'll let you take her out."

The old man rose heavily. "I'll go up to your house with you now. There is no reason to postpone anything until tomorrow. You never know when a sudden storm will come."

He followed Manoel down the stairs and out upon the pier. "I suppose," he said, "that the sea is in our blood, yours and mine. It gets into the blood of people who live by it, whether it's in Ireland or Portugal or here in Massachusetts. You will be a sailor, as your father is and as I have been."

"I hope so, Captain Peter."

"I want you to remember this: the sea has a law, and it is the law of the Christian. Help the other man when he needs your help. You know that law already. Keep it in your mind, and you will be a good man."

"A good sailor."

"A good devoted American," said Captain Peter.

Then, together, the old man from an old fishing town of Ireland and the boy whose people came from an old fishing town of Portugal went up the hill. As they went, they began to sing the old sea song that so many men have sung as they went through the streets of the town:

> Come, all you young fellows that follow the sea,
> With a yeo-ho! We'll blow the man down!
> For happy young sailors we're going to be,
> With a yeo-ho! We'll blow the man down!

Captain Peter lost his breath and the tune at the first landing, but Manoel was still singing as they climbed the hill. The day was bright, the sky was blue, and the ocean danced. Why wouldn't a boy be happy?

Do you enjoy watching or taking part in plays at your school assembly programs? Most boys and girls do. Would you like to write a play for a school assembly?

The story you have just read would make a good play. Here are some things you need to think about before you write the play.

1. How many acts shall we have in our play?

2. Shall we make a summary of the story and present only the most important parts of each act, or shall we present every detail—everything the characters think and say?

3. How many characters are there in the entire play? in each act? Who will be the principal characters?

4. How shall we choose the characters for the play?

5. What scenery and costumes will be necessary?

ACT I

A street in the fishing town

Manoel meets Mrs. Kelty on the way to the wharf. They talk. Manoel explains the meaning of the Blessing of the Fleet; how he feels toward Mrs. Kelty; why he wants to be a cross-bearer.

ACT II

At the shore

The procession passes. Manoel talks with Captain Peter.

Can you finish the play now?

Fisherman's Song

Spread the nets out in the sun;
Come, work, my lads, together!
Mend the strands now, one by one,
Oh, work, my lads, together!

Ship the dories, hoist the sails!
Oh, work, my lads, together!
Out to meet the northern gales,
We'll sail, my lads, together!

BLANCHE JENNINGS THOMPSON

The Mermaidens

The little white mermaidens live in the sea,
In a palace of silver and gold;
And their neat little tails are all covered with scales,
Most beautiful for to behold.

On wild white horses they ride, they ride,
And in chairs of pink coral they sit;
They swim all the night, with a smile of delight,
And never feel tired a bit.

LAURA E. RICHARDS

Fishing Fleets

Have you ever gone fishing?

In a brook or a river or a little lake?

Or even in a great ocean?

Have you ever caught minnows for bait?

Or perch or trout or catfish?

Then what did you do with it?

Did you bring it home and ask your mother to cook it for dinner?

In a bigger way that is what thousands and thousands of people all over the United States and its territories are doing. Some of them fish for pleasure, as you do. Others fish as a way of making a living.

Most of the fishing is done by men working together in the fishing fleets.

They bring in many kinds of fish, for every year people want more fish. More than one hundred and sixty kinds of fish—fish from the Atlantic, the Pacific, the Gulf of Mexico, Chesapeake Bay, the Great Lakes, and from smaller lakes and rivers—are sold in our American markets.

Fishes—little fishes and big fishes, red and white and gray fishes, and fishes that shine like silver—make one of the principal foods of men.

Even before history was written men caught fishes. They found that some of them made good food. In time they traded the fish they caught with other people who had other kinds of food to trade. That was the beginning of the fish trade, one of the great trades in our world.

Every year Americans are eating more fish, but most of the fish caught are never used for food at all. Some fish taken off the East and the West Coasts are used for making cooking fats, chicken feed, and paints. Fish are also used in the making of oils, soaps, perfumes, buttons, shoes, purses, and hundreds of other things for everyday trade. Fish caught by American fishermen go to more than a hundred different countries.

There have been American fishermen ever since the beginning of the early settlements along the Atlantic seacoast. More than two hundred years ago fishing for cod was an important industry there. It is still important, but to it have been added many other kinds of fishing. The most exciting of the fishing industries, the search for whales, is no longer one of the great American adventures, but it is still a real industry.

One of the great fishing places of the world is the place known as the Grand Banks. The Grand Banks are off the coast of Newfoundland. For many, many years fishermen from America have been going there for fish, although it is a long way from their homes.

The trip is nearly always hard. There are fierce storms and many wrecks. Men are often lost. The work is so hard and the dangers so great that the fishermen of the Grand Banks are known everywhere as men of great courage.

Along the shores of Chesapeake Bay lives the oysterman. His work is not quite so dangerous as that of the deep-sea fishermen. He does not have to meet as many storms as do they, but his work is hard and long. The oyster fisherman is also an oyster farmer, planting his farm on the floor of the bay with oyster "seeds."

Off the coast of Florida, men go out in search of great fish that give battle, but this fishing is for pleasure rather than for trade. On the Gulf of Mexico may be seen the boats of the sponge fishers, as well as those of the fishers for shrimp. From the Great Lakes come the famous whitefish and perch. From northern lakes come fish which are only caught by being brought up through the ice. From the mountain streams of the West comes mountain trout.

On the Pacific Coast the great catch is the salmon. Sometimes great nets catch the salmon as they come back from the sea into the rivers where they were hatched. Sometimes fleets of big boats bring their catch of shining salmon to the big canning factories of the coast towns.

Every year new ways of fishing are tried. In many places motorboats have taken the place of the small fishing dories. Big nets have taken the place of hundreds of lines. Fleets of fishing boats that once had to wait for wind are now driven by steam.

The men of the fishing fleets still work for their livings, however, on the sea that is their old friend, their old enemy. To earn a living for themselves, their wives, and their children, they work from dawn until dark, and sometimes through long nights. Theirs is an old trade, an honored trade. Christ Himself blessed and worked with the fishermen of Galilee; and Christ still sets His blessing upon the fishers of the fleet.

Below you will find a new way to write an outline. It is called an idea line. The major ideas, or important details, are given to you as headings to columns written across the page. On your paper draw a form and copy the headings given in the sample below. Then fill in the minor ideas, or subtopics, just as you do when you fill in an outline. If you need to do so, refer to the story to fill in the details correctly.

Use the idea line to help you to make a report to the class or to help you to answer questions about the story.

Reasons for Fishing	American Markets Sell Fish from	Some Uses of Fish	Kinds of Fishing on Atlantic Coast	New Ways of Fishing
1. For pleasure	1.	1.	1.	1.
2. To earn a living	2.	2.	2.	2.
	3.	3.	3.	3.
	4.	4.	4.	
	5.	5.		
		6.		
		7.		
		8.		
		9.		
		10.		

Broad Stripes and Bright Stars

I. *Dreams of the Future*

Jerry and Beth and John David were sitting near the big guns on the Sea Wall at Annapolis.

Beth was tossing little stones into the water. John David was reading a book. Jerry was watching the boats out on the water.

Some of the boats were small. There were oyster boats like the one in which their father was at work. There were sailboats where the pupils of the Naval Academy, called midshipmen, were at practice. There were pleasure boats out in deeper waters.

Some of them were big. There was the ferry to the Eastern Shore. There was a boat carrying oil, steaming north from the ocean. There was a great, gray battleship that stood proudly in the harbor.

There were little boats running out from shore to the ships of the Navy. Men with two and three service stripes on the left sleeves of their dark-blue uniforms passed the Sea Wall on their way to or from the little boats. White-uniformed sailors went by. Midshipmen of the Academy kept coming and going. As they passed, all of them saluted a big man who walked up and down, up and down, near where Jerry and Beth and John David were sitting.

He had a broad gold stripe beneath the narrower gold stripes and the bright gold star on his sleeve. His

uniform cap had more gold on it than had the caps of the men who saluted him. Jerry and Beth and John David paid no more attention to him than they did to any of the others except that once, as he went by, Jerry noticed how deeply blue were the man's eyes.

"They look like the sea and the sky," thought Jerry.

Perhaps this idea came to Jerry's mind because he had been thinking of the sea and the sky. "I'd like to be on that battleship," he had been telling himself, "when she goes down the bay and out into the open sea where there would be nothing but sea and sky. I'd like to be an officer on her. More than anything else in the world I'd like to be an officer in the Navy of the United States."

Then he sighed, for he did not know how he could

make this happen. He was a Crabtown boy, the son of an oyster fisherman. Crabtown boys, who lived in another part of Annapolis, did not often get into the Naval Academy. "But I'd certainly like to be a midshipman," Jerry said aloud wistfully.

"When you are old enough you can join the Navy," John David said without looking up from his book.

"I'd like to be a midshipman," said Jerry.

"You will have to pass a lot of examinations when you finish high school. You will have to ask a man in Congress to put you on the list for the Naval Academy. How can you do that?" asked John David.

"There is another way, Jerry," Beth said. "I read the other day that once a year the President of the United States chooses a hundred sailors from the fleet. He lets them come to the Academy here. Do you suppose you could be one of them?"

The big man passed again just then. She stared at him as if she thought of asking him. The big man smiled at them as if the sight of two barefooted boys and a barefooted girl on the Academy Sea Wall pleased him, but he did not speak.

"I guess maybe," Jerry said, "I'm only dreaming dreams when I think about getting into the Academy. I suppose I will just be an oysterman like Father when I grow up."

"There is nothing against being an oysterman," said Beth.

111

"You don't make much money," said Jerry.

"That isn't everything," declared Beth.

"I think it is fine to be an oysterman," Jerry said, "if you like to be an oysterman. Father likes it, but I want to be a midshipman and then an officer and then an admiral."

"Admiral!" John David cried. The big man turned in his walking but moved on again as John David added, "Why, that's the highest position in all the Navy! How do you think you would ever get to be an admiral?"

"That is what I don't know," Jerry said. "I just said that is what I want to be."

"If Jerry wants to be a midshipman," Beth told John David, "you have no right to make him think he can't be. This is the United States of America."

The big man stopped and looked at them. He smiled understandingly at Beth. "You are quite right," he said to her. "This is the United States of America, and any boy who wants to be a midshipman of the Navy of the United States has certainly a chance to win his way to be one."

"There!" Beth told John David.

Someone on the pier called to the big man. "In just a moment," he said. "Let's see, what time is it now?" He took from his pocket a gold watch that gleamed as brightly as the gold star on his sleeve. Then, as an officer saluted him, his own right hand lifted to his cap.

112

As if it had wings, the gold watch flew from between his fingers and whirled into the waters of the bay.

"Oh!" cried the big man.

"Oh!" cried Beth.

"Oh!" cried John David.

Jerry said nothing at all. He couldn't. At that instant he was already in the water, diving down to where the bright object had sunk. In a moment he was up again with the watch. There was water in his mouth so that he could not speak, but he held out the watch to the big man. "Whew!" He tried to get his breath as he climbed up over the Sea Wall.

"Are you all right?" the big man asked.

"Sure, I'm all right. That wasn't anything."

"It was quick thinking. It was more than that. It was forgetting yourself to do something for someone else. I cannot tell you how grateful I am to you," said the officer.

"Is the watch hurt?" John David asked anxiously.

The big man looked at it. "There may be water in the works," he said, "but I think it can be fixed. It is a good watch," he went on. "It was my father's. It was, I think, the one valuable thing he had. He gave it to me the day I left for Annapolis." He stared hard at Jerry. "You're the boy who wants to be a midshipman, are you not?"

"Yes, sir."

"How old are you?"

Jerry told him.

"Where do you live?"

"Here—in Annapolis. We are Crabtown people, so I suppose I haven't much chance of getting to be a midshipman," said Jerry wistfully.

"Crabtown? Crabtown?" the big man roared. "How often do we have to tell those young midshipmen not to use that word? And why shouldn't you have the chance to make yourself what you want to be? Listen to me, youngster." He took hold of Jerry's wet shoulder. "I am going to tell you the story of a boy who didn't have as much chance as you have."

114

II. With Work and Prayer

John David and Beth and Jerry listened as the big man told them the story of a boy he had known.

"He was a boy on a farm in Iowa," the big man said. "Do you know where Iowa is?"

"It's in the Mississippi Valley, sir," said John David.

"It is—and it is a long way from Annapolis," continued the officer. "This boy had never seen a ship. He'd never seen a boat except a rowboat on a little stream near the farm. He lived far out from a town, and his people were so poor that he had only a few books.

"One of them was a book about the American Navy. In it he read stories of the heroes of the American Navy. It told the story of the American flag floating over American ships. It told the story of the courage of the men of the American Navy."

"I like books like that," said Beth.

"He liked the book," said the big man. "Every day, as he went to school in a little red schoolhouse or as he worked out in the wheatfield or in the cornfield, he kept thinking about those men. He told himself that someday he was going to be one of them.

"He didn't know what he had to do to join the Navy. Annapolis was just a name to him. He had never seen a midshipman or an officer or even a sailor. But he kept on thinking about the Navy.

115

"As he grew older he found other books, books about ships and sailors. He found stories in newspapers. He found people who knew something about the Navy and about how boys could get into it. He studied and he worked. After a while he found out that there was a man who lived near him who knew a great deal about the Navy. This man was a member of Congress. He went to see this man, and the man gave him good advice. The boy took that advice and kept on working and studying. Then, one day, he came here and took the examination for the Naval Academy."

"Did he pass it?" Jerry asked.

"He passed it, but he had studied so hard that he had strained his eyes. The doctors who examined him said that he did not have good enough eyesight for the Navy. That was the hardest hour of his life, that hour when he came out of the doctor's office. He felt that he had failed in the one thing he wanted to do."

"What did he do then?" asked John David.

"He went out of the gate back there and walked along the street, not knowing where he was going. Then he came to a church."

"St. Mary's?" asked Beth.

"St. Mary's," nodded the big man.

"That's our church," said Jerry.

"That day St. Mary's was his church, too," said the officer. "There, all alone, he poured out all the sorrow and disappointment of his heart to God. He prayed

116

to Him for grace, for courage to face his future. God heard his prayer and gave him courage and strength. He gave him, in time, better eyesight and another opportunity to get into the Academy."

"Then what happened to him?" Jerry asked.

"Well, he completed his studies, and one day in June, when his class graduated, he pulled off his collar, as all the midshipmen used to do, and cheered and cheered because now he was an officer. Then he packed his uniforms and went off on duty to far China."

"Where is he now?" Jerry asked.

"Oh, he is around Annapolis. He is still proud that he got into the Navy."

"Is he a captain yet?" John David asked.

"He has been a captain. He is an admiral now."

"Admiral?" Jerry cried. "Why, that is the highest position in the whole Navy!"

"That is why I told you about him," the big man said. "I wanted you to know that if a boy from an Iowa farm can become an admiral in the United States Navy, a boy right here in Annapolis has just as good an opportunity."

"Do you really think, sir," Jerry questioned him, "that I would have a chance to get into the Academy?"

"You will get into the Academy, youngster, if you study and work the way that boy did."

"And pray," said Beth.

117

"And pray," said the big man slowly. "You run into the shallows pretty fast if you don't pray."

Another man in a dark-blue uniform, with gold stripes on his sleeve not so broad as those on the big man's, came up the stone walk. "They are ready for you, sir," he said.

"Coming," said the big man. He held out his hand to Jerry. "I am going out to sea now," he told him, "but when I come back next year, you will find me in my office at the Academy."

"I'll remember you, sir." Jerry wondered why he felt suddenly both glad he had come to know this man and sorry that he would not see him again for a while. "I shall never forget you."

"I won't let you." The big man walked away. Sailors and officers stood at attention as he moved towards a motorboat that lay at the foot of the steps from the Sea Wall.

The Stars and Stripes floated from the mast, and beneath it waved another flag, a blue flag with four white stars set in the shape of a diamond. Jerry stared at the blue flag. "Why, that's—that's—" He clutched Beth's arm as he spoke to a sailor just going by. "Who is that who was talking to us?" He pointed to the big man who was standing now beside the four-starred banner.

The white-uniformed sailor looked where Jerry pointed. "I thought everybody knew him," he said. "He's the admiral of the battle fleet."

CAN YOU PICTURE THE PEOPLE AND PLACES YOU READ ABOUT?

In this story there are many pictures made with words. Here are some descriptions, or word pictures, taken from the story. See how many more word pictures you can find. Copy the sentences you select from the story on your paper. Perhaps you would like to make a drawing of one of them.

1. Jerry and Beth and John David were sitting near the big guns on the Sea Wall at Annapolis.

2. There was a great, gray battleship that stood proudly in the harbor.

3. Then, as an officer saluted him, his own right hand lifted to his cap.

4. The white-uniformed sailor looked where Jerry pointed.

119

Luck

What bring you, sailor, home from the sea—
Coffers of gold and of ivory?

When first I went to sea as a lad
A new jack-knife was all I had;

And I've sailed for fifty years and three
To the coasts of gold and of ivory;

And now at the end of a lucky life,
Well, still I've got my old jack-knife.

WILFRED GIBSON

Wings for America

On the lonely sands of Kitty Hawk in North Carolina, on a cold windy day in December, 1903, two brothers stood ready to try out their first airplane. A few men had gathered to watch the flight. The machine looked a little like a box kite, but it had propellers, an engine, and wings. Its pilot had to lie flat on the wing which held the motor.

The younger of the Wright brothers, Orville, climbed onto the plane. The wind gave the plane a lift, and it was off. Then by its own power it rose slowly, slowly from the earth. Up, up it went. It nosed and dipped. Once it came suddenly down toward the earth. Then it rose again.

For the first time a machine heavier than air had made a successful flight. It had stayed in the air just twelve seconds, but it had flown!

People had always wanted to fly. Men had written about flying, had drawn pictures of flying machines, had even tried to fly, but always without success.

These stories of man's desire to fly excited these two American boys, Orville and Wilbur Wright. The Wright brothers played at flying. In the high March winds they sailed their well-made kites. As they grew older, they studied about flying. In their father's big library they read many books about airplanes. In their workshop, with the help of their mother, who was

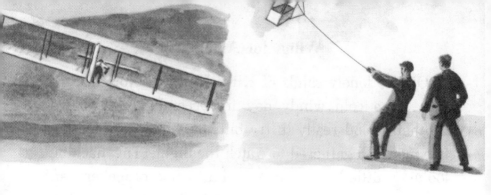

clever in using tools, they built kites that they learned to fly in the breeze.

Orville and Wilbur Wright did not fly their kites for fun. They wanted to know what made the kites fly. Very carefully they watched every movement as the kite floated in the still air or twisted in a sharp breeze.

The boys understood that God, knowing all things, made the bird able to fly. The brothers believed that if they could find God's laws for flying, they could build a machine so that man too might fly.

In the fields, in the yard near their bicycle shop, during the early morning, all through the late afternoon, Orville and Wilbur studied birds. They watched them "take off" and soar through the air. They kept a record of what they saw. Day after day, month after month, they searched to find answers to the questions that would not leave their minds.

Little by little the brothers began to understand the mystery of the flying bird. With what joy they started work on their birdlike machine, the glider! All night long and into the early morning in the workshop of their home in Ohio, they measured and sawed and hammered on the strange machine.

Finally the Wrights built a glider which proved to be successful. It was this glider, into which they had built an engine, that made the famous flight at Kitty Hawk in 1903.

The brothers returned home eager to improve their already successful invention. Five years later, with the improved plane, Wilbur Wright went to Europe, where interest in airplanes was high. Before delighted crowds he flew the handmade plane. At home Orville flew the plane before the people of his own country.

The governments of several nations honored them. The American government bought the first plane, for army use, from the Wright brothers.

Aviation is now one of America's greatest industries. Today Americans talk airplanes, think airplanes, dream airplanes, make airplanes. Searchlights stab the sky, motors roar, silver wings soar high by day and by night because once, on a December day over the sands at Kitty Hawk, two Americans made the dream come true that man would one day be master of the air.

Many magazine articles, books, and stories have been written about airplanes. This is not only an interesting subject, but it is also one about which new things are being discovered.

You will probably enjoy seeing how many facts you have learned about airplanes by taking notes from the story you have just read about the Wright brothers. Then try adding to your list of information by reading more on this topic from other books.

Note only the important facts. Use as few words as possible.

The Wright Brothers

1. Date of first flight
2. Appearance of plane
3. Machine first worked on
4. Wanted to find
5. Helped by
6. First plane bought by
7. Aviation today
8. Dream that came true

After you have prepared your notes, perhaps you will enjoy giving a report to your classmates about the Wright brothers. This might be done in the form of a contest to see who can give his report in the most interesting manner. You can add to the interest of your report by telling something you have read from another book. Pictures make a talk interesting too.

Wings and Wheels

Ahoy and ahoy, birds!
We cannot have wings
And feathers and things,
But dashing on wheels
With the wind at our heels
Is almost like flying—
Such joy, birds!

Oho and oho, birds!
Of course we can't rise
Up and up to the skies;
But skimming and sliding
On rollers, and gliding,
Is almost as jolly,
You know, birds!

NANCY BYRD TURNER

IV

The Sower and the Seed

"Behold, the sower went out to sow. And as he sowed, some seed fell by the wayside, and the birds came and ate it up.

"And other seed fell upon rocky ground, where it had not much earth; and it sprang up at once, because it had no depth of earth; but when the sun rose it was scorched, and because it had no root it withered away.

"And other seed fell among thorns; and the thorns grew up and choked it, and it yielded no fruit.

"And other seed fell upon good ground, and yielded fruit that grew up, made increase and produced, one thirty, another sixty, and another a hundredfold."

Then he said, "He who has ears to hear, let him hear."

MARK 4, 3–9

Grace for Freedom

Our mother teaches us to say
For every meal on every day,
"Bless us, O Lord, and these thy gifts
Which we shall now receive."
Our father says that we should say
A prayer on every single day
For all the blessings that are in
The Faith which we believe.

But, most of all, he says that we
Should thank God for our liberty,
"Bless us, O Lord, and this, our land,
Where we all have the right
To live our lives as Christians should,
To grow up strong, and kind, and good,
And work and play beneath the sun
Of freedom's holy light."

A Game in an Orchard

The children were playing "Run, Sheep, Run" in the orchard. Eleanor Brent sat on the old stone wall, watching them, pretending to play with them, although she could not join in their game. For Eleanor, who read to them, who told them stories, who let them ride her pony, who loved them all as they loved her, could not run with them, could not climb the trees, could not jump the fences.

Eleanor Brent was lame.

There had been a time when she had felt far apart from them when they had raced among the trees and through the fields of the big Brent farm in the orchard country of Maryland. Then Henry had found a way to bring her into the games. "Eleanor is our umpire," he had said. "She can keep the score."

"Eleanor is our umpire," all the other children repeated.

After that Eleanor played every game with them, although she did not always feel that she was really one of them.

Eleanor played with Henry and Martha, whose father had come from Germany and who showed the workmen how to care for the soil and how to grow better apples.

She played with Tim and Judy, whose father had come from Ireland and who was the tree doctor of the orchard, the man who made sick trees well.

She played with Rosa and Tony and little Carlotta, whose father had come from Italy and who ran the big machine that loosened the soil of the orchard. He also drove one of the big trucks that took the apples to market.

All of them were in the game now, and Eleanor watched every move of it. Tim was captain of the boys. Rosa was captain of the girls.

Tim was better than Rosa at finding places where the children on his side could hide. The girls were better at running. The score was almost even when a turn came for Tim's side.

The girls on Rosa's side stood facing the trees. They shut their eyes as Tim tried to find hiding places for the boys. He stood just in front of Eleanor, pointing up into the spreading branches of an apple tree.

She shook her head to warn him not to send the boys up into that tree.

It was the most valuable tree in the orchard. Eleanor's father was very proud of it. So were the fathers of all the other children. They didn't want anything to happen to any of the trees, but they were more careful of this tree than of any of the others. They had often told the children that they must not climb the trees in this part of the orchard.

"Don't send them up there," Eleanor whispered to Tim, but Tim waved the boys to hide in the tree.

The boys climbed up. As they went, they broke a branch. Eleanor sighed when she saw them do that. She knew that breaking branches often injures good trees. The boys climbed so high in the branches that they thought the girls could not see them, but Judy had sharp eyes. She saw the broken branch and stared up into the tree. "I see them!" she shouted and raced back toward the goal.

"Run, my good sheep, run!" Tim ordered.

The boys came down the trunk of the tree so fast that they broke another branch, but the girls reached the goal first.

"We've won!" Rosa cried. "We have won the whole game, haven't we, Eleanor?"

Before Eleanor could reply, Henry's father hastened over to the children. "What are you doing?" he asked. Then he saw the tree. "Who did that?" His voice was

131

stern and harsh, and his eyes were angry. "Who broke these branches from that tree?"

No one spoke.

"If you had anything to do with this damage," he said to Henry, "I shall punish you as I have never punished you before. How often have I told you that you have no right to hurt the property of others?"

Henry said nothing.

"Who did that?" their father asked Martha.

Martha did not speak.

"Who did that?" he asked them all.

No one answered.

"You saw it done, Eleanor," he said. "You know that even the tree doctor may not be able to save this tree. You know how your father will feel about it. Who did it?"

"We all did it," Eleanor said.

"You couldn't have been with them. Who went up that tree?"

"All of us didn't go up the tree," she said, "but all of us were playing the game."

"None of the girls went up the tree," said Tim. "Some of the boys went up because I told them to go. I am the captain; so it is all my fault. I am responsible."

"I'm captain on the opposite side," Rosa said. "It was all in the game, and so it is just as much my fault as it is Tim's."

"We were all in the game," said Eleanor stubbornly.

132

"We all play together. We have our good times together. We have to take our bad times together. We
must all take punishment for this."

The children waited while Henry's father sent for
Tim's father, the tree doctor.

"It is pretty bad," he said. "You'd better show it
to Mr. Brent."

They waited nervously until Eleanor's father came.
They listened while the other men told him about the
injured tree. He examined the broken branch and then
turned to face the group of children.

"Who did this?" he asked quietly.

"We all did it," Eleanor said. "We were all playing together. It is everybody's fault."

"I see," her father said calmly.

He carefully examined the tree again. Then he looked at Eleanor and the other children. Tim stepped toward him. "We boys did it, sir," he said frankly, but Rosa spoke. "We girls were in the game with them. If it was the fault of one person in the game, it was the fault of everyone in the game. We are all in this together, and we should all be punished together."

"That is a pretty large order," said Eleanor's father seriously. "Look here, let's get this straight. You boys and girls know, don't you, that these apples are God's gifts to us, but that we have to take care of them so that there will be money for food and houses and clothes for all of us?"

"Yes, sir," they said.

"Then why don't we make a bargain with each other to give them this care?" he asked. "Why don't you children promise me that you will protect the trees just as we men try to protect them?"

"We will do that, sir," they answered in chorus.

"You have stood together in your playing. Will you stand together in this?" Mr. Brent asked.

"Yes, sir," they promised.

"Then we shall cancel the punishment this time. If it happens again—that's different."

"It won't happen again," they promised.

All of them, Tim and Henry and Tony, Rosa and Judy and Martha and little Carlotta, came up and sat

beside Eleanor on the old stone wall. Not one of them said anything until their fathers went away. Then Tim spoke.

"That was mainly my fault," he said.

"It was just as much mine," said Rosa.

"It was more my fault than any of yours," Eleanor said. "I could have stopped you, for I was umpire, and I didn't."

"You tried," said Tim.

"I did not really try," said Eleanor. "I was afraid you would think I was not truly one of you if I stopped you."

"But you are one of us," Rosa said.

"We were all partners in the game," said Judy. "You were a partner, Eleanor, just like the rest of us."

"A partner?" Eleanor smiled at them happily. "That is better than being an umpire."

"Of course it is," they told her.

"A partner, a partner with you," Eleanor said, as she looked at each one of the children. "That is what I have always wanted to be."

Partners and equals, citizens of the Free State of Maryland and of the United States of America, they sat together on the old stone wall as the sun began to go down beyond the trees of the orchard.

DISCUSSING THE STORY

In order to make sure that you understand this story, listen carefully while the following points are being discussed. Try to take a fair share in the discussion. Maybe it will be your question or answer that will help someone else.

1. In what ways did this group of children co-operate?
2. What did you like best about Eleanor?
3. Of what importance were the trees in this story?
4. Did the fathers of the children do their duty?
5. In what other ways could this story have ended?
6. Can you find a synonym, or a word which means the same, in the story for these words: *hurts, quietly, cross out?*
7. Perhaps you can suggest an antonym, or a word which means the opposite, for the words *opposite, punishment, hastened?*
8. Can you find the sentences which have the other word that will match these homonyms or words that sound alike but are spelled differently and have a different meaning: *there, threw, hour, one, hole.*
9. Each word below has more than one meaning. Use the glossary in this book and write sentences to show different meanings for each of these words: *score, stern, soil.*

A Comparison

Snow falls softly, but
Apple blossoms look like snow,
They're different, though.
Snow falls softly, but it brings
Noisy things;
Sleighs and bells, forts and fights,
Cozy nights.

But apple blossoms when they go,
White and slow,
Quiet all the orchard space,
Till the place
Hushed with falling sweetness seems
Filled with dreams.

JOHN FARRAR

Even people who knew very well
all that he did for his fellow men
would be likely to ask you,

Who Was Jonathan Chapman?

Jonathan Chapman was one of our nation's great citizens. He helped more people than anyone has counted. He helped thousands of Americans to get better farms, better homes, better ways of living.

Very few persons, even while he lived, knew that this helper was Jonathan Chapman. But they knew him very well by another name. Because of his way of helping other Americans they called him Johnny Appleseed, and Johnny Appleseed became a name in American history.

Jonathan was born near Boston a few weeks after Paul Revere had made his famous ride. He grew up in the way of most boys of that time and place. He listened to older men and women telling of their hopes and dreams for freedom. He marched along the roads with other boys. He made wooden guns and watched from behind stone walls for red-coated soldiers. He went through the woods, looking for signs of the enemy.

When he was eight years old the War for Independence ended. Other boys went about ordinary tasks, but Jonathan added to his farm chores a task of his own. Every hour he could spare he spent in the woods. He

138

made friends with the squirrels and the chipmunks. Birds ate from his hand. A gray wolf which he had rescued from a trap followed him tamely. He learned about wild berries and about plants from which medicine was made.

As he grew older, he gave more time to the little orchard on his family's farm. He was most interested in the apples. He had read about them in the Bible which he always carried.

Three books of the Bible mention apples, but the apples of the Bible were probably the fruit we call apricots. Jonathan did not know this. "Comfort me with apples," the Bible had said; and Jonathan Chapman began to give that comfort to his fellow men.

When he was a young man, he walked toward the Western frontier. He started an apple orchard near Pittsburgh on the great highway then crowded with settlers seeking homes in the West.

He had very little idea of the lands beyond the Ohio River, but he was sure that the settlers should have apple trees. He saved apple seeds to give them, putting them in little bags made of deerskin. When his own orchard could not give him all the seeds he needed for the passing settlers he walked many miles to a cider mill and searched through the pulp there to get more seeds.

Finally he realized that many settlers were taking other roads to the West. They too would be needing apple orchards, he thought, and so he set out, with a great bag slung on his back, to take seeds to people beyond the Ohio. People along nearly every road of the new settlements came to know him, as he tramped, winter and summer, with his sacks of apple seeds. "Johnny Appleseed," they called him, and counted him their friend.

Johnny Appleseed proved his friendship for the settlers in more ways than by giving them seeds for planting. He carried messages to them and for them. He did errands for the busy mothers of families. He taught boys about the trees and plants he knew so well. Once he saved the lives of hundreds of settlers.

The Shawnee Indians, who knew him well, made him a member of their tribe. They were usually friendly to the whites, but once, aroused by what they thought was an injustice, the Shawnees went on the warpath. Johnny Appleseed came to their camp on the night before the Indians were to attack the whites of the settlements. Alone, he ran over the roads and trails, warning men and women to prepare for the attack.

The danger was greater because the young nation was fighting another war with England, and the British were giving guns to the Indians. It was necessary to warn the American soldiers at an Ohio fort. Johnny Appleseed took on the task. For two days and two nights he ran through the woods and over the prairies, reaching the fort in time to give the warning. Then he went back to take care of wounded Indians.

Even though he helped in time of war, Johnny Appleseed was a man of peace. He never shot a wild creature. "God made them," he said, "and they have a right to live."

He never wanted anything but a little food and a few clothes to cover him, ragged breeches and a coffee-sack shirt. Sometimes he traded his apple seeds for breeches. A settler once gave him a pair of yellow and a pair of blue. Johnny cut them and sewed them so that he had two mixed pairs, half blue, half yellow. His only shelter was in the woods, although settlers often invited him to stay in their cabins.

141

Sometimes he used a horse or a canoe to travel, but most of the time he walked, carrying a hoe, a cooking pan, and his precious sack of seeds. For fifty years he tramped along the frontier and through the wilderness, helping all who needed his help.

As he grew old, he saw the growth of the country, a growth he had greatly helped. He saw wagon tracks become highways, cabins become brick houses, little clusters of saplings become great orchards.

He saw the children to whom he had brought toys become men and women. He heard their children and their grandchildren call him Johnny Appleseed, and he smiled at them as he had smiled at the children of the frontier. For strange, shabby old Jonathan Chapman was truly a friend to man, an American who helped the growth of his nation by his belief in using and spreading the gifts of God.

CHOOSING THE BEST SUMMARY

On page 143 you will find three summaries of the story you have just read. Read them carefully to decide which summary best tells the story in a few words. The following questions will help you to decide:

1. Does the summary include the important ideas?

2. Does the summary include too many minor details?

3. Does the summary include the major ideas that the author wanted you to remember?

Be able to tell exactly why you have selected the summary that you think the best one.

1. Johnny Appleseed was born in America. He loved trees and wanted to plant as many as possible in the western part of our country. Seeds of apple trees were given to other people to plant. Soon he had given away all the seeds he could spare. He never wanted to harm any living thing and was satisfied to live on the berries and apples he could find in the woods.

2. For over one hundred and fifty years people in our country have been honoring Jonathan Chapman. Besides doing ordinary farm chores, Johnny Appleseed spent much time in the woods, making friends with the animals and plants. He realized that he could help many people by giving them apples from his trees and seeds to start their own orchards. His friendship for the settlers and Indians was proven by the risks he took to protect them. He watched the people of this nation use the gifts of God to help their country grow.

3. Jonathan Chapman, who was called Johnny Appleseed by the American people, spent his life taking care of apple trees and being good to everyone. The pioneers, the Indians, and even the animals and plants were his friends. He never carried a gun. As he traveled through the western part of the country, he listened and talked to whomever he met so that in time he became a sort of living newspaper for the people in the wilderness. To everyone who came to him he gave a bag of apple seeds so that they too might grow orchards of this fruit that is mentioned in the Bible.

Roads Go Ever Ever On

Roads go ever ever on,
Over rock and under tree,
By caves where sun has never shone,
By streams that never find the sea;
Over snow by winter sown,
And through the merry flowers of June,
Over grass and over stone,
And under the mountains in the moon.

Roads go ever ever on
Under cloud and under star,
Yet feet that wandering have gone
Turn at last to home afar.
Eyes that fire and sword have seen,
And horror in the halls of stone,
Look at last on meadows green
And trees and hills they long have known.

J. R. R. Tolkien

Blue Ribbon at the Fair

I. *Off to the Fair*

Teresa awoke first. Nearly always she awoke before her twin sister and had to call Emma. As a rule she called her at once, for Teresa did nothing without Emma, just as Emma did nothing without Teresa. But today Teresa wanted to think for awhile, all by herself, of what they were going to do that day.

For this was the day of the Elkhorn Fair. The Elkhorn Fair!

Last year Teresa and Emma had been there. They had gone with their father and mother and with William and Elizabeth in the big car that they used only for special events and for Mass on Sundays and Holy Days. They had enjoyed every minute of that day in Elkhorn, but not as they were going to enjoy today!

Last year their father had shown many things at the fair. He had shown some of the finest dairy cattle in the county, the beautiful cows he raised on .their big dairy farm in this Wisconsin valley. His cattle always won prizes, blue ribbons and red ribbons, all bright with gold. Last year he had won a first prize. He had won other prizes, too, for the big yellow cheeses which he made in the cheese factory.

Their mother had won prizes, too, prizes for chocolate cakes and strawberry jam and sauerkraut.

William had been very happy because he won a prize for the young bull he had entered in the 4-H Club contest; and Elizabeth would have won a prize for the pickles she had made if she had not put a little too much spice in them.

That had been exciting—but this year, today, would be far more exciting, far more wonderful. For Teresa had something of her own to show. She had a calf entered in the 4-H club contest!

The 4-H Clubs are, everyone knows, the most important clubs in the United States for farm boys and farm girls. The government of the United States has said that these clubs are fine for making better farms, better citizens, and better communities. The clubs get their name from the four words beginning with the letter H—head, heart, hands, and health—which are in the pledge the members take. This is the pledge:

I pledge { my Head to clearer thinking,
my Heart to greater loyalty,
my Hands to larger service, and
my Health to better living, for
my Club, my Community, and my Country.

Every member wears a 4-H Club pin. It is a green pin that looks like a four-leaf clover. On each clover leaf is a white letter H.

The aim of the 4-H Clubs is "to make the best better." Every member tries to do that, and there are over two million members in the United States and Canada. It is an honor to be a member of a 4-H Club.

Was it any wonder that Teresa wanted to win a 4-H Club prize with Brownie?

Teresa remembered happily how her father had told her that the calf would be her own if she took care of him. Her brother had laughed and said that she was too little.

"The twins are small," her father had said, "but they can do as much as any girls of ten years."

Suddenly Teresa knew that she had gone as far without her twin as she wanted to go. "Emma!" she called. "This is the day of the fair. Let's dress fast!"

They dressed quickly. They put their feet into socks and shoes and put their arms into dresses as if they were going through exercises. They knelt down beside

147

each other and said their morning prayers, with their voices sounding so much alike that they were like one voice. They hurried downstairs. They blessed themselves at the same moment as they stood before the table. And together they started to say, "Mother, we—"

"One at a time," their mother laughed.

"We go to the Elkhorn Fair today," Teresa said.

"Teresa is going to enter Brownie in the contest," said Emma.

"Brownie will win a prize," said Teresa.

"Maybe second prize," said Emma.

"Maybe first," said Teresa.

"That will be fine," said their mother, "but finish your cereal. You will have to hurry to do all your chores before we leave. You must be ready in twenty minutes."

"We have only ourselves to get ready," said Teresa. "Brownie has gone in the truck."

"We'll meet Brownie again at the fair," said Emma.

With William and Elizabeth they rode on the back seat of the big car past wide fields where herds of fine cattle grazed. Sometimes they sang little German folk songs which their mother had learned when she had been a little girl in Germany. Sometimes they sang,

> My country, 'tis of thee,
> Sweet land of liberty,
> Of thee I sing.

Sometimes they counted birds on the fences or cried

148

out when they saw the crimson berries near the fence posts. Every once in a while they reminded William and Elizabeth that Teresa was going to win a prize with Brownie.

"Don't count your chickens before they're hatched," William warned them.

"Oh, I am sure to win some kind of prize," said Teresa.

"Even if it is only second," said Emma.

The town was happy and lively when they drove down the wide street with tall elm trees on each side. People in cars and people on foot were moving fast, all going toward the grounds on the other side of town where the fair was being held. People shouted and waved to one another. Teresa and Emma saw some children who went to the same school as they.

"We'll see you at the fair," the twins cried. "Our father is taking us all," they went on. "We are all in the contests."

"I didn't put too much spice in my pickles this time," said Elizabeth.

"I'm afraid the bull I am entering in the contest this year isn't as good as last year's," said William.

"The cake is good," said their mother, "but there may be too much sugar in it."

"If the cattle are as fine as they were last year, I'll be satisfied," said their father, "even if I don't win any prizes."

"Not-win-any-prizes?" said Teresa and Emma together.

"Not-win-any-prizes," he repeated. "Winning prizes isn't the most important thing in life, my children."

"But what is?" asked Teresa.

"Doing right, always doing right by other people. It is fine to try to be the best, but it is not fine to try to get ahead by hurting others.

"My grandfather taught me that," he went on as he turned the car toward the fairgrounds. "My grandfather was a good man and a great man, although only the people who lived here near him knew it and appreciated him.

"He came to this country nearly a hundred years ago with other men who wanted freedom they couldn't get in the old country, Germany. They found that freedom here, and they showed their thanks by doing everything they could for this, their new country.

"My grandfather taught me that the only way we can hold freedom is by doing good to all our neighbors; and because he was a good Catholic, he knew that every man was his neighbor."

"Did he ever win a prize?" asked Emma.

"The best prize of all," their father said, "the prize of having people call him a good man."

"I want to be good," said Teresa, "but I should like to have Brownie get a ribbon, too."

II. *The Best Prize*

In the fairgrounds flags were flying, and a band was playing. A merry-go-round and a ferris wheel were whirling round and round. Men and boys were selling sandwiches and lemonade and soda pop and ice cream. Everyone was smiling. Everyone was happy.

"Oh, this is grand, grand, grand!" shouted Teresa and Emma.

After he had parked the car, their father hurried off to the building where the farm machinery was being shown. William went off to the circle where the 4-H Club boys were meeting. Elizabeth joined a group of older girls. Teresa and Emma stayed with their mother at the booth where her cakes and jellies were being shown. They begged her to let them walk around the fair.

151

"But be careful," she warned them.

They walked, hand in hand, past the great cheeses which were piled high on the counters. They passed the tables which were covered with tall cakes of all kinds. They came to the booths where doughnuts were piled high like little mountains of brown rings, and they bought doughnuts. They passed the shining white counters where white-coated men and boys were selling cold drinks, and they each drank a bottle of soda pop, sipping it through straws.

"That was good," they said.

On the merry-go-round Teresa rode on a horse and Emma rode on a zebra. Then they rode together on the ferris wheel. It was a warm day, and the twins were hot and thirsty. They each drank a tall glass of ice-cold lemonade, and then they went back to their mother.

Their father came, after a little while, with William and Elizabeth, and they all went together to a big building where crowds of people were already having a midday dinner. Teresa and Emma were not very hungry, but they ate soup and ham and potatoes and green corn and blueberry pie with ice cream.

"The 4-H Clubs have the first shows this afternoon," their father told Teresa. "You will have to bring Brownie out of the stall and get him ready. Are you going to lead him in the parade?"

"Of course I am going to lead him," said Teresa.

Brownie's smooth coat was already shining when their father led him out from the stall; but Teresa brushed him and brushed him, until Brownie got tired of being brushed and began to pull away from her.

At last all the children who had animals to show took their places in the line that was waiting for the parade. There was one little girl with a lamb. There was a boy with a pig. There was a boy with a sheep. There was a girl with a sheep, too. Then came a half-dozen calves but not one of them was as well brushed, as shining of coat, as well behaved as was Brownie.

"You are sure to win the prize," Emma said to her sister.

There was a long, long wait in the big shed that led out to the show ring where the parade would take place. The sun grew hotter and hotter. After a while Teresa began to feel a little dizzy. So did Emma.

"I feel sick, Teresa," said Emma.

"We'll be out of here soon," said Teresa.

They weren't, though. Teresa stood holding the strap which led Brownie. The sun grew hotter, but the shed grew darker.

"Oh, Teresa," gasped Emma, "I'm terribly sick, and I feel faint."

"Oh, Emma, you can't be too sick," said Teresa. "I must lead Brownie out myself, or I can't have the prize. But I will not leave you."

"I can't help it," Emma said. "I'm too sick to go out." She stared at Teresa with tear-filled eyes. "You take him out, Teresa."

"Oh, Emma, I can't do that. I can't leave you alone when you are sick."

"Oh, Teresa, you must!"

"But if you're sick, Emma—"

"I can stay alone."

Just then a shrill whistle blew. "Everybody ready," a man called. "March!"

"I can't leave you when you are sick. I won't leave you," Teresa cried.

"But Brownie won't win unless you take him—oh, Teresa, go on!" begged Emma.

"I can't go! I won't go! Oh, Emma, don't faint!" she sobbed aloud as Emma fell against her.

Swiftly the parade of the pigs, the sheep, and the lambs moved out toward the show ring. Then the calves were led away. Beyond the door of the shed Teresa could see the crowd. Then she heard the cheering. Someone was winning the 4-H Club prize for the best calf in his class. Tears came into Teresa's eyes as she stared regretfully at Brownie. "You could have won," she murmured, "only—only I couldn't leave Emma when she felt so ill. She is my twin, you know."

A long time later, it seemed to her, their father found them. "Why didn't you march in the parade?" he asked Teresa.

"I was sick," said Emma, "and Teresa wouldn't go without me."

"What did you eat?" their father asked.

"Nothing much," said Emma, "except some cheese and—"

"A little cake and—"

"Some doughnuts and—"

"Some soda pop—"

"And lemonade once."

"And that dinner of ham and potatoes and corn and blueberry pie and ice cream?" He did not smile, but he added, "It is just as well, I think, that you haven't had cider and popcorn."

"I don't mind for myself," Teresa said, "that I did not win the prize, but Brownie—"

"Brownie will live through it." Their father stared thoughtfully from one girl to the other. "Well," he said slowly, "it is a difficult lesson for you, but, at that,

I'm proud of you. You certainly stick together, and
that is more important than any prize. That is loyalty."

"I wanted a prize," said Teresa.

"Everyone does," said her father, "but everyone
cannot win the prize. There is one thing, though, which
everyone can win."

"What is that?" Teresa and Emma asked together.

"He can win good citizenship. He can do that by
doing what you did today—staying with someone who
needed you—being loyal to someone."

"I'd have done the same for Teresa," said Emma.

"I'd do it all over again," said Teresa.

"I think that your great-grandfather would have
liked that," their father said. "That is what he would
have called good Christian spirit."

Answer these questions *Yes* or *No* to show your opinion. It will be a good idea to write the reasons for your answers on another sheet of paper.

Do you think

1. that Emma and Teresa were sorry that they were twins?
2. that the 4-H Clubs are worthwhile?
3. that the aim of the 4-H Clubs might be followed by everyone?
4. that the twins tried to be helpful to their parents?
5. that the fair was a dull place to go?
6. that their father was sure that he would win a prize?
7. that the grandfather's prize had any value?
8. that the girls were wise in eating a little of everything?
9. that Teresa should have left Emma to go with Brownie?
10. that it is all right to want to win a prize?

ON BEING THOUGHTFUL

This story told you how Emma and Teresa tried to help each other. Can you add other examples of their thoughtfulness to this list?

1. As a rule Teresa did nothing without Emma, just as Emma did nothing without Teresa.
2. They rode together on the ferris wheel.
3. "You are sure to win the prize," Emma said to her sister.

157

Cornstalks

Row after row the cornstalks stand
Across our wide and windy land.
They stand in solemn thought that they
Have heavy duties, day by day. ı
They stand in pride, with plumes unfurled,
Because they help to feed the world.

Each year they rise with hope newborn,
The heralds of the golden corn,
They lift their heads in morning sun,
And hold them high when day is done,
They stand in pride above the sod
Because they do the work of God.

Wheat Mills and Wheat Fields

In the heart of our country grow great fields of yellow grain, millions and millions of acres of golden riches for the use of man. Men plant these fields.

The sun and the winds and the rains come to ripen the seeds and make them grow for the harvest.

Men and machines cut the golden grain. They take it to the mills. The mills grind it into flour for our daily bread.

Our daily bread.

Every day we pray to God for it.

Through the wheat fields God answers our prayer.

The wheat fields used to be prairies. Indians lived on them. Buffaloes crossed them. As the settlements of the white man moved West, the buffaloes were killed and the Indians moved on to less settled country.

The white men made the prairies into farms. For many years each farmer grew just enough wheat for the use of his own family. There was no way to send it to distant cities for sale. When the grain was ripe, he cut it and took it in wagons to the mill. There the miller ground it, sometimes between two huge stones.

Then the railroads were built. Farmers grew more wheat, because now they could send it on the railroad to big mills in faraway cities. The mills made the wheat into flour and shipped that flour to all parts of the world.

Wheat has been grown in our land since the days of the first colonies. Mills were widely spread through the pioneer lands. The first power mill to grind wheat in what is now the United States was a windmill built in Cambridge, Massachusetts, in 1692.

The mills in the early settlements ground mostly for the farmers of their own neighborhoods, but after a while shippers began to send American flour out of the country. One of the men who sent flour from his own mill was George Washington. The flour he sent was so good that the sign "George Washington—Mount Vernon" on a barrel was proof of its fine quality.

George Washington was one of the men who discovered how to make his farm better. All his neighbors in Virginia grew tobacco, but he thought that this hurt the soil and so he grew other crops. He sent to England for a new kind of plow of which he had heard. He himself invented a new tool for planting wheat.

160

After Washington's time men used a tool they called a "cradle" for cutting down the wheat. All men who used these cradles said that the work was too hard. Then Cyrus McCormick, who, many years later than Washington, also lived on a Virginia farm, invented a grain-cutter. This cutter, called a reaper, made the greatest change in farming that has happened since men began to farm. For the reaper was a machine, made of knives and drawn by horses, which went up and down a field in a small part of the time it would have taken several men to cut the grain.

Since the McCormick reaper was invented, many important changes have been made in the way grain is harvested. The use of gasoline engines on farm machines has made harvesting much easier. A wonderful machine called a "combine" cuts and threshes the grain at the same time.

All the improvements used for the planting, the cutting, and the threshing of wheat have been used with corn and other grains. The American cereal industry has become one of the most important industries in the world.

BUILDING AN OUTLINE

See if you can complete the outline of this story given on page 162. The four main topics are shown by Roman numerals. Choose the subtopics which belong under each main topic.

Wheat Mills and Wheat Fields

I. Two reasons for growing more wheat

   A.

   B.

II. Making flour

   A.

   B.

III. Helps for cutting wheat

   A.

   B.

   C.

IV. Results of progress made

   A.

   B.

SUBTOPICS FOR THE OUTLINE

1. Same methods used with other grains
2. A "cradle" cut down the wheat
3. Building of railroads
4. Power mills such as a windmill
5. Mills made wheat into flour
6. George Washington's ideas
7. Reaper invented by Cyrus McCormick
8. Growth of American cereal industry
9. A "combine" cuts and threshes at the same time

Snow in the City

Snow is out of fashion
But it still comes down,
To whiten all the buildings
In our town;
To dull the noise of traffic:
To dim each glaring light
With star-shaped feathers
Of frosty white.
And not the tallest building
Halfway up the sky;
Or all the trains and busses,
And taxis scudding by;
And not a million people,
Not one of them at all,
Can do a thing about the snow
But let it fall!

RACHEL FIELD

163

They Worked and They Sang and They Prayed

I. *The Blizzard Comes*

The children were singing as the school bus rolled down the road through the snow-covered wheat fields. They were all singing, Ben and Tom and Lucy and all the other boys and girls on their way to St. Francis' School.

"Merrily we roll along, roll along, roll along," they sang.

"It is a good thing it is winter," Jim Strong, the bus driver, said. "You would frighten the birds if you sang like that when the windows were open."

"It would be all right to frighten the crows, wouldn't it?" Tom asked. "I don't like crows."

"I like meadowlarks," said Lucy. "I like violets. I like to see the wheat coming up in the springtime."

"I like summertime," Hilda said. "I like the strawberries we pick in the garden. I like to watch the men work in the fields."

"I like harvest time," said Tom. "I like to see the wheat grow golden. When the wind blows it looks like a golden sea. I like to watch the big combines go over the fields and get the grain ready for market."

"I like winter," said Ben. He scratched off some of the frost from the bus window. The snow outside was so thick that he could not see the fields beside the road. "I like snowstorms," he added.

"The weather report on the radio said there would be snow today," Tom told them.

"That will be grand," Ben said. "If the snow is deep enough, we can take the toboggan up on the hill behind our house."

"It will be deep enough," the bus driver said. "See the way it is coming down now. This is a real blizzard."

"Look at Lucy!" Tom cried. "Lucy is afraid of blizzards."

"I'm not afraid of blizzards, but my mother told me last night about a storm her mother saw once out here. I certainly wouldn't want to go through a storm like that. People froze on the roads. Cattle died in the fields. It was terrible." Lucy shivered as she remembered her mother's story.

"The pioneers had a dreadfully hard time," Hilda said.

"They worked hard," said Tom. "They came here when these wheat fields were nothing but prairies."

"Indians lived on them," said Lucy.

"Buffaloes crossed them," said Tom.

"The buffaloes were killed, and the Indians moved farther west," said Ben. "Then the pioneers plowed the prairies and planted wheat. Sometimes the wheat grew all right. Sometimes heat killed it. Sometimes grasshoppers came in clouds and ate the grain."

"What did the people do then?" Hilda asked.

"They kept on working and hoping," Lucy said, "and they sang."

"Sang?" Tom and Hilda and some of the other children cried.

"Yes, they sang. My mother says that when everything went wrong, her mother used to sing."

"What did she sing?"

"Oh, lots of songs," said Lucy. "There was one called 'Old Dan Tucker.' They sang hymns, too. My mother says she learned 'Mary, help us, help, we pray' when the grasshoppers swarmed like black, whirling clouds over the wheat."

"They prayed, too," said Ben. "My grandfather says that no one does very much unless he prays. He says the pioneers worked and sang and prayed."

"That is what has made United States a great country," said the bus driver. "You youngsters don't know how lucky you are to be living in a country like ours."

"Oh, yes, we do!" they shouted.

"Well, I'd like to see you prove it."

"We could if we had to," said Tom. He scratched off more frost from the bus window. The snow was not coming down so rapidly now, but the sky to the east was dreary black. "Maybe we can't get to school today," he remarked.

"Of course we will get to school," said Ben. "Don't frighten the girls."

"We are not afraid," all the girls cried, as a voice outside the bus called, "Need any help, Jim?"

"No, thank you," the driver said.

"Who is that?" Tom asked.

"Ed Clark," answered Jim. "He is carrying the mail today."

Ben moved nearer to the driver. "Why does Mr. Clark think you need help, Jim?"

"He saw me stuck back on the road," Jim said. He raised his voice. "We'll be all right, Ed, thanks!"

"So long!" the postman called.

"What would happen if you got stuck, Jim?" Ben inquired.

"I'd hate to think of it, Ben. This looks to me like a pretty bad snowstorm. If it keeps on like this, you youngsters will have to start for home at noon so that you can get home tonight."

" 'Jingle bells,' " Hilda began to sing, and the other children took up the melody. " 'Jingle bells, jingle bells, jingle all the way,' " they sang, until suddenly the bus stopped with a terrible jolt.

"What has happened, Jim?" Ben cried.

"We struck something on the road," Jim said.

"What is it? What is it?" they cried.

"I don't know. I'll see," Jim said calmly.

"Is it—somebody?" asked Hilda.

"No," Jim said. He stood up and moved to the door of the bus. "It's a drift. We'll see if we can get through it."

He got out on the road and tried to turn one of the big wheels. Suddenly he cried out in pain. "Will you help me, boys?" he asked.

"Sure, Jim," the boys cried. They all leaped off the bus, but Ben asked, "What's the matter, Jim?"

"I don't know yet, Ben," Jim said. "I hurt my

side, I think." Even in his pain he pulled himself up to the steering wheel only to find that it would not turn. "Something has gone wrong with the wheel. Oh!" He turned white and moaned painfully again.

"Won't the bus run, Jim?" asked Ben anxiously.

"I am afraid not. Oh!"

"He is hurt. Jim is hurt," Lucy said.

"It's just my side. I'll be all right." Jim's voice grew weaker, and he slipped down to the floor of the bus. "Don't be frightened," he told the children.

"What shall we do?" Lucy sobbed.

"He will be all right," Ben said. "Get some snow, and we'll rub his face. Do you feel better now, Jim?"

"A little," Jim said faintly. "Don't worry. But— one of you must go for help. I couldn't drive even if I could start the bus again."

"Where shall I go?" Ben asked.

"Go to Wilson's house," Jim told him. "It's the nearest—but it's three miles from here."

"I'll go," Ben said.

"Oh, you can't, Ben!" Lucy cried. "Look at the snow now! This is a blizzard, a terrible blizzard."

"Someone has to go," declared Ben.

"I'll go with you, Ben," offered Tom.

"No," Ben said, "you'd better stay here. You're the biggest boy, next to me. Take care of the others."

"We'll sing while you're gone," said Lucy.

"We'll pray, too," said Tom.

II. *The Answer to Prayer*

Ben heard the children singing as he started through the snowdrifts. He went off bravely; but he knew, even before he was out of sight of the school bus, that he was in danger.

The wind shrieked and howled as Ben faced the storm. The snow beat down on him. He stumbled into the frozen ruts of the road and had to climb out again. He fell against fences that were buried in the snow. His feet and his arms ached. His eyes hurt so badly that he could hardly see. The snow stung his face as if it were icy needles. Time and again he lost his way in the roaring blizzard.

All the time, as he struggled through the drifts, he thought of Jim and the children in the bus. He remembered that he had taken on a job. He told himself that he had to finish it and so he kept on.

Back in the bus the children kept wondering what had happened to Ben.

"Do you think he will get to Wilson's house?" Lucy asked.

"Sure, he will," said Tom. "Old Ben knows his directions, doesn't he?"

"Jim, do you feel any better?" Hilda asked the driver anxiously.

"Not much. I couldn't steer that wheel yet, even if there were nothing the matter with it."

"Could I drive it?" asked Tom.

"No one can drive it. It will take the workmen to repair it."

"What if Ben gets lost?" Hilda asked. "Shall we have to stay here all day and all night? Nobody will be coming out in a storm like this. Oh, dear!" She began to cry.

"Why don't you children sing?" Jim asked.

" 'Merrily we roll along,' " they started, but Lucy stopped them.

"I think it would be better," she said, "if we prayed."

The children began to say the Rosary.

They were praying as Ben struggled through the snowdrifts, trying to find his way to Wilson's. Sometimes he was far off the road, for the snow was high over the fences. He knew that his face was almost frozen. He couldn't see three feet in front of him. He struggled along in the way he thought he should go, but he couldn't be sure he was moving in the right direction. As he went, he too prayed.

" 'Our Father, Who art in Heaven, hallowed be Thy name.' Oh, God, please help me find Wilson's. 'Thy kingdom come, Thy will be done—' oh, dear God, please show me the way— 'on earth as it is in Heaven. Give us this day our daily bread—' and oh, please, God, let me get help for all of them— 'and forgive us our trespasses as we forgive those who trespass against us, and lead us not into temptation, but deliver us from evil—' and, oh, God, is this the way? 'Amen.' "

Then, suddenly, through the storm he saw the outlines of a house. Wilson's!

"Oh! Oh! Mr. Wilson! Mr. Wilson!" he called and fell against the door.

A man opened the door and looked down at him. "What's this?" he asked. "Why, Ben! What has happened?"

"The school bus," Ben gasped. "It's stuck, back on the road. Three miles!"

"You don't mean that you have walked those miles through this awful storm?" asked Mr. Wilson.

"Somebody had to come. Jim is hurt," explained Ben.

"Come in, come in!" the man said excitedly. "I'll take the truck. How many of you are out in that bus?"

"Fifteen—and Jim."

"I'll get them."

"I'll go with you. Will you take them on to school?"

"I'll take them directly home. The radio says that this is the worst blizzard in twenty years. You have saved the lives of all the people in the bus by coming out in it. You are a hero, Ben."

"Hero—nothing," Ben said. "I just did what anyone would do. What do you suppose they are doing now in the bus?" he asked, as the man started the truck through the drifts.

"We'll soon find out," Mr. Wilson said.

As they came up to the bus, they heard the sound of singing.

"Maybe they're singing, 'Merrily we roll along,'" Ben said.

They weren't.

The children were singing, "Mary, help us, help, we pray," as the truck came up beside the school bus.

"Climb in!" Mr. Wilson shouted to the children as he helped Jim climb to the high seat. "Everyone here?" he asked.

"Everyone!" the children shouted happily. For they were safe, and they were going home.

Number your paper from 1 to 10. Read each question, then write the word or phrase that completes the sentence correctly. When you have finished, check your work by rereading pages 164–173 of your book.

1. Where were the children going in the school bus?

    to church   to school   to a picnic

2. What time of the year was it?

        springtime   fall   winter

3. What kind of a storm did the bus driver say they were going to have?

        hail   blizzard   wind

4. Who were the people that had had a hard time?

    farmers   pioneers   hunters

5. What did the pioneers do when trouble came?

    worked   sang and prayed

      worked and sang and prayed

6. Who was Ed Clark?

    bus driver   mailman   policeman

7. What did the bus strike on the road?

      a drift   a rock   a person

8. Why did Jim call for help?

      he was afraid   he was in pain

        he wanted company

9. What did Ben do as he struggled through the storm?

      prayed   laughed   cried

10. Why did Mr. Wilson say that Ben was a hero?

  he wasn't afraid   he saved the lives of others

      he liked adventure

Daily Bread

The wheat grows high upon the fields
Where farmers work. They sow the seed,
And tend the grain, and reap the crop
Because they have the world to feed.

The miller turns the wheat to flour,
The baker works by day or night
To measure flour, and mix the dough,
And see that everything is right.

Now when I buy a loaf of bread
I see how people, far and near,
Have worked through days and worked through nights
To bring it to the grocer here.

This is the bread of every day,
The bread we eat to keep us living,
But there's a better Bread of Life,
The Holy Bread of Christ's own giving.
It is the Bread which is Himself,
Which makes us love and help each other.
Oh, God, make this, our Daily Bread
For me, my sister, and my brother!

V

The House by the River

"Everyone therefore who hears these my words and acts upon them, shall be likened to a wise man who built his house on rock. And the rain fell, and the floods came, and the winds blew and beat against that house, but it did not fall, because it was founded on rock. And everyone who hears these my words and does not act upon them, shall be likened to a foolish man who built his house on sand. And the rain fell, and the floods came, and the winds blew and beat against that house, and it fell, and was utterly ruined."

MATTHEW 7, 24–27

Father Marquette Looks Down the Mississippi

I saw you when the land was young.
    I knew you were a river great;
And so I named you after Her
    Who is the One Immaculate.
I asked the Queen of Heaven to bless
    Your shining path down to the sea,
I asked her aid for men who sought
    To make a new land strong and free.

I watch you now. The land is old.
    Great cities rise beside your stream,
But still I see within your course
    The ancient glory of my dream,
A nation lifting praise to God
    For all His gifts of liberty,
O Mary, Mother of the World,
    Keep this, your land, forever free!

MARY SYNON

There are few friendships greater
than that of a boy for a dog,
and particularly for a dog like

Biff

More than anything else in the world Charles wanted a dog. "Just any kind of a dog," he told his mother. "All the other boys at school have dogs. I don't see why I can't have one."

"It is because we live here on the mink farm," his mother explained.

"I should think a dog would help to protect the minks," Charles said.

"Your father says that the barking of a dog disturbs the young minks so much that it is a real danger," his mother reminded him.

"My dog wouldn't hurt them."

"The minks don't know that, Charles. And you know how hard it is to raise them. We can't risk any loss. Don't you see that?"

"Yes, I see that," Charles said, "but, just the same, I wish I had a dog."

All the way to school, as he went down the road with Sara and Dan and Jean, he kept telling them that any dog he owned could not possibly hurt the minks which his father raised for the fur market. Then, after awhile, he began to tell other people how much he wanted a dog. He told Sister Mary Camilla. He told Sister Mary Agnes, the principal of the little

179

wooden school which stood beside the great river. He told Mr. Benton, who owned the fox farm.

Mr. Benton said that his son had a dog he wanted to give away, but that Charles would have to promise that he would give the dog a home.

"I'm afraid I can't do that," Charles said.

That afternoon he went to see Old John, who had been a hunter and a trapper before there had been any fox or mink farms in the valley. Old John still went out in the woods to hunt and trap for the market.

Ever since Charles could walk, the old man had been his friend. He used to tell him stories of trappers and hunters and how they had helped to push forward the nation. Old John had a dog, a very old dog.

"Wouldn't you like a nice young dog in your house?" Charles asked him.

"For my own?" asked Old John.

"Well, not exactly. You could use him, though."

"I am satisfied with Cappy, my own dog," Old John said.

"Would you mind if I let my dog stay here?" asked Charles shyly.

"That is different," said Old John. "Why didn't you ask me that in the first place?"

The next afternoon, after school, Charles went up to Mr. Benton's and found the dog. He was a big, young dog, and Charles realized that he would have to give most of his spending money to Old John to pay

for the dog's food; but he was so glad to own the dog that he was willing to do that.

"We've got a fine dog," he told the old trapper.

"Not as good as Cappy, but he'll do. What are you going to call him?"

"I don't know yet."

"What do you think of Rover for a name?"

"I don't want him to be a rover and roam around. I think I'll call him Biff."

"Well, he is your dog," smiled the old man. "Call him what you want."

Biff grew and grew until he was the biggest dog in the village. When Charles's father saw him he told Old John that he felt he should pay more for what the dog ate than Charles was able to pay, but Old John said no. "It is a bargain between Charles and me," he said.

Biff used to wait for Charles every morning at the big tree on the road between the mink farm and the village. When he saw the children coming, he would jump around and bark for joy.

"It is a good thing he isn't up on the farm," Sara would say. "He would kill a mink with every bark."

"Biff wouldn't hurt anything," said Charles.

When they came out from school Biff was always waiting patiently by the gate. He would run along and romp with Charles. Sometimes they walked for miles along the riverbank. Charles would toss sticks into the stream, and Biff would bring them back to him.

"I am safe with Biff," he told his mother. He always took Biff back to Old John's before he started for home. "Good night, Biff," he would tell the dog, as he stroked the rough fur on Biff's head. "Be good until tomorrow."

One Saturday Charles went up the river with Biff. They had come near a deep place in the stream when Charles heard a cry. "Someone needs help," he told Biff. They ran along the bank until Charles saw a man struggling in the water just beyond a log which had fallen into the stream. "He is going to drown," Charles shouted. "We've got to help him!"

He crept out on the log. The man was not calling now, perhaps because he was weaker.

"I can't get out that far," Charles thought. Then he spoke to Biff. "You can do it," he told him. "You

182

can go out and bring him in. Bring him in to me as if he were a stick. Good Biff! Go to it, Biff!"

Biff leaped from the riverbank and swam out to the drowning man. He gripped his jacket in his strong teeth and started slowly back to the shore.

"Oh, God, please help Biff save him," Charles prayed. Once he thought both dog and man were going to be whirled down the swift stream, but Biff held steady and brought the man ashore. "Good Biff," said Charles. "Good Biff!"

Then he saw the man whom Biff had pulled up on the riverbank. He was Old John.

For a while he lay so very quiet that Charles was afraid he was not going to open his eyes again; but gradually he opened them. "I'll be all right," he said weakly, "thanks to you."

"Thanks to Biff," Charles said.

"Thanks to you both, and thanks to God. I don't know what happened to me. I must have had a cramp. I couldn't swim. I thought I was gone. Then you came."

"I wouldn't have been here," Charles said, "if it hadn't been for Biff, and I wouldn't have had Biff if you hadn't let me keep him at your house. So it is your own reward, Old John."

"Well," said the old man after he was completely dried out at home, "Biff can stay with me as long as you please, Charles."

183

"I think that will be all his lifetime, Old John, or as long as minks are afraid of dogs. Don't you think minks are rather silly, Old John?"

"Well, maybe if you were a mink you would be afraid of dogs, too."

"Perhaps I should."

"The same thing is true of people. You can't judge them until you know what they know and feel what they feel."

"What would you call that feeling?"

"I don't know its name," said the old man. "I know that it has been a good American idea since I was a boy. My father taught it to me, and his father taught it to him."

WHAT DO YOU WISH?

Pretending can be a great deal of fun if it is done in the right way. Perhaps you would enjoy making a wish in the form of a story. If you will write the answers to these questions carefully, you should be able to tell the story of your wish to the class.

1. Have you ever wanted very much something that you couldn't have? Was the reason you couldn't have it as important as the reason why Charles couldn't have a dog?

2. Old John helped Charles to realize his wish. Has anyone ever helped you to make a wish of yours come true?

3. Have you ever made a bargain with anyone? Did you keep your part of the bargain?

The Old Bridge[1]

The old bridge has a wrinkled face.
He bends his back
For us to go over.
He moans and weeps
But we do not hear.
Sorrow stands in his face
For the heavy weight and worry
Of people passing.
The trees drop their leaves into the water;
The sky nods to him.
The leaves float down like small ships
On the blue surface
Which is the sky.
He is not always sad:
He smiles to see the ships go down
And the little children
Playing on the river banks.

HILDA CONKLING

[1]Reprinted by permission of the publisher, J. B. Lippincott Company, from *Silverhorn*, by Hilda Conkling. Copyright, 1924, by J. B. Lippincott Company.

Our American people have built
many great churches, but none of them
worked with finer faith than the people of
the cabin country who built the

Church in the Cotton Fields

Winfield is ten years old. He lives in a cabin on a cotton plantation just north of the land at the mouth of the Mississippi River. That land is called the river delta.

When Winfield was four years old the Mississippi, rushing and tumbling and leaping in spring flood, swept over the land that his father had just plowed and planted with cotton seed.

Winfield fled in fear. So did his father and mother and his sisters, Rose and Annie, and his brother Terry.

When the waters of the river slipped back within their banks, his family came back to the cabin. His mother cried when she saw the mud left by the flood, but his father hitched the mule before the old plow and started out again to plant more cotton seed. That year they lived on salted meat and coffee and bread and fish.

Two years later came the dry season. From too much water they were cut down to no water at all. The tender cotton plants dried out in that long, hot summer. The cotton blossoms died. The children went without shoes that year.

When Winfield was eight years old, little white

186

worms ate into the cotton crop. They dug into the stalks and into the husks and into the seeds of the plants that had been so straight and so strong.

That was the year when Winfield's father lost the little plantation. He had borrowed money from the store to pay for tools and for seed and for food. When the crop failed, the store asked him for money. He had none. With his shoulders stooped from worry and his head bent low with trouble, Winfield's father hitched the mule to the old cart and drove to a town ten miles away. He sold the farm to pay his debts.

They stayed on in the shabby little cabin. Winfield's father received tools and seeds and supplies from the new owner of the land in exchange for his work. He had little pay. That year again they lived on salted meat and bread and fish. They had no coffee.

That was the year when Father John came to the river delta. Winfield will never forget the morning when he first saw Father John.

It was almost the end of the season, and the boy was picking cotton in the field near the river road, dragging his sack after him, when an old black car drew up at the fence rail. Winfield pulled off his wide-brimmed straw hat and stared silently at the man who was getting out of the car to speak to him.

Father John leaned against the fence rail and questioned the bashful boy. He asked him about his father and his mother, and about all the boys and girls who

lived along the river. He wanted to know if any of them had been baptized. He asked if they had enough to eat and enough to wear.

Winfield stood first on one bare foot and then on the other, but he answered the young priest. He heard Father John sigh. He saw the sorrow in Father John's eyes as he told the stories of the cabins along the river. Even before Father John rode away with a promise to return, Winfield knew that he had found a friend.

There was no Catholic church in the community. There never had been one along that stretch of river road. "We will build one," Father John had told the boy. "We will build a church and a school. They will belong to all the people."

So, helped by the priest's holiness and friendly kindness, the people of the delta built the church.

Winfield's father led the other men to the best lumber in the swamps, and there they cut down the trees. They hauled them to a sawmill, where the trunks were cut into boards. They carried them back again, up the road past Winfield's cabin, to the high ground chosen by Father John for the church.

They never stopped to think, as they labored for the young priest, that not one of them was a Catholic. But Father John knew, as he labored beside them, that he was working for their souls.

"Some day you will all be Catholics here," he told Winfield. "Saint Isidore will help me to lead the way."

Then he told the boy about Saint Isidore the Plowman. The boy, his eyes wide with wonder, listened to the story of the farmer who had lived many hundred years ago.

Winfield told his brother Terry about Saint Isidore and his feast day. He told Rose and Annie. He told his mother. He told his father.

"Saint Isidore lived a long time ago in the far country of Spain," Winfield told them. "He was a poor farmer like our own father, and he worked in the fields. He was so good that all the great people of the city looked up to him.

"He helped everyone. He took care of the poor and the sick. He was kind to orphan children, and he

189

shared with them the little he had. He taught them how to plant and plow and reap.

"He did so much work that people said that angels helped him when he plowed. He was a poor farmer, but when he died, the people of Spain were sad. For days and nights thousands of men and women and children came to see him for the last time. They said, 'Isidore was a saint.' The Catholic church called him a saint, and so he has been Saint Isidore to all the whole wide world."

"When is the feast day of Saint Isidore?" asked Winfield's father.

"Father John says that it comes in March," Winfield told him.

His father made a promise. "The church will be finished on that day," he said.

Everybody worked. Winfield's father and the other men from the river plantations sang as they hammered and sawed wood and drove in nails to build the church. Winfield's mother and all the other women from the cabins painted and varnished the floors and the benches. Winfield and his brother Terry and even Rose and Annie carried great pails of water.

They worked by day and by night. On the evening before the feast day of the saint of Spain, the golden cross was set in place on the steeple of the church in the cabin country. The church was finished. Winfield told again the story of Saint Isidore.

Before the sun was in the sky on Sunday morning, Winfield was on his way to the first Mass in the new church. Beside him walked his father and mother and Rose and Annie and Terry. After him, on horseback, on muleback, in wagons, and in old cars, came their neighbors and friends.

They heard the new bell.

They entered the church they had built, the church which was their own.

They stood silently, or knelt clumsily, as Father John read the service of the Sacrifice of the Mass.

Then, in the gold and white of his vestments, he turned to speak to them. He thanked them for their help. He told them of his desire to serve them. His voice was deep and low as he went on. He knew their problems, he said. He had been a boy on a farm, and so he could speak of crops and failures. Then he told them of the joys of farm life, the look of the wide sky, the songs of the birds, the friendliness of animals, the kindness of neighbors.

He held out to them, as their eyes turned toward the little pulpit, a hope of escape from the long discouragements. He told them of ways to control the little white worms and to fight failure and waste.

He told them of the school he would build for the children, and he told them of his hopes and his dreams.

Then, with tears in his eyes, he told them about faith and about God. He told them of God's love for

them, of their place as brothers under God the Father. Men would one day understand that, and everyone would be better and happier.

He began to pray.

Their voices, not yet familiar with the words, were slow to repeat them. "Our Father, Who art in Heaven, hallowed be Thy Name," he said.

"Our Father, Who art in Heaven," they answered him.

As he finished the age-old prayer he stood on the steps that led toward the rough stone altar and blessed them. "May God bless you," he said.

A light, brighter than sunrise over the Mississippi, shone in the eyes of Winfield, and of his father and his mother, and of Rose and Annie, and of his brother Terry.

"Amen," they said.

Sometimes we can get a better understanding of a story when we have a clear picture in our minds as to just when or about what time a certain event took place. Read the following sentences carefully. Copy them on your paper. If the happening has completely passed, write the word *Then* after it. If the event is still taking place or can still take place, write the word *Now* after it.

1. When Winfield was four years old he was frightened when the Mississippi overflowed.

2. The Mississippi often overflows.

3. A dry season often follows a wet season.

4. Father John came to the river delta.

5. Winfield was picking cotton when he first saw Father John.

6. Father John said that he would be helped by Saint Isidore.

7. Winfield's father was unsuccessful on his plantation.

8. Stories of God's love are told to the people.

9. People learn new ways to fight discouragements, failure, and waste.

10. Their voices were not yet familiar with the words of the Our Father.

11. The feast day of Saint Isidore is March 22.

12. Some of the joys of farm life are the friendliness of animals and the kindness of neighbors.

13. It was the end of the season when Father John first went to the river delta.

Church Lets Out

Sweet and low sounds the organ,
Faintly through open church portals
Like some heavenly music,
Escaping through protecting clouds,
The divine moment lingering
Between earth and heaven—
All this impressed on rugged faces—
Friendship in their roughened grip,
Love in their tired eyes,
A firmness in their walk,
As church lets out.

JEANNETTE V. MILLER

boy who had been born a slave
d a great service for all
mericans when he became

The Peanut Doctor

What do you do with peanuts?

Eat them, of course.

But what else is done with them?

Peanuts are used in making many foods: peanut butter, salad oil, meal, bread, coffee, soft drinks, peanut milk, and cheese. They are used in making many other products which we find in our homes.

Nearly all these uses were found by one man, George Washington Carver. In all, this great scientist found over three hundred uses for the peanut.

George was the son of slaves. His mother worked for a man named Carver, while his father worked on a plantation far away. One night his mother and little George were stolen by raiders. Their owner, Moses Carver, sent out a search for them, but only the baby was found. Moses paid the finder with a race horse which he valued at three hundred dollars.

The baby grew up in the Carver home, loved by both Moses and Sue Carver. He helped them both, Moses in the fields and Sue in the house. They taught him all they knew, and he taught himself far more. He could make sick plants healthy. He learned how to carve wood. He was, the neighbors said, the brightest boy in the Missouri country where they lived, but he was not satisfied with what he could do. "I want to go to school," he told Aunt Sue.

The Carvers let him go, telling him to come home whenever he wished. He set out alone, a very small Negro boy of ten years. He walked all day to the nearest town. The school was closed when he reached it.

He found a place to sleep in a nearby barn. In the morning Aunt Maria, a kindly Negro woman, found him. She gave him breakfast, sent him off to school, and told him to come back to her for his dinner.

Aunt Maria taught the lad how to wash and iron clothes. "You're going places," she told him, "going far." She changed his name from Carver's George to George Carver. They read the Bible together, and they prayed together. She wept when he told her that he wanted to go to school in another town, but she told him to go.

George Carver worked his way through the new school by washing and cooking for people in the town. He made himself ready for another school, but when he reached there the principal told him that the school was for Indians, not Negroes.

He finally reached a little Iowa college. He had only ten cents when he came to the town, but he was ready and willing to work. He found an old shack in which no one was living and started a laundry. A friendly merchant let him have a washtub, soap, an iron, and an ironing board. George promised to pay for these things as soon as he earned the money.

When he had saved a little money, he entered the art school. His art teacher, seeing his great love for growing things, advised him to study plant life. It is fortunate for the world that George followed that advice.

At about this time he read of the work which another man of his race, Booker T. Washington, was trying to do at a school in Alabama. When Washington wrote, asking George Carver to come and teach at his school, Carver believed that his work was to be for his own people. He did not then know that, by that work, he would be helping all the world.

In Alabama George Carver became interested in the peanut. He was in cotton country, and he saw the difficulties which men had with that crop. The whole South depended on the cotton crop. When it failed, all the people, white and black, suffered. The young scientist tried to find a way to help them.

First of all, he showed people near the school how to plant and care for other crops. He showed them how to raise nearly all the food they should eat. This was good, but it was not enough. Then he realized that the climate and soil were just right for growing peanuts. He showed farmers how to raise bigger and better peanut crops; but after they raised them, they could not sell them. No one wanted so many peanuts.

Another man might have become discouraged and given up. George Washington Carver—he had added the Washington because he admired Booker T. Washington so greatly—set out to find other ways in which the peanut could be used. He worked day and night in "God's Little Workshop," as he called the room where he carried on his studies. He tried first one thing and then another. From this work he discovered the many uses of the peanut.

His work changed the South to a place of many more opportunities for the workers. The change helped the Negro workers, but it also helped the whole community. It helped, too, the nation, and in time, the entire world. Today we have many products we might not have had, had it not been for the work of this

Negro scientist. There are today a thousand uses for the peanut, all of them helpful to man.

Doctor Carver studied other plants. He made wallboard from banana stems and nut shells. He turned cotton stalks into paper. From the stems of a vegetable he made rugs and ropes. He made more than a hundred products from the sweet potato. When people asked him how he could do so much, he would say that he was only an instrument in the hands of God.

George Washington Carver refused great sums of money from companies which wished him to leave his college and work for them. Honors piled upon honors for him, from England as well as from the United States. Through it all he remained the simple man who had run a laundry in an Iowa town to pay for his education. For George Washington Carver not only did great deeds, he was also a great man.

It is important to read words accurately. A single word can change the meaning of a sentence or paragraph. In each of the following sentences there is one word that is not true.

Number your paper from 1 to 10 and divide it into two columns as shown in the sample. Read each sentence carefully. Then write the word that is wrong on the first line in the first column and write the correct word on the first line in the second column.

Sample

Wrong Word   *Correct Word*

1. _ _ _ _ _ _ _ _ _ _ _ _   _ _ _ _ _ _ _ _ _ _ _ _

2. _ _ _ _ _ _ _ _ _ _ _ _   _ _ _ _ _ _ _ _ _ _ _ _

1. Peanuts are used for making few products.
2. George Carver became a great artist.
3. He earned his way by making clothes.
4. George was the owner of slaves.
5. He was the laziest boy in the Missouri country.
6. Aunt Maria and George read the paper together.
7. He had ten dollars when he came to the town.
8. His music teacher advised him to study plant life.
9. When George Carver went to Alabama the whole South depended on the peanut.
10. There are today about a dozen uses for the peanut.

Sight

I see skies more bright and blue
Than any skies beheld by you,
I see trees so tall and high
Their green leaves brush against the sky,
I see birds (and hear them sing)
Like rainbows that have taken wing;
I see flowers fairer far
Than any in your garden are,
These lovely sights you'll never find,
Because—my dear, you *see*; I'm *blind*.

CORA BELL MOTEN

Would you like a boat ride?
Then come with two children
of Louisiana when they go for

A Paddle in a Pirogue

I. *Jean Finds the Way*

The Mississippi River runs into the Gulf of Mexico in one great stream and a hundred little streams. The little streams wander through the flat fields and swamps of Louisiana. The people, because they are the children of French settlers, call these streams bayous.

Jean lives in this country of the bayous. Not a day passes that Jean does not ride in a boat. Sometimes he rides in a flat-bottomed boat with his father, who stands tall and straight even as he paddles. More often Jean paddles his own boat. This has been carved from a tree and looks like a canoe. In the country of the bayous these small boats are called pirogues.

Jean, who is twelve years old, has paddled his pirogue for a long time. In the bayous everyone knows how to paddle a pirogue.

When Jean and his sister Madeleine go to bed, they hear the sound of owls in the dark forest. The noises of the night are louder than the voices of the children as they talk before they go to sleep.

One morning, before Jean was awake, Madeleine heard a noise on the bayou. She dressed quickly and ran to the door, but her mother was there before her.

202

"What is it?" she called to a man who stepped from a boat at the little wooden wharf.

"I am the druggist in the town above you," he said.

"Oh, yes, sir," said Jean's mother. "Can I do something for you?"

"The doctor telephoned me to take medicine to your sister, but—"

"Aunt Pauline?" Madeleine cried.

"Is she ill?" her mother asked the druggist anxiously.

"Not seriously, but I cannot go all the way," the druggist replied. "Will you take it to her?" he asked Madeleine's mother.

"I shall see that she gets it," promised the woman.

The druggist went back to his boat, and her mother turned to Madeleine. "I cannot leave the baby," she said. "You and Jean must take this medicine to Aunt Pauline."

"It is far," said Madeleine.

"God will help you," said her mother. "I shall call Jean now. You can start as soon as I give you breakfast. You will enjoy the trip."

As Jean picked up his paddle, the movement of the boat made little waves in the water. They lapped against the green shore. Here and there the children saw living things in the water below. They saw the silver fin of a fish as it flashed before them. They heard the splash of a frog that had jumped from a root into the water. Madeleine thought she heard a deeper splash.

"An alligator, Jean! I saw his eyes! He was looking at me!" she cried, delighted that such a thing could happen so early on the trip.

"No, no, Madeleine!" Jean tried to quiet her.

"Yes, yes!" She was sure. "I saw the water. I saw the alligator move!"

Jean did not even glance into the deep waters. "Alligators never come so near the village," he said. "Sometimes they are seen beyond the turn, but never here."

"You know everything about the bayous," Madeleine admitted a bit sadly.

"I know where the loveliest flowers grow," Jean boasted. "I'll show you." They moved forward, and Jean held the pirogue close to the shore. "See, Madeleine! There they are!"

Morning-glories covered the banks. Some of them —blue and pink and lavender—proudly lifted their bright heads toward the wide blue of the sky. Some of them—yellow and white and violet—bent low to touch the dark water of the bayou.

"I'd like to reach out and pick a pink one," Madeleine sighed, as she saw their beauty.

"You would upset the boat," Jean warned her.

Beyond the flowers there was a little settlement. Houses, a store, a school, and a church were built on strong posts that held them high above the marshy ground, so that floodwater could not sweep over them when the bayous flowed over the banks. Wind and weather had beaten against the unpainted sides of the buildings and now, soft gray and green, they looked as if they had grown in the woods like the morning-glories.

"There is Suzanne!" said Madeleine.

Suzanne turned at their call. She was decorating the shrine that rested under its glass case in front of the high house. The flowers in her hand made a bright picture against the gray-green of the house.

"Where are you going?" she called.

"To Aunt Pauline's," the children answered her.

The pirogue moved on. They passed the little gray church with its steeple and cross lifted high above the village. Long ago the church had been built by people who had been driven from their homes in Canada and who had come to Louisiana. They had built new homes in the new country. Through the years, even when a visit from a priest came but once or twice in many months, the people kept the Faith and passed it on to their children.

They passed the store. "There's Martin. He's my best friend." Jean shouted at him.

The boy looked up at the call. He set down the boxes he was carrying from his father's store and rushed toward the pirogue. "Good morning, Jean! Good morning, Madeleine! Will you come in?" he asked.

"Not this time, Martin," they told him. "We are hurrying to Aunt Pauline's. She is ill."

They reached the place where the bayou divides into many streams. Jean hesitated for a moment.

Madeleine had once heard of someone who had been lost in the bayous. "Jean, where are you going? This is not the right way. We shall be lost." She was close to tears. "It is dark here."

It was dark. Gray Spanish moss, hanging from the trees, drooped low in the water and made the bayou dark. Cranes, birds with long bills and longer legs, flew across the thick clouds of moss or stood silently in the still, black water.

"This is the right way," said Jean, but his voice was small and full of fear.

"There is not a boat in sight," Madeleine sobbed, as she burst into tears.

"I have been here many times. People born in the bayous do not get lost," said Jean bravely.

Only Madeleine's tears answered him as they moved on through darker stretches.

"Can't we turn back?" Madeleine begged.

At that instant Jean had caught sight of a speck of light through the trees. "We are on the right stream," he said. "I knew we were safe."

II. A Happy Day

Jean and Madeleine came out of the bayou into a great open space where the water ran over flat land. The sun shone again.

"Are we nearly at Aunt Pauline's?" asked Madeleine.

"We are almost there," said Jean.

Through low branches of the trees Madeleine caught sight of something white. "It is Aunt Pauline's sunbonnet!" she cried.

The woman on the bank saw them. Even before Jean could fasten the boat to the landing, she was down to meet them. "Jean! Madeleine!" she greeted them.

"We thought you were ill," said Madeleine. "We have brought your medicine."

"Thank you," said Aunt Pauline. "I am already better. Now I know I shall soon be well."

They followed Aunt Pauline in her starched cotton dress with its collar of homemade lace. Through the garden, with its little shrine of Aunt Pauline's favorite saint, they passed, dancing happily beside the aunt they loved.

"It is good to be here," said Madeleine.

"I am happy you have come," said Aunt Pauline.

They followed her into the kitchen. The floor was as white and as clean as the fresh curtains that blew in the soft southern breeze of the morning.

"I smell something good," said Jean, his dark eyes sparkling.

"So do I," Madeleine clapped her hands.

They knew what Aunt Pauline had made. Fruit tarts! They moved closer to the table. There were the tarts, golden-brown and filled with fresh, sweetened berries. Aunt Pauline lifted the tray.

"Thank you! Thank you!" The children reached out and took the tarts.

"There is milk for you, too," said Aunt Pauline, hurrying around the kitchen. She poured out two great glasses of milk, rich with yellow cream.

The happy day went on. In the late afternoon Jean and Madeleine left Aunt Pauline.

"We must be through that awful swamp before dark," said Madeleine, remembering its dangers.

Aunt Pauline came down to the pirogue with them. She gave them a roll of fresh butter for their mother. Jean and Madeleine were delighted, for they loved nothing better than to bring a surprise for her. They kissed Aunt Pauline.

"Thank you for a lovely day," they said in farewell.

Jean paddled the little boat down the canal, and then they passed into the dark bayou. They were no longer afraid, because now they knew the way. They came again to Suzanne's village, but neither Suzanne nor Martin was in sight. As they floated along, they talked of many things.

"Will you work in the bayous when you grow up?" Madeleine asked Jean.

He smiled a little. "Of course," he said. "I shall be an engineer and have the biggest power pump of all. Then the best rice in all Louisiana will grow on my land."

They passed a number of blue and white water lilies. "Stop a moment, Jean," begged Madeleine. "I must gather these for Our Lady's shrine in front of our house."

"You never forget Our Lady, Madeleine," said Jean.

"She never forgets me," said Madeleine.

As the afternoon shadows grew long, they came to the bayou that flowed through their own village. They were nearly home. Quiet hung over the dark water until they turned into the last mile. Then the bells rang out in the distance. Church bells! The Angelus!

Jean stopped paddling, and the children blessed themselves. *Ave Maria!* Hail Mary! they prayed to Our Lady and to Her Divine Son.

The bells stopped. As Jean paddled the pirogue, Madeleine sang softly. At last they came to their own landing, home to their father and mother, home once more in a country where Our Lord lives in the heart of the quiet villages and in the hearts of His faithful people.

In this story there are many pictures made with words. How many word pictures can you find? Perhaps you may be able to make some illustrations of this story in your art period.

Here are some word pictures taken from the story you have just read.

1. Sometimes he rides in a flat-bottomed boat with his father, who stands tall and straight even as he paddles.

Can you see Jean's father? Is he dark or fair? What color are his clothes? How does the boat look? Where is Jean sitting?

2. Suzanne was decorating the shrine that rested under its glass case in front of the high house.

Can you see this picture? What material is the house made of? wood? brick? stone? What color is Suzanne's dress? What is she using to decorate the shrine? Do you see any trees or bayous in this picture?

See how many word pictures you can find in this story. Copy them correctly from the story. How else could you say each word picture? Try to put each sentence into your own words. Can you make as vivid a picture as the author? Can you find ten pictures in this story?

Child's Evening Hymn

Now the day is over,
Night is drawing nigh,
Shadows of the evening
Steal across the sky.

Now the darkness gathers,
Stars begin to peep.
Birds, and beasts, and flowers
Soon will be asleep.

Jesus, give the weary
Calm and sweet repose;
With Thy tend'rest blessing
May mine eyelids close.

Through the long night watches
May Thine angels spread
Their white wings above me,
Watching round my bed.

When the morning wakens,
Then may I arise,
Pure and fresh and sinless
In Thy holy eyes.

S. BARING-GOULD

Sugar Beets and Sugar Cane

Every American is said to eat every year as many pounds of sugar as he weighs. How many pounds of sugar do you eat in a year? Perhaps you eat much more than that, if you like candy. Too much sugar is, of course, bad for both young and old, but the right amount supplies the body with a much-needed food.

Americans eat more sugar than any other people in the world, but the use of sugar is much older than our nation.

Even before America was discovered the people of Europe were bringing sugar overland from Asia by caravan. This journey took many months. The trade in sugar and spices was so great that Columbus was looking for a way by water to help carry the bags and barrels from the East.

For a long time nearly all sugar came from sugar cane. Then a man from France and a man from Germany found ways to make sugar from beets.

The first American cane sugar was made in Louisiana before our War for Independence. The first American beet sugar was made about a hundred years later. In the United States the making of both cane and beet sugar is a great industry.

Most of the sugar cane for American use is grown in Louisiana, Florida, the islands of Hawaii, and in islands where the climate is warm. Most of the beets used for sugar are grown in California, the Rocky Mountain states, and other states, even as far east as Ohio.

In sugar factories the sugar syrup, which is taken from either cane or beets, is whirled around at very high speed in machines which throw off the liquid and leave the sugar.

You know sugar best as a sweetener of food and of drink, but there are many other uses for it. It is used not only for sweetening chewing gum, ice cream, and candy, but it is also used in making tobacco, soap, and many other products.

There was a time when sugar was so scarce and the price so high that only the very rich could afford to buy it. Today the price is much cheaper and nearly everyone can buy it, certainly everyone in the United States.

The use by man of the sugar beet and the sugar cane as a source of a much-needed food is another example of God's care for His children. He has given to His children the ability to discover, to improve, and to use the gifts of His goodness.

CAN YOU COMPLETE THIS IDEA LINE?

In the idea line below you are given some major ideas and some minor ideas. Can you supply those that are missing? Copy this idea line on your paper. You may use your book as you fill in the blank spaces.

Look at the idea line. If you can answer these questions, it will help you to fill in the blank spaces.

1. From what two sources do we get sugar?
2. In what countries or states is sugar cane grown?
3. From what product are the articles listed in the third column made?
4. What three abilities has man made use of with the gift of sugar?

Kinds of Sugar	Where Our Sugar Comes From	- - - - - - - - - -	Abilities Given by God
1. _ _ _ _ _ _ _ _	1. _ _ _ _ _ _ _ _ _ _	1. Sweetener	1. _ _ _ _ _ _ _ _
2. _ _ _ _ _ _ _ _	2. _ _ _ _ _ _ _ _ _ _	2. Chewing	2. _ _ _ _ _ _ _ _
	3. _ _ _ _ _ _ _ _ _ _	gum	3. _ _ _ _ _ _ _ _
	4. _ _ _ _ _ _ _ _ _ _	3. Ice cream	
	5. _ _ _ _ _ _ _ _ _ _	4. Candy	
	6. _ _ _ _ _ _ _ _ _ _	5. Tobacco	
		6. Soap	

The Cathedral of St. Louis

I know I shall remember
When it is time to die
Those towers, that cross, at evening
Against the mellow sky.

And life shall leave me lightly
(I shall not know nor care)
Like a chime of bell notes drifting
Across the shadowed square.

CARL CARMER

When a lonely boy finds a friend
—or maybe two friends—he may
learn a great deal about his
home town and have a

Happy Saturday

I. A Lonely Boy Finds a Friend

Louis Adams had nothing to do that Saturday morning. He came out of the old house into the brightness of the New Orleans sunshine and moved lazily across Jackson Square.

He liked the Square, for he had the pride in it of a boy whose people had long lived near it. He waved to the statue of General Jackson that seemed ready to ride, day or night, against any enemy of our country. He threw peanuts to the pigeons that flew around the statue and watched the tourists who were already taking pictures of the old cathedral.

Once he saw two boys together and moved toward them; but when he came near them, he saw that he did not know them. "I wish," he thought, "that I did not go to school away off on the other side of town. If I went to school here in the neighborhood, maybe I'd know a boy who lives near me. We could have fun."

He did not know how to say it, but he was lonely. An only child, he often felt apart from other children. He had no brother. He had no cousin in the city, although he had many out of town; for his mother, who

217

was one of an old French family of Louisiana, had many sisters and brothers on plantations along the river. He had no playmates away from school; and this was Saturday, and school was miles away.

The wind from the Gulf of Mexico was blowing across the Square. It blew through dark green leaves, and tossed pink blossoms, and bent the high branches of the palm trees. It snatched the little red cap that Louis wore and tossed it around the statue of General Jackson. Louis ran after it, caught it, and pushed it down hard on his head. "I beat you that time, Mr. Wind," he told the breeze from the Gulf.

He heard someone laugh. One of the tourists, he thought, had seen his chase. He turned around to laugh with him. That was when he saw the boy with the monkey.

The boy was about his own age, but they did not look like each other. Louis was thin and fair with quiet blue eyes. The other boy was stout and dark with black eyes that flashed fire. Louis, even on Saturday morning, was well dressed. The other boy wore no jacket. His trousers were old, his shirt was not clean, and his dirty sneakers were ragged.

"I could not play with him," Louis thought. Then the boy smiled, and Louis walked near to him.

"Is that your monkey?" he asked.

"Sure," said the boy.

"What do you call him?"

218

"Beppo."

"Have you had him long?"

"My father brought him to me two years ago from South America. He works on a banana boat."

"I know the banana boats," Louis said. He did not say that his father owned the Adams Line of banana boats that brought back the great bunches of fruit from countries to the south.

"My father gets home today," the boy said. "The banana boat gets in soon."

"I know," Louis said. His father had said this morning that the *Francis Adams*, one of the big boats of the fleet, was due.

A little group of tourists closed in around them. The boy slid the monkey from his shoulder. The monkey began to dance, then ran up the leg and arm of one of the tourists. The man laughed, but a woman screamed.

219

"Beppo!" his owner called, and the monkey ran back to him.

"What's your name?" Louis asked him.

"Angelo. What's yours?"

Louis told him. Angelo started away from the Square.

"Do you mind if I go with you?" Louis asked.

"Come on," said Angelo. The monkey ran ahead of them toward the French market, near the Square.

There was a crowd at the market. Women in sunbonnets sold chickens and hams. Fishermen sold shrimps and oysters. Women in big aprons sold long loaves of hot bread which held fried oysters, a food which, for no reason that anyone knew, they called the peacemaker. Other women sold popcorn balls and pralines. And there were great piles of fruit—oranges, apples, bananas, pineapples.

Suddenly Beppo snatched a banana from a bunch. "Here, Beppo, Beppo!" Angelo shouted.

"Beppo, Beppo!" Louis echoed.

The monkey paid no attention to them. He began to eat the banana until they came close to him. Then he ran fast, but Angelo ran faster. He had almost caught him when Beppo raced up a tall telephone pole.

"Come down, Beppo!" Angelo ordered, but the monkey would not come down.

The man who owned the fruit stand from which Beppo had taken the banana stood beside the pole.

He shouted, "Thief, thief," and shook his fist at the monkey. The crowd in the market began to laugh. The man turned and shook his fist at them. They laughed all the more.

"I'll go up after Beppo," Louis said to Angelo.

"Maybe he'll bite you," said Angelo. "Better let me go after him."

"No, let me," pleaded Louis.

He started to climb the pole. It was hard, at first, but after a little while, he found the trick of making his knees hold him as he pushed up. The monkey, still holding the banana skin, watched him carefully.

At last Louis came near the top of the pole. He reached out to take Beppo. The monkey threw the banana skin straight into his face. It struck his eyes and, for a moment, he could not see. That was the moment when Beppo ran down his shoulder, down his arm, down his leg, and down the pole. Angelo caught him as he reached the foot of the pole. The crowd in the market cheered.

"I guess we'd better get out of here," Louis said. "Beppo might take another banana."

"You will pay me for that banana," said the man who owned the fruit stand.

"I have no money," said Angelo.

The man muttered. Louis reached down in his pocket and brought out a coin. The man gave change to Louis. "Now, go away," he grumbled.

221

II. *Adventure in the City*

The boys went from the market into a wide street paved with heavy blocks of stone. They had to push their way past wagons and carts that jammed the place.

Angelo held Beppo tightly. "You won't get away again," he told the monkey.

To their right Louis and Angelo could see the masts and smokestacks of ships. "What are you going to be when you grow up?" Angelo asked.

"Why, I don't exactly know," said Louis. He would, he thought, be a businessman like his father, but that was a little hard to explain. "What do you want to do?"

"I'm going to be a sailor," said Angelo.

"On a banana boat?"

"No, on one of the big passenger boats. I'm going to Europe, and Asia, and Africa, besides South America."

"Maybe we could go together," suggested Louis.

"Maybe we could," Angelo replied.

They came to a long platform which ran between some tall warehouses and the boats. They could see the tall elevators where grain was stored as it waited to be placed on the ships for countries which needed it. They could see the big oil tanks which held oil for the many oil boats they called tankers. Everywhere men were busy, loading the ships with goods to go to foreign lands, or unloading the ships that had come in from other countries. Sugar to go out, coffee to come in, wool and cotton to go out, bananas to come in, Louis thought.

There were great piles of lumber on the docks, most of it mahogany from the West Indies. There were all sorts of strange fruits and vegetables.

"If you knew everything that comes in here and goes out of here, you'd know a lot about the world," Louis told Angelo.

"Sure," Angelo agreed.

A little crowd of sailors on one of the big boats saw Beppo and began to whistle to the monkey. Angelo tried to hold him, but Beppo leaped away from him and ran to the boat.

"Catch him, catch him!" the boys shouted, but the sailors kept whistling for Beppo to come to them.

A watchman on the dock would not let the boys follow the monkey. "But he's mine," Angelo cried. "I must get him. What can we do?" he asked Louis.

"Ask for the captain," Louis said.

At first the watchman refused to call the captain. Then he let the boys pass him. They went into the boat and found their way up toward the deck by following the shouts of the sailors. On the deck they met a man in uniform.

"What are you boys doing here?" he demanded.

"We want our monkey," said Louis. "Your men are holding him."

"Follow me," the officer said.

They went with him until they came directly under the place where the sailors stood. Beppo was eating something the men had given him. He would not come down to Angelo. "Bring him," the officer ordered the sailors. One of them caught the monkey and came down with him. The officer reached out, and Beppo tried to bite him. "Take him," the officer told Angelo, "and take him fast."

Angelo held the monkey tightly as they went off the deck and back to the dock. The watchman frowned at them, and Beppo moved toward him. "Take that brute away," cried the watchman.

"He's not a brute," said Angelo. "Beppo behaves all right if you treat him all right."

"Where do we go now?" Louis asked his new friend.

"Do you see those masts?" Angelo pointed to a boat that was moving through the harbor toward an open space a little way beyond them. "I think that's our banana boat."

"The *Francis Adams*? She's due today."

"How did you know her name?"

"Oh, I heard it." He was not going to risk Angelo's friendship by telling him that the boat was named for one of his own family.

The banana boat was just reaching the Adams Line dock when the two boys and Beppo arrived. Machinery was in motion. Men were shouting, both on the dock and on the boat. There was a keen excitement about the scene which thrilled Louis. Why, he wondered, didn't his father meet every boat of the Adams Line? Why hadn't he brought him here? "This is grand," he told Angelo.

Angelo was so busy watching the boat that he almost let Beppo slip. He gave a happy shout as he saw a big man come to the rail.

"Papa," he cried. "Papa! Here I am!"

The man looked from one side to another. Then he saw Angelo and shouted in answer. "My son, my son!" he cried. "How are you? And how is Mama? And the baby? And Tony? And Maria?"

"Fine, papa, fine. And here is Beppo," Angelo pointed excitedly to the monkey perched on his shoulder.

225

"Ah, Beppo!" The big man raised his hands above his head. "Keep him with you," he said. "Do not let him come among these bananas."

Already the dock workers were starting to unload the great bunches of bananas. Machinery was bringing them up from the depths of the ship and setting them on the dock. Workers lifted them to carts and trucks, and other workers carried them away. All the bananas were green, for ripe bananas would spoil on the long journey to New Orleans. Soon they would ripen, and people all over the country would be eating them.

"I guess we'll have to go," Angelo said, after they had been pushed aside by the workers and after Beppo had struggled to get more bananas. Green or not, the monkey liked them.

This time they went around the French market, not into it, although Louis wanted to buy doughnuts for them all. "We'll come another Saturday," he thought.

As they came from a narrow street into Jackson Square, the cathedral clock was striking twelve. People were going into the old church. "Do you think we could take Beppo in?" Louis asked Angelo.

"I often have," said Angelo.

There was a priest at the door, and Louis spoke to him. "May we carry our monkey into the church?"

"If you promise to hold him tight," the priest said. "After all, God makes monkeys as well as boys."

There were many people in the old cathedral. There were boys who had just come from band practice. There were some of the women in sunbonnets whom the boys had seen in the French market. There were men in overalls and men in uniforms whom they had seen on the docks. There were white men and black men and brown men. Here, at noon, they had all come together in this old church, to pray to God in hope, in thankfulness, in faith.

"Why, we are all alike," thought Louis. "We are all praying to God in His house."

Angelo held Beppo tightly. The monkey did not move until the two boys came out into the Square.

"Well, I've got to go home now," Angelo said. "I've got to tell my mother that the banana boat is in. We'll have a party tonight, now that my father is home."

"I hope I'll see you soon," said Louis.

"Sure," Angelo said. "Let's meet here in the Square next Saturday."

As Louis started home, he looked back from the edge of the Square and saw Angelo, with Beppo on his shoulder, turn into a narrow street behind the church.

"Oh, boy," he thought. "This has been a wonderful day. I've found a friend, a friend with a monkey."

HOW DIFFERENT YET HOW ALIKE?

Living with people becomes more interesting as we learn to understand each other better. No two persons are exactly alike in everything, but there are still many ways in which we do resemble each other. In this story, Louis and Angelo have a number of things in common, but they are very different in other ways. Can you list the ways in which they differ from those in which they are the same?

	Louis	*Angelo*
Age:		
City lived in:		
Color:		
Size:		
Clothes:		
Pet:		
Father's occupation:		
Tried to rescue:		
Wanted to become:		
Church visited:		
Point of courtesy:		

Universe[1]

The Universe is all the skies
Reaching far beyond your eyes.

The Universe is all the seas
Spreading in unseen degrees.

The Universe is all the earth
Besides the spot that gave you birth.

If you can with your small eye
Know one star in all the sky:

If, of all the seas there be,
From one beach you know the sea:

If, of all the land on earth,
You can know one meadow's worth:

You might do a great deal worse
To understand the Universe.

ELEANOR FARJEON

VI

On a Thousand Hills

"I am the good shepherd. The good shepherd lays down his life for his sheep. But the hireling, who is not a shepherd, whose own the sheep are not, sees the wolf coming and leaves the sheep and flees. And the wolf snatches and scatters the sheep; but the hireling flees because he is a hireling, and has no concern for the sheep.

"I am the good shepherd, and I know mine and mine know me, even as the Father knows me and I know the Father; and I lay down my life for my sheep. And other sheep I have that are not of this fold. Them also I must bring, and they shall hear my voice, and there shall be one fold and one shepherd."

John 10, 11–16

The Moon-Sheep[1]

The moon seems like a docile sheep,
She pastures while all people sleep;
And sometimes, when she goes astray,
She wanders all alone by day.

Up in the clear blue morning air
We are surprised to see her there,
Grazing in her woolly white,
Waiting the return of night.

When dusk lets down the meadow bars
She greets again her lambs, the stars!

CHRISTOPHER MORLEY

[1]From *Chimneysmoke* by Christopher Morley, copyright, 1921, 1949, by Christopher Morley, published by J. B. Lippincott Company.

God gave all men the right
to use His gifts reasonably;
and there should be no
different laws for

Big Ditches and Little Ditches

The Colorado is a mighty river. Once it was a wild and wandering stream which sometimes burst its banks and flooded the lands. Now it roars and rushes through deep canyons and over wide plains toward great dams which hold it in control. Man has learned to make the river serve the country through which it flows.

Young Jack Miller had never seen the Colorado; but the river was as real to him as the pony he rode over the dry roads near the lettuce ranch in the valley. For on the lettuce ranch he and Tomas, the Mexican foreman, earned a living; and the lettuce crops depended upon the water which came through canals and ditches from the Colorado River.

Young Jack's father and mother had settled in the valley before the ditches had been dug. They had found life hard in that desert country. Year after year their crops had failed because they had no water. They knew the value of irrigation, for the Spanish missionaries had long ago taught its use in the Southwest; but there had been no way then to bring the waters of the great river to the valley.

Then the government of the United States began to help the ranchers of the dry Southwest.

233

Government engineers found a way to control the wild waters of the Colorado. They built a great dam. Above the dam they made a lake, where they stored the waters of the river. Then, as the thirsty land needed water, they opened great gates and let the water flow downward.

The engineers built a canal, the All-American Canal, to carry water to the ditches which took it to the ranches. From this canal ranchers, both in the United States and in Mexico, could get water to irrigate their fields and orchards.

By the use of this water the ranches began to blossom. Figs and dates, oranges and lemons, grew big. Truck gardens grew vegetables and berries in winter seasons when prices were high. The valley began to ship its products to the cities of the North and East.

The Miller ranch began to pay. For a few years everyone was happy, the Millers and Tomas, their Mexican foreman, and Joanna, his wife. Little Jack laughed and played as the lettuce grew. Then his parents died, and the boy was left an orphan.

Father Hackett, the pastor of the church in the nearest valley town, wanted to send Jack away to school. The priest was the boy's guardian, and he thought a boarding school the only place for Jack; but the boy begged to stay in the valley.

"I can run the ranch with Tomas and Joanna," he told the priest.

Because Father Hackett knew that Tomas and Joanna were good and kind and faithful, he let Jack stay with them.

"But running a ranch is a big job for the three of you," he said.

"Everyone helps us," Jack told him; but the real work of the ranch fell on Tomas and himself.

It was hard work. Through long, hot days they dug and planted the ground. The rows had to be even and straight. Through other hot days they sprayed the young plants. They weeded and they hoed. Then, at last, they gathered the lettuce. They packed it for market in crates. They put the crates on the old truck and drove to the railroad. There, beside the track, they sold it.

235

Everyone in the valley town knew Jack and Tomas. The mayor, the lawyer, the doctor all spoke to them when they met them and spoke of them afterward.

"That's a fine boy," the men told Father Hackett.

There was one man in the valley who did not like Jack and Tomas. He was Jarvis Lunt. He was their neighbor and he should have been their friend, but he wanted the Miller land. He had tried to buy it at a low price when Jack's father and mother died. Father Hackett, who was Jack's guardian, had refused to sell it to him.

"I shall get it sometime," Lunt had said to the priest.

"We shall see that he never gets it," Jack told Tomas.

"Beware of him," said Tomas. "He is a bad man, a very bad man."

Lunt made trouble for them in many ways, but it was not until he bought the land south of their ranch that the trouble grew dangerous. For through this land ran the big ditch which brought water from the canal to the Miller place.

"He will steal the water which should be ours," said Tomas.

Any one of the ranchers along the ditch could take off enough water for his own fields. Sometimes men took too much by accident and cut off the supply of their neighbors who were not as near the canal as they were. Jarvis Lunt meant to take it. He knew that without water the Miller ranch could not pay. It would have to be sold. Then he would buy it very cheaply. No one else would want a ranch that would not pay.

Day after day the plants in the fields wilted and drooped. "We cannot go long without water," Tomas told Jack. "In this dry land there is no hope of a crop unless man brings water to the roots of the plants."

"Lunt has no right to take the water away from us," Jack said.

"He has no right," the Mexican said, "but he is a big man, a rich man."

"We'll fight him," the boy said.

"Bad, bad," moaned Tomas as he looked at the wilting lettuce and the dry ditches. "We can do nothing without water."

"We shall get the water," Jack said; but he wondered how he could get it.

He rode into town to see Father Hackett. "I don't know what can be done," said Father Hackett, "but I shall find out."

"I knew you would," said the boy. "You always find ways to do everything."

"Not always," said Father Hackett, "and when I do, it is only because so many people are kind."

He put on his wide-brimmed hat and went out with Jack into the hot street. They passed the mayor and the judge. Jack wondered why the priest did not ask

237

them about what could be done. The priest kept on until they came to the office of the irrigation engineers. There he took Jack in with him and stood before the desk of a tall man who wore high rubber boots. Father Hackett spoke to him for a few moments and then turned to Jack.

"Tell this man your story," he said.

The tall man listened carefully while Jack told of Lunt's method of keeping water from the Miller ranch. Then he spoke slowly. "This man Lunt," he said, "has the right to take off enough water for his own use. If he takes a pint more than that, he can be punished."

"How can we know that he takes more than he should?" Father Hackett asked.

The tall man smiled. "There are ways to measure that," he said. "I shall see that they are used."

He kept his word. On the next day other men in high rubber boots came out to the ditch which ran through the Lunt ranch to the Miller ranch. They

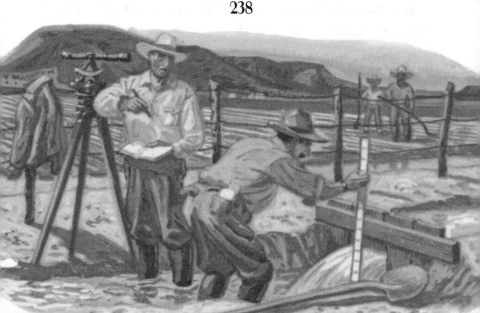

worked all day with instruments whose names Jack did not know. The boy and Tomas watched them as they set down notes in little books. They went away; but, in a little while, other men came and told Jarvis Lunt that he could not use the amount of water he was taking from the ditch. Lunt shook his fist at them, but within an hour the water began to flow again through the Miller fields.

Tomas laughed when he saw it. "Fine, fine," he said to Jack.

"Isn't it wonderful, Tomas," Jack asked him, "how big people like Father Hackett and the engineers help the little people like us?"

"Sure, sure," said Tomas. "Big ditches carry water to little ditches, and the big river carries water for them all."

HOW WELL CAN YOU EXPLAIN WHAT YOU MEAN?

Can you explain clearly what the phrases given below mean? Read them carefully. Then try to put their exact meaning into your own words. Be able to explain them orally to the class. Using them in sentences may help to explain their meaning.

1. the value of irrigation
2. through deep canyons
3. government engineers
4. began to blossom
5. stored the waters
6. ship its products
7. packed crates
8. Jack's guardian
9. beware of him
10. wilted and drooped

The Pasture

I'm going out to clean the pasture spring;
I'll only stop to rake the leaves away
(And wait to watch the water clear, I may):
I shan't be gone long.—You come too.

I'm going out to fetch the little calf
That's standing by the mother. It's so young
It totters when she licks it with her tongue.
I shan't be gone long.—You come too.

ROBERT FROST

There are not so many now as
there once were; but cowboys
still ride the Western plains
and still work with

Bulls and Brands and Broncos

Many American boys and girls have never seen a
real cowboy, but to them and to many who are not
Americans the cowboy means our United States. He
is the Lone Ranger. He is Hopalong Cassidy. He is
the Range Rider, and he is the man who rides the horse
Trigger. He is freedom. He is the land of the young.

The cowboy is in motion pictures, in television, and
on the radio; but he is also on the plains of the West,
all the way from Mexico to Canada, and from the
Missouri River to the Pacific Ocean.

He wears a wide-brimmed hat to protect him from
the sun. He ties a handkerchief around his neck loosely
so that he can draw it over his mouth if he has to face
a storm. He wears blue jeans now, although he used
to wear buckskin breeches. He wears high-heeled boots
because the heels hold him better when riding. These
boots make walking hard, but the cowboy does not
walk far. He rides.

The Spanish, coming northward from Mexico,
brought with them horses and cattle, both bulls and
cows. They also brought the cowboys to ride the
horses and herd the cattle. The cowboy did not need
many tools for his work. He needed only a horse and

241

saddle, a bridle, and a lariat. His bed was a blanket spread under the Western stars. With these the cowboy built the great cattle industry of our land.

The Spanish cattle ran wild over the Texas plains and became tough, long-horned animals. They were hard to catch and hard to hold. At first, they belonged to anyone who could catch them; but in time, they were caught and held and owned by men or companies of men.

To prove ownership, the owner had to mark the cattle he had bought or captured. To do this, the owner used the Spanish method of branding. He chose a special mark for his own and had it burned upon the hides of the cattle he claimed.

There are hundreds of brands, marking both great

and small herds of cattle. There are so many that there is a museum of brands in a town in Texas, and books have been written about these brand signs and what they mean.

The branding was a big job. The unmarked cattle were driven by the cowboys into a fenced space called a corral. They were thrown upon the ground and tied. The branding iron, which had been heated in a fire, was set upon their hides. The branding iron could only make certain kinds of marks,—straight lines, circles, triangles, squares. For this reason the brands were fairly simple. Letters that were easy to make were used. One, and seven, and eleven were used more often than three or eight. Once the cattle were marked, it was easy to prove ownership.

243

For a time the market for beef and for hides had to be near the plains or ranges where the herds grazed. But the building of railroads to the north of Texas opened the chance of new markets in the cities of the North and East. The railroads were still a long distance from the ranges, and so the cowboys had to drive the great herds of cattle over the trails to the railroad.

This opened the famous trails, especially the Great Texas Trail, sometimes called the Chisholm Trail. Another trail was the Goodnight-Loving Trail, which was named for two men of those names. Still another was the Santa Fe Trail.

The cowboys who rode these trails used good, well-broken horses, but part of their work was catching and training wild horses. Some of the horses were small and wiry. They bucked and plunged so hard that their riders gave them the Spanish name for *wild*, bronco; and the word has come to mean any small, ready-to-fight horse. Broncos have to be "broken," made ready to take on a rider without throwing him off, usually over the bronco's head. Once they have been tamed, they usually make good horses.

The cowboy of today no longer makes the long drives up the great trails because railroads now run near the cattle ranges. Demand for more tender meat has caused a change from the tough Texas longhorns. Cattle are now shipped from the far ranges to farms in the Middle West, near the big stockyards, where they are fattened for the market. Branding methods have been greatly improved.

In the West, however, there are still cowboys. Sometimes, from a train window, you may see a man sitting easily upon his horse. It makes a picture of the West that the traveler will not forget, for the cowboy is the West.

HOW MUCH DO YOU REMEMBER?

After you have read "Bulls and Brands and Broncos" once, try to answer the following questions. Number your paper from 1 to 10. Be sure to write your answers in complete sentences. When you have finished writing your answers, read the story again. Did you get them all right?

1. Has every American child seen a real cowboy?
2. Who brought the bulls and the cows to the West?
3. How was the ownership of cattle proven?
4. What kind of brands were usually used?
5. Why could the markets for beef and cattle hides be changed from the plains to the cities?
6. What were the names of some of the trails over which the cattle had to be herded?
7. What other work did cowboys do besides riding horses?
8. Why were some horses called broncos?
9. Do the cowboys still have the long drives up the trails?
10. What do we still think of when we think of the West?

Cattle Country

I'm the land of wider ranges,
I'm the land of shorter grass,
I'm the country of the campfires
Where the great herds used to pass;
I'm the land of plain and mountain,
Land of mesa and of hill,
I'm the land of Heigh-ho Silver
And the land of Buffalo Bill.

I'm the land of ropes and saddles,
Clinking spurs and lariats whirled,
Cowboy chaps and wide sombreros,
I'm the rodeo of the world.
I'm the land of drives and roundups
Where the branding irons are pressed,
I'm the land of dust and desert,
I'm the wide and wondrous West.

Long ago the roving Spaniard
Followed north the flying birds,
Brought me men and brought me missions,
Brought me horses, brought me herds;
Left me these as sign and token
Of his passing on his quest,
Gave me faith and way of living
For the building of the West.

Men from eastward found my cattle,
Men from northward rode my land,
All the way to purple Rockies,
All the way to Rio Grande,
Rode my trails to every border,
Chisholm, Goodnight, Santa Fe,
Learned my ways and learned my language,
Strong and harsh and brave and gay.

Gone the wideness of my ranges,
Turned my older, brighter page,
But the cattle still are milling
Through the fields of purple sage.
Still the missions top the hillsides,
With the crosses on their spires,
Still the padres light the mesas
With the glow of holy fires.

I'm the land of toil and danger,
I'm the land of liberty,
I'm the old, old cattle country,
I'm the young land of the free,
I'm the land of dream and longing,
I'm the land of sun-baked sod,
But my Rockies touch the heavens,
And my trails lead up to God!

Mary Synon

The children's children of the Spanish
settlers keep up the old Faith and the
old courage of their people. They prove
it in times like the one when

Margarita Rides at Night

I. The Sheep Ranch

If you saw the Otero children riding their ponies
along the trails of their father's big sheep ranch, you
would think of them only as children who liked pleasure and excitement more than anything else in the
world. You would be wrong, and you would think
quite differently if you knew what Margarita Otero
did not so long ago.

It happened the night after Margarita rode alone
with her father over the whole wide range of the sandy
hillsides which were the sheep pastures.

They had set off happily that morning, with Margarita
on her pony, Star. Her mother had called good-by to
them, while her two little brothers, Marcos and Carlos,
had shouted after them that some day soon they too
would ride the range.

Margarita and her father had ridden slowly along
the pastures while her father examined fences and the
shelters for the sheep. They had stopped at houses
made of sun-baked clay to talk with the families of
the sheep herders. They had visited the home of the
ranch foreman, Roberto, whose little boy lay ill, and

248

Margarita's father had given orders for the child's care. They had called on an old woman who remembered the time when Archbishop Lamy lived in Santa Fe. "He was a saint of God," she had told Margarita. "He blessed our land by living among us."

They went then to the great pasture at the foot of the mountain. They made their way over one trail so narrow that Margarita held back her pony in fear.

"Steady, now!" her father warned, as they saw the canyon below them, and he showed her how to guide the pony. "Well done!" he praised her, as they came to the end of the trail.

"I should be afraid to do that alone," she said.

"You won't have to ride it alone," her father said, "until you've learned much more. I will teach you."

In the great pasture some of the men were repairing fences and building sheds for the protection of the flocks from the wild storms that sometimes swept over the mountains. Others were leading sheep toward the stream which ran through the valley, while the faithful black and white sheep dogs barked at the sheep which lagged behind and drove them into line. The wide pastures were dotted with hundreds of sheep, nibbling the short grass.

"We need rain," Margarita's father said, looking at the dry soil and the yellowish-brown grass of the pasture.

"We shall have it soon," Margarita said.

249

"Give us time to get home," her father laughed.

"Let's not go back yet," Margarita begged.

She loved the pasture, she thought, better than any other part of the ranch. In May and June, when the sheep were sheared, it was a busy place. The men drove the flocks to the workers, who cut off the long woolly coats which had grown through the cold winter. Then everyone worked so hard that there was little time for anyone to explain anything to Margarita.

"I like sheep," she told her father.

"So do I," he said, "but they are a lot of work."

"I should like to take care of some little lambs."

"Perhaps I shall let you do that when they come."

250

"And have them all for my own?" Margarita asked eagerly.

"All for your own—but you will have to learn to care for them. No one has the right to neglect anything or anyone placed under his care."

"I wouldn't forget them," Margarita promised.

They turned back toward home, but they took another trail and not the narrow one over which they had come.

"This trail takes longer," her father said, "but you have had enough hard riding for today."

"Oh, Father, look at the sky!" Margarita cried, as they came to the top of a hill. Above the green of pines and juniper, above the deep red and purple of the mountains, it shone in clear blue. "Like the cloak of Our Lady," Margarita said.

Her father frowned. "See that cloud over there," he said. "We shall have to hurry to be home before the rain." They rode swiftly toward the big house.

"Hello!" Marcos and Carlos called to them, as they came into the patio just before the breaking of the storm. Margarita leaped down from her pony, but her father turned his horse toward the road again.

"You are not staying?" her mother asked. "It is going to be a terrible storm."

"That is why I cannot stay," he said. "I must take all the men to the far pasture. We shall need every one of them."

"Be careful," her mother warned. "You know what the doctor said about your heart."

"I'll be all right. I can't ask the men to do what I would not do myself."

"I understand," she said, waving to him as he galloped off; but Marcos grumbled, "I don't see why Father couldn't stay. Look at that storm!"

II. *The Ride in the Storm*

The storm rose as Marcos and Carlos and Margarita watched with their mother. Heavy, dark clouds scudded over the mountaintops and pressed close to the house. Trees bent before the rush of the wind. Rain drove hard against the buildings. Once Margarita thought she heard the bleating of the sheep, but it was only old Pluma, the sheep dog, barking.

"I am worried about Father," she told her mother.

"He will be all right," her mother said; but she led them all to the tiny chapel which had been in the house since it had been built long years before. There they knelt, Marcos and Carlos and Margarita, saying with their mother an old prayer of the Church for the pilgrim and the traveler.

For hours the storm raged. Margarita read story after story to Marcos and Carlos so that they would not worry about their father, while their mother went about her usual work in the house. Then, at last, the wind died down and the rain stopped. It was night before their father came home.

He was tired when he came in. "The sheep are safe," he said, "and the men all right. I had to leave them all at the far camp."

"Are you all right?" his wife asked anxiously.

"All right," he told her.

He was not all right, but Margarita did not know that until hours later. She was sleeping when her mother called her. "Margarita, dear, wake up! Margarita, you must do something for me quickly. Your father is very sick. I have telephoned the doctor and he is on his way, but I cannot reach Father Gabriel by telephone. The boy at the rectory says he has gone on a sick call to a camp that is beyond our own far camp. Margarita, dear, I wish I had someone else to send, but there is no one. Will you ride—as fast as you can—up to our camp for Roberto? He will go for Father Gabriel and bring him here. God keep you, darling!"

"I will go, Mother," Margarita said. She dressed faster than she ever had before and ran to the stable. She had never been there alone in the darkness, and for a moment fear shook her. "Our Lady, help me," she prayed, and moved through the darkness toward her pony's stall.

Star whinnied a little, then fell silent as she spoke to him. "You will have to be patient with me," she

253

told him. He pushed his head against her shoulder as she led him out of the stall. "I don't know how I am going to get you saddled," she said, "but I am going to do it."

Saddle him she did, and put on his bridle with its silver star. "Now we are going to ride," she told him as she swung up onto his back and rode out into the country that had been so bright that morning.

Ride, ride, ride!

Mile after mile slid away beneath her as she rode the pony through the cool darkness of the New Mexican night. The storm had long since passed, but clouds hid the stars which might have guided her. On and on she went, faster and faster, until the road narrowed into the trail that had frightened her when she had come into it with her father.

"Oh, how can I do it?" she thought and pulled in

254

the rein. "I can't," she sobbed. For a moment she
waited, trying to see the trail. Then she threw back
her shoulders. "Go on, Star," she told the pony.

Slowly, step by step, the pony moved. Sometimes
Margarita thought that in a moment they must plunge
down off the trail into the canyon below. It was so
dark that she did not know when the trail grew wider.
It was the pony's speed that told her they had passed
the danger. "Oh, thank you, God!" she sobbed.

They sped then over the road to the great pasture
where tiny lantern lights guided her to the camp.
Roberto, who was taking his turn watching the sheep,
stood beside the fence as she turned in from the road.
Swiftly she told him her reason for coming. Just as
swiftly Roberto saddled his horse.

"While I go for Father Gabriel," he said, "one of
the men will take you home." Suddenly he turned
back to her. "How did you come?" he asked her.

"Over the trail Father showed me this morning," she answered.

"Not that trail?" he cried. "And after the storm!" He stared at her in wonder. "No one else in New Mexico would have attempted it tonight. Not even your father!"

"I rode it for my father."

"For your father," said Roberto, "and for God. That is the Spanish way."

"That is the American way," said Margarita.

For that ride Margarita is known all over the sheep country of New Mexico. People speak of her as the girl who braved danger to bring the priest to her father, and they point her out as she rides with her father again over the bright roads. Marcos and Carlos say they would have done the same had they known how to ride as Margarita rides. Margarita knows that they would.

For the blood of the Otero children is the blood of those Spaniards who fought for their country and their Faith. Through the years they have lived in New Mexico, their people have kept in their hearts love of the land and love of God.

Today, on the mountains and hills of New Mexico, they are willing to live and die for this nation of ours as bravely as did their grandfathers and great-grand-fathers in Spain so long ago for the flag of their country and the Cross of Christ.

The events in this story are given in the following list. If you arrange these events in order, you will have an outline of the major ideas in the story. Then you can tell the story by looking at your list of events. Number your paper from 1 to 8. Find the first event and write the letter that is before it after number 1.

a. The children's father returned safely.

b. Margarita and her father rode over the sheep pastures.

c. Margarita started out alone to the camp to get Roberto.

d. Margarita's father became very ill.

e. They saw the storm clouds gathering.

f. They rode over a narrow mountain trail.

g. The children prayed for their father's safety.

h. Margarita's father left just before the storm broke.

Sheep Corral

Near my mother's hogan
Is the sheep corral,
A bare, brown place
Fenced with poles.

There is a tree
For shade.
There is a shelter
For lambs
In the sheep corral.

257

The sheep stand together
In their corral.
They stand close
To each other.
I think
Sheep like to know
That they are many.

Sometimes,
I play that way.
I play
That there are many children
All around me,
All about me.
When I am herding
And I cannot see my mother,
It is good
To play
That many children
Stand together with me,
And that all outside
Is my corral.

ANN NOLAN CLARK

Among the great pioneers of America
have been the Catholic missionaries;
and no one of them has been braver than

The Shepherd of Santa Fe

On a blazing hot day in August more than a hundred years ago, two weary men rode their weary horses up the Santa Fe Trail. Friends from their childhood, they had come a long way to this far Western mountain country. They had crossed an ocean and more than half a continent. They had suffered illnesses and shipwrecks. They had gone hungry and thirsty on this last, the most difficult part of their journey. They had escaped death by minutes.

Both of these brave men were French missionary priests. Both of them had labored in parishes in Ohio. Both of them lived only to love and serve God; and both of them would win fame as pioneer bishops of the great West.

One of them, John Lamy, was already the Bishop of Santa Fe. He had been made a bishop in Cincinnati and had set out for Santa Fe by way of New Orleans, since the season for travel on the overland trail was past. In New Orleans he found his sister ill in her convent. Because of this he missed the boat he was to take. He found passage on another, a miserable vessel which sank as it was reaching the Texas shore. Bishop Lamy saved only his life and his books.

259

He missed meeting his friend, Father Joseph, who was to go with him to Santa Fe. He left word that Father Joseph was to follow him and joined a group of soldiers. He was injured, and the soldiers had to go without him. Father Joseph overtook him, and together they joined another troop. The soldiers could go only part of the way with them, and the priests had to go on alone.

The journey was difficult and dangerous. The roads were poor. There was little water, and most of it was bad. There was no protection against enemy Indians or against white robbers, but they rode on and at last came in sight of Santa Fe.

The town, set high in the mountains of New Mexico, was the wildest town of a wild West. Crimes of all sorts took place within it. Most of its people loved and feared God, but they also feared the gamblers, the robbers, and the murderers. Most of its people were Catholics, but there were few priests; and the Mexican bishop did not often come to Santa Fe. The people welcomed Bishop Lamy gladly.

Quietly Bishop Lamy set about making Santa Fe a better place. He gave out no orders, but he made men and women wish to make themselves better. In a little while the town began to show this spirit. His people began to help him as he helped them. He rebuilt churches that had fallen into decay. He built schools, a hospital, and an orphanage. He brought the Sisters across the plains to help him care for children and the sick of the community.

He helped to build good roads. He asked the railroad company to employ native New Mexicans for its work in building new railroads. Knowing his love for them, his people gave him their love.

The governors of the territory became his grateful friends. The generals of the Army asked for and received his help. The great Army scout, Kit Carson, gave him loyal friendship. Only once did they disagree. That was the time when Carson favored the moving of the Navahoes by the government from their homes. Bishop Lamy felt that this was unjust. He was glad when the government moved the Indians back a few years later.

261

Arizona was added to his parishes. He made many and long journeys in order to meet and know his people. Often he had to ride on roads where every rock might be hiding an Indian warrior ready to kill a white man. He usually traveled alone, riding one horse, leading another. He carried his food with him, hard-boiled eggs and crackers, for he did not like what he called "the blessed bean" and "holy porridge."

Stories of the bishop's kindness are still told in Santa Fe. A Jewish merchant of the town was taken ill as he was returning with a wagon train. The leaders of the train forced him to leave his wagon; and, fearing that he had a deadly fever, they placed him in a trapper's sod house. They were leaving him, sick and alone, when Bishop Lamy passed by. Hearing the rumor about the sick man, he went to him and brought him to his wagon.

"I may have the fever," the merchant warned.

"We do not fear it," said the bishop. "We will take care of you."

In time Bishop Lamy became an archbishop. When he died, his body lay in the cathedral he had built. Thousands of men and women looked for the last time on the great archbishop who had been their guide, their friend, their leader, the Shepherd of Santa Fe.

CAN YOU TELL THE DIFFERENCE BETWEEN A FACT AND AN OPINION?

A *fact* is something that is known to be true. It is usually stated in a very definite way. An *opinion*, on the other hand, is what one thinks or believes about something. Everyone's opinion does not have to be the same as everyone else's. We are allowed to form our own *opinions*, but we should learn how to form wise ones. We can do this by letting our reading guide us in our thinking and in choosing correct and worth-while facts.

How good are you at telling the difference between a fact and an opinion? Read each of the sentences below. If the story tells you the answer, you may call it a *fact*. If you have to decide for yourself from your reading, call it an *opinion*. If it is a fact, put an F after the statement. If it is an opinion, put an O.

1. Bishop Lamy and Father Joseph were friends from their childhood.
2. Both of these men were French.
3. Both of them were always happy.
4. They did not fear anything.
5. Most of the people in Santa Fe were Catholic.
6. Bishop Lamy met many dangers when he went across the border into New Mexico.
7. He was a man who did not talk very much.
8. He rebuilt many churches that had fallen into decay.
9. He helped everyone.
10. Stories of the Bishop's kindness are still told in Santa Fe.

First Christmas Night of All

That first Christmas night of all,
No lights were in the dreaming town,
No steeples shook their tidings down,
   No carols raised their call.

But music broke upon a hill,
And all the dark was strangely stirred
With beauty of bright angels' word—
   A word that echoes still.

And in a dim and dusty stall
A little light began to glow,
That Christmas night so long ago—
   First Christmas night of all!

NANCY BYRD TURNER

Many lovely Spanish customs
live in our Southwest. One
of them is the game that
Mexican children play on

Christmas Eve

I. *The Statue in the Shop*

Christmas Eve had come to the Southwest.

It was not the white Christmas of the North, where snow lay on fields and streets, where frost covered windows and roofs, and where little stars twinkled far away in a high, cold sky.

It was a warm Christmas, with bright red flowers blooming beside the roads and with big stars seeming to float just above the dark line of the hills on a deep, blue sky. It was an evening that must have been like that night when the shepherds watched their flocks near Bethlehem.

In the towns the Christmas lights of red and blue and gold shone up and down the streets. In the dark blue twilight they shone on palm trees and pepper trees. They shone on wide streets and narrow streets, from big houses and little houses. They seemed to shine everywhere except in a little patio in the Mexican part of the city behind the old church.

That patio was strangely dark. A boy, standing in its shadows, moved whenever anyone turned in from the street.

265

Men and women and other children passed him, all of them carrying packages—big packages, little packages, Christmas packages. The boy pushed closer to the wall as a tall girl came under the street light just outside the patio; but when she came close to him she turned toward him.

"Pedro?" she said, "what are you doing out here?"

"I am waiting for Lolita," the boy explained.

"Lolita? Where is she?" Rita glanced quickly about the shadowy patio.

"She has something to do. She went to do it."

"After dark?" Rita asked in surprise.

"She could not go before dark," explained Pedro.

"Did *Mamacita* let her go?"

"*Mamacita* did not know she went. Oh, please, Rita, you won't tell her that Lolita went out of this patio, will you?" pleaded the boy.

266

"I won't tell her," promised Rita, "but you must come in with me. It is almost time for the procession."

"But Lolita and I are to lead the Christmas Eve procession," Pedro said. "*Mamacita* said so. We are the youngest. We will walk ahead of everyone, of her and of Father, and of you and Maria and Ramon."

"Then Lolita had better hurry. Where did she go?"

"I cannot tell you," said Pedro.

"Do you know?" Rita asked, as they came to the door of their own bungalow in the patio.

"Oh, yes," he said, "I know."

He knew very well where Lolita had gone. More plainly than the dark patio before him he could see the bright shop where he and Lolita had seen the statue of Our Lady of Guadalupe.

It was a little shop which they had seen for the first time one day when they had gone shopping with their mother. *Mamacita* was buying a prayer book for Maria. He and Lolita were staring at books and rosary beads and pictures when Lolita had said, "Oh, Pedro, see her!" and had pointed to the statue.

It was a little statue, but it looked like the big statue in the church. There was the same rich red in Our Lady's dress, the same deep blue in her mantle. Even the veil that covered her soft brown hair looked the same. Lolita had stared at the statue with big eyes that grew bigger.

"Oh, *Mamacita*, isn't she beautiful!" she had cried.

Their mother had turned around. "The statue is lovely," she had said, "but it is expensive."

Lolita had looked at the mark that told its price. The statue was expensive. Pedro knew as well as she did that their mother could not afford to buy it. Their father worked hard in a factory where pottery was made. Their mother worked, too, at fine needlework that she sold to one of the shops in the open market. Sometimes, after she had sold her work, she gave money to Pedro and Lolita for their own spending.

"Perhaps I can save enough to buy the statue for *Mamacita*," Lolita told Pedro.

Pedro had known that she could not. Lolita had given up buying the orange-flavored ice cream she liked so well. For a month she had bought no little sweet cakes from the bakery that had such bright yellow and pink cookies in the window. She had pulled threads in a towel and put beautiful needlework upon it. She had sold it in one of the shops, but she had not yet enough money for the statue.

"If only I could buy it for *Mamacita* for Christmas!" she had kept saying to Pedro.

She had gone without a ride on the ferris wheel when they had gone to the *fiesta*. She had saved the money that her father had given her for the merry-go-round.

"I am saving every penny for the statue," she had told Pedro.

"I'll go without ice cream, too," he had said to her.

"No," she said. "This must be all my own gift. Sister Ruth says that no gift is truly good unless we give up something to make it."

She had given up far more than she had kept for herself; but Christmas Eve had come, and Lolita still did not have enough money to buy the statue.

"It is too bad," Pedro had told her just before dark. "What else could you get for *Mamacita?*"

"Nothing else," Lolita had said, "that she will like half so well." Her eyes had filled with tears. Then she had turned sharply to Pedro. "I am going to try once more," she had said. "I am going back to the shop."

"But, Lolita!"

"Don't tell anyone where I have gone. I shall be back in time for the procession," called Lolita as she hurried off.

II. *The Christmas Eve Procession*

Swift as a bird Lolita had gone out of the patio. She had not yet come back. As Pedro followed Rita into the house, he sighed in worry. Where was Lolita? Wouldn't she be back in time to lead the procession with him? Wouldn't she be back in time for *la piñata*, that Christmas game of all Mexican children?

He tiptoed after Rita into the dark house. Like the patio it was quiet, but even in the stillness and the darkness Pedro knew that all the family, except Lolita, were there.

Mamacita's voice rose. "Who has come?" she asked.

"It is Rita," the girl answered.

"It is Pedro," said the boy.

"Where is Lolita?" asked *Mamacita*. "It is almost time for the procession to begin. She is to lead it with you, Pedro."

"She is not here," whispered the boy.

"She should be here. We cannot wait for her."

"Must I—walk alone?"

"You must," declared *Mamacita* firmly.

"But can't we wait for Lolita?"

"No," said his mother. "Lolita knows that when darkness comes on Christmas Eve and the big bell rings at the church, we walk in procession. Have you children your candles ready to light?"

"I have," said Rita.

"I have," said Ramon. "I am holding mine in my hand."

"When do we start?" asked Pedro.

"When the bell rings."

For a few moments they all sat close together in silence. Then, through the soft night, came the sound of bells across the park, bells in the tower of the old church which had been built by the padres many years ago.

"It is the signal," said *Mamacita*.

"It is now time for the procession," Pedro's father said, and he began to answer the church bell by ringing a little bell in his hand.

The little bell rang through the room.

It echoed through the house.

It rang out into the patio.

Other bells, in other houses around the dark patio, answered it. Then all the bells in the Mexican houses began to ring.

"Quick, the candles!" cried Maria.

Rita was the first to light her candle. Pedro could see her eyes shine in the soft light. Ramon lighted his candle. Then his father lighted one.

"Maria will lead the procession with you," his mother told Pedro.

"Where is Lolita?" Maria whispered to him.

"She will be here," he said, but fear came back to him.

271

Lolita had to cross a busy avenue to get to the little shop. What if a car had struck her? There were always so many cars on the avenue, and there would be more than ever tonight. Silently he began to pray for his sister's safety.

"Oh, God, please take care of Lolita," he prayed.

"Now we are ready for the procession." *Mamacita* rose from her chair.

Pedro and Maria lifted the statues from the top of the table. Maria took the statue of Our Lady, a beautiful statue but not so beautiful as the statue of Our Lady of Guadalupe that Lolita had so much wanted for their mother. Pedro took the statue of Saint Joseph. They held the statues high.

The rest of the family fell into line behind them. They moved two by two out into the patio in an age-old custom that the Mexicans had brought with them from Mexico to the States. This was the procession of Christmas Eve. It reminded men of that little procession of the first Christmas Eve when Saint Joseph had looked for a shelter in Bethlehem for Our Blessed Mother.

Mamacita began to pray. Her husband and the children answered her. Rita began to sing an old, old Christmas hymn.

Statues and candles in their young hands, Pedro and Ramon and Maria raised their voices in a prayer of welcome to the Christ Child. They sang it with all their hearts. Surely a door must open soon, *Mamacita* prayed, and make room for the lovely Lady of Heaven.

Other people were coming out into the patio from other little houses. Men and women and older children followed the little boys and girls who carried other statues of Saint Joseph and of Our Lady. They fell in line behind Pedro and Maria and their sister and brothers and their father and mother. They all moved around the patio, going from door to door of the bungalows.

Before every door Rita and the other older girls sang the old hymn. Before every door the younger children joined in it. Before every door mothers repeated the prayer, but all the doors stayed shut.

273

They came to the door of the last house. Twice they knocked on the door. The door stayed shut. They knocked the third time.

"Open for the Queen of Heaven," said the mothers.

"Open, open!" they pleaded.

The children held their breaths.

Slowly the door began to open. The light, coming into the darkness of the patio, made them all blink. Maria stepped through the door and into the house. Pedro followed her. They carried the statues of Saint Joseph and of Our Lady carefully. Gently, as the others sang a Christmas carol, they placed the statues within a hay-filled manger in the corner of the room.

Mamacita came close to them. "God care for all in this house tonight," she prayed.

"God and His angels care for all here," everyone prayed after her.

"God, please take care of Lolita," Pedro prayed.

Rita blew out her candle. Ramon and Maria and their father and mother and all the others blew out theirs. Suddenly lights went on in the patio.

"*Piñata! Piñata!*" the children cried. "Now it is time for *la piñata*! We shall play *la piñata* at Pedro's house!"

All the children of the patio ran to Pedro's house, but Pedro followed them slowly. What fun would there be in *la piñata* without Lolita? And where was Lolita? Had something happened to his sister?

III. *La Piñata*

As the lights went on in his own house, Pedro saw Lolita. She was running into the patio even faster than she had run out of it. In her hands she was carrying a package wrapped in paper, a package bigger than the statue of Our Lady which Maria had carried in the procession.

"Oh, Pedro, I have it!" she cried. "I thought I did not have enough money, but the lady in the store said that it cost less tonight because it had been so long in the window. I had money enough to buy it for *Mamacita*. Help me hide it until I can give it to her after we have played *la piñata!*"

"You have missed the procession," Pedro told her.

"I am sorry. All the year I have thought of how I should walk with you, but I had to do this for *Mamacita*."

"Has anyone seen Lolita?" her mother called.

"I am here," said Lolita, hiding the statue so that her mother would not see it. "I am sorry I am late."

"*Piñata, piñata*," the children were shouting. They skipped around the room as Lolita joined them.

Above them, hanging from the ceiling, was the *piñata*, a great clay jar filled with candies and Christmas gifts for all the children of the patio. It was covered with a bright paper doll which smiled down upon the little children.

275

They knew the fun of the game. Every Christmas, as long as they could remember, they had rushed into the fun. Blindfolded, they would stand and take aim at the clay jar with a long stick. When the jar was broken the gifts would tumble out onto the floor and then all of them would scramble to pick them up.

"*Piñata! Piñata!*" Their happy shouts filled the house.

Rita, because she was the oldest, stepped forward. The noisy room grew suddenly quiet. Which child would have the first chance? Rita looked from one to another.

"Take me!" cried Pablo.

"Take me!" shouted the others.

Older people from houses around the patio came in to see *la piñata*. They crowded against the walls of the brightly lighted rooms and they laughed with the children.

Again Rita, her dark eyes smiling, looked around at one child after another. Her eyes rested the longest on a roly-poly boy with big black eyes and a merry face. "Pablo!" she called.

The others cheered, "Pablo! Pablo!"

Rita blindfolded Pablo. Then she put a long stick in his hand and turned him around and around.

Pablo held the stick tightly in his fat little fist. He struck out with all his might toward the spot where he thought *la piñata* hung, but *la piñata* was not there.

"Higher, Pablo, higher!" shouted the children.

Again and again he aimed at *la piñata*. He whirled so hard that he turned himself around.

"Your turn is up, Pablo," said Rita, as she untied the scarf over his eyes.

Maria had a turn. Lolita had a turn. Pedro had a turn. Still *la piñata* was unbroken, and the paper doll covering the clay jar smiled down at them.

"Only Ramon is left," said Rita, and she tied a hard knot in the blindfold around his eyes.

Ramon swung once with the big stick. He swung twice. He swung three times, and with a loud whack he struck the clay jar. It broke into a dozen pieces as the smiling paper doll sailed through the air. With screams of delight the children ran to gather the candies and the little gifts that were scattered over the floor.

"Look at my gift!" Lolita fairly sang, as she held up a pair of dainty ear-rings made of straw.

"I have a piggy bank!" Pedro laughed, as he unwrapped a smiling little china pig trimmed with pink roses and broad gold bands.

"I have an airplane," Ramon exclaimed with joy, "an airplane with an American flag painted on it!"

"O-o-o-o-h!" Pablo reached for a furry little toy donkey with a pack on its tiny back.

"A blue bracelet!" Maria cried happily as she slipped it on her arm.

"A bottle of perfume!" Rita held it close to her.

Pedro moved closer to Lolita. "Is it not time to give *Mamacita* her gift?" he asked.

"We shall get it at once," Lolita said.

Together they raced back to the other room for the paper-covered gift. Lolita carefully lifted it out from where she had hidden it in the dark.

She sped back toward *Mamacita*, Pedro running ahead of her. His voice rang through the happy excited talk of the neighbors and the other children. "Happy Christmas, *Mamacita*!" he cried.

Mamacita looked up from the table covered with little cakes and candies. She saw Pedro. Behind him, bearing the package with its bright ribbon, she saw Lolita. Her dark eyes shone at them. "Happy Christmas!" she welcomed them.

Lolita stood on tiptoe to kiss her mother. "A merry

278

Christmas from Pedro and me," she said as she handed her the precious gift.

"It is all from Lolita," Pedro said.

Mamacita untied the crimson ribbon and carefully folded it before she placed it on the table. She took off one fold of tissue paper. She took off the second fold, and she unwrapped the third. Then, for all the people to see, she raised in her strong hands the children's gift, a statue of Our Lady of Guadalupe, beautiful in a rich red robe and a deep blue mantle.

"It is like the picture of Our Lady in the church!" she exclaimed. "It is beautiful!"

Mamacita set the statue down and put her arms around Lolita. "You must have worked hard to save enough money to buy this for me," she said.

"And she has nothing left for the *fiesta* tomorrow," Pedro said.

Lolita's father lifted her high on his shoulder. "Do not worry about the *fiesta*," he told her.

"I don't," she sighed happily. "More than anything else I wanted *Mamacita* to have a statue of Our Lady of Guadalupe."

"You shall ride on the ferris wheel at the *fiesta* too," he promised.

From out in the patio, bright now with lights from a dozen windows, came the sound of music and laughter. Someone began to sing. A violin caught up the melody. Through the happy hours the Mexicans sang and danced while the stars, bright in the sky, looked down upon them as they had once looked down upon another Christmas Eve in Bethlehem.

Just before midnight the first bell of the church rang out, sending across square and city street a call to the faithful. The song stopped. The violin grew still. The bell rang again.

Their father waited as *Mamacita* drew her dark coat close to her and threw a silken shawl over her dark head. "Come, Rita," she commanded. "Come, Maria and Ramon and Pablo and Lolita and little Pedro! It is time for us to go to midnight Mass."

They moved out of the patio and into the wider street and across the park to the old church. The candles were already lighted on the altar. Two by two, they went into the church that had been built by other Mexicans when they had come to a new land that was now their own.

280

In this story there are several words from the Spanish language. These words are underlined in the sentences below. If you read the sentences containing them very carefully, you can perhaps tell their meanings. Then try to rewrite them in words that we generally use. It would also be interesting to look for the meanings of the words in the glossary of this book.

1. Did _Mamacita_ let her go?
2. Wouldn't she be back in time for _la piñata_, that Christmas game of all Mexican children?
3. The old church had been built by the _padres_ many years ago.
4. Suddenly lights went on in the _patio_.
5. "You shall ride on the ferris wheel at the _fiesta_, too," he promised.

FINDING OUT ABOUT CHRISTMAS CUSTOMS

This story described one of the Spanish customs at Christmas time. Almost every land has its own special Christmas customs. Many of these customs have been brought to our own land by people of other countries. You can learn more about these interesting customs by referring to the encyclopedia. The following topics will give you the information: Christmas in Other Lands, Christmas, Christmas Customs in the New World and in the Old. Remember to take notes so that you can report to your class.

As the children of Spanish America walk in the Christmas Eve Procession they sing songs which are older than our American history. Group after group, they take up the song which tells the story of how Saint Joseph and Our Lady sought for

Lodging

Saint Joseph

Will you give shelter
To pilgrims two?
A simple lodging
We ask of you.

Innkeeper

Even though you may be
Tired as you say,
We take no strangers
From the highway.

Saint Joseph

You can see that my wife
Can travel no more.
In God's name open
Your hard-locked door.

Innkeeper

My inn is crowded,
We've nothing today.
Do not be foolish,
Keep on your way.

Saint Joseph

We cannot go on
As far as the city.
God will reward you
If you will have pity.

Innkeeper

Will you move out of
The outer yard?
If you annoy me,
I'll call the guard.

282

Saint Joseph

My name is Joseph.
In Nazareth town,
I'm a carpenter
Of good renown.

Saint Joseph

The Queen of Heaven
Lady of Light,
Asks you for lodging
For this one night.

Saint Joseph

My wife is Mary
Of David's line,
She will be mother
Of a Son Divine.

Saint Joseph

May God save you
From all distress,
And bless you for
Our happiness.

Chorus (from without)

Enter, dear pilgrims,
A welcome awaits.
Our hearts open to you
Their hard-closed gates.

Innkeeper

About your name
I care nothing at all.
I have nothing for you
Within this wall.

Innkeeper

If she is a queen,
(Which I must doubt),
Where is her court?
Why is she out?

Innkeeper

Enter, dear pilgrims,
End all this strife.
I did not know you
And Mary, your wife.

Innkeeper

We wish you a long
And happy life.
Enter, good Joseph,
And Mary, your wife.

Chorus (from within)

This is the night
Of happiness bright
Because we can shelter
The Mother of God.

VII

Treasures of the Earth

"Do not lay up for yourselves treasures on earth, where rust and moth consume, and where thieves break in and steal; but lay up for yourselves treasures in heaven, where neither rust nor moth consumes, nor thieves break in and steal. For where thy treasure is, there thy heart also will be. . . .

"No man can serve two masters; for either he will hate the one and love the other, or else he will stand by the one and despise the other. You cannot serve God and mammon."

MATTHEW 6, 19–24

Shells in Rock

I've been along the quarry road,
And I have watched men digging wells,
And everywhere it was the same—
The stones were full of little shells.

And they are packed away in rock;
They're under sand and under clay;
And someone said that they were left
When the ocean went away.

I saw them in the stones that make
A church, and in a bridge.
They're hidden in the solid rock
But they show along the edge.

You see them in foundation stones;
They show in creeks and waterfalls;
And once I saw them on the jail—
More little shells in walls.

We walk on them when we walk on roads;
And they're packed under all the hills.
Suppose the sea should come back here
And gather up its shells.

ELIZABETH MADOX ROBERTS

Red Willow's Gift of Silver

[See page 292 before you begin to read this story.]

Navaho country was home to Red Willow. He knew every high red rock and every deep dry canyon. He knew where the evergreen trees stretched out their dark arms along the mesa. Long before anyone else saw them in the Spring-Moon-Time he would find the pink blossoms of the cactus on the edge of the desert. The eyes of Red Willow were bright, but the smile of Red Willow was brighter. Out in Navaho country he was always the first to cry a word of greeting when the tribes gathered for the sheep-shearing or the roundup of the horses. It was then that Red Willow welcomed his friends, Beautiful Boy, and Round Boy, and Little Warrior.

Far off, under the blue sky Red Willow would glimpse the red velveteen shirts and the green trousers of the Navaho boys as they rode toward him from the far corners of the reservation. Even before the horses and wagons would come down the high cliff road Red Willow would see the velveteen jackets of the girls and their wide skirts trimmed in bands of purple.

"*Ei-yei!*" he would shout.

"*Ei-yei!*" they would answer.

Life in the Navaho country was happy for Red Willow.

It was pleasant in the morning to wake to the

warmth of the hogan and see his mother, No War, stirring the fire under the heavy iron kettle of steaming corn.

It was brave to ride on his burro through the brightness of the desert with his father, Old Wagon.

It was wise to listen in the desert starlight to the stories of his grandfather, White Hair, who had been young when the Navahos had thundered their rage against the white man.

It was good to go to the mission of the Sisters of the Blessed Sacrament, who had come from the white man's country to teach the Indian.

It was fine to stand at the forge of Painted Bowl and learn the old man's way of working with silver. Day after day, as the sun beat down upon the mesa, Red Willow would make bright silver plates for his

broad leather belt. He would make round silver buttons for his high red moccasins, and gleaming silver ornaments for his burro's bridle. Tap-tap-tap would go Red Willow's hammer on the bar of silver.

Once he had made a heavy necklace for his mother. It was bigger and stronger and had more blue stones than any other necklace No War wore. She was proud of him, his mother said. Some day, she told him, he would be a great silversmith among the Navahos.

"I shall be the best silversmith," declared Red Willow.

One day, as he watched Father William and the stronger men of the Navahos building the new church at the mission, the boy spoke to the priest. "Soon," he said, "I shall make something for this church of God."

"Will it be a rug?" asked Father William. "I have seen many beautiful Navaho rugs."

"The women weave them," said Red Willow. "It cannot be a rug."

"Will it be a painting such as the Kiowas make?" asked Father William.

"I am no Kiowa," said Red Willow.

"Will it be like the pottery of the Pueblos?" asked the priest.

"It will not be pottery," said the Navaho boy. "You will know, Father, on the day when I give it to you, the day when you finish the church."

"That will be the Feast of the Annunciation," said Father William.

"My gift will be ready," said Red Willow.

Even as he went his way to the forge of Painted Bowl the boy knew that his gift would be more beautiful than anything yet made by a Navaho. It would be a gift that would last long after White Hair and Father William and even Red Willow himself were gone from the life of the mesas and the canyons and the desert. It would be a gift that would rest upon the altar of God for all men to see the faith of the Indian.

Red Willow set to work. Tap-tap-tap went his hammer on the forge. All through the Months-of-the-Big-Snow the boy worked. Even when the men of the reservation spent their hours in the building of the church Red Willow stayed at the forge.

Into the chalice he put the finest silver his father had mined from the earth. Within the cup of the chalice he pounded gold which his grandfather had brought a long time ago from Mexico. Below the rim of the chalice he set the most beautiful stones of blue which his mother had gathered.

On the Eve of the Feast of the Annunciation Red Willow was still working. He was too busy to go to the top of the cliff and shout greeting to Beautiful Boy, and Round Boy, and Little Warrior, who had come for the procession which would that night go into the church. There was still work to be done on the chalice.

Only when the first sound of the mission bell rang out across the darkness did Red Willow finish his task. Then, running out into the first warm spring air of the March night, he raced toward the procession of Indians that was forming outside the church door. Then, and not until then, did he see the smoking lanterns of the men and the dust in the road from the horses and wagons. Then, and not until then, did he see the campfires on the edge of the circle of hogans. Then, and not until then, did he see the cross which a man of the tribe lifted high above the heads of the crowd.

"Wait!" cried Red Willow. "Wait for me!"

His mother moved on with a lighted candle in her hand. "Hurry," she called to the boy. "We are about to follow Father William into the new church."

Red Willow ran past the Navahos with their hundreds of flaming candles. Father William, bright in his golden cope, already was moving up the church steps. The new bells of the mission were ringing in joy.

"Wait!" cried Red Willow.

Father William saw him then. "What is it, Red Willow?" he asked.

Red Willow held up his arms with his gift. "It is my gift to God," he said.

Father William lifted the chalice. Its silver and gold and blue shone in the glow of the hundred candles and the torches and the campfires. Higher and higher Father William lifted it. There was a light in his eyes

291

brighter than all the golden lights on the altar within the church. "Some day," he said, "when the bishop comes here to our mission, he will consecrate this work of your hands."

In the desert night, with a gladness he had never before known, Red Willow moved beside Father William into the church of the desert, the church which was built for the glory of God among the high red cliffs and the mesa and the deep dark canyons of the Navaho country.

CAN YOU LOCATE ANSWERS TO QUESTIONS BY SKIMMING?

Before you read the story, number your paper from 1 to 10. Write on your paper the exact time when you start to do the exercise. You may write your answers in short phrases, or you may write just a single word to answer the question correctly. Write down the exact time when you finish the exercise. How many minutes did it take you to finish the exercise?

1. Where was Red Willow's home?
2. Who was White Hair?
3. Who was Old Wagon?
4. Who was No War?
5. What community of Sisters taught the Indians?
6. What things did Red Willow make of silver?
7. What metals were used in making the chalice?
8. What was the name of the priest who built the church?
9. What day was the church finished?
10. What was Red Willow's gift to God?

Copper

Copper for pennies, and copper for pans,
Copper for faucets, and copper for cans,
Copper for kettles, and copper for cars,
Copper for fences, and copper for bars,
Copper for windows, and copper for doors,
Copper for printing, and copper for floors,
Copper for hundreds and hundreds of things,
There's even copper in airplane wings.
Copper from Mexico, and from Peru,
Copper from Asia and Africa too,
But of the copper men take from the mine
None has the brightness, the gleam, and the shine
Of copper the underground miners still get
From the diggings they know as the Old Calumet.

Men who work in mines
work in great danger;
and one of them was saved by

The Donkey Who Found Daylight

I. *Meet Peter and Goldie*

Peter was a little gray donkey. He lived in the depths of a black coal mine where he had been born.

He had never seen a little girl or a little boy, for he had never been out of the mine. He knew only the thin, pale men who came down the black shafts to work in the mine. They all wore shining little lights in the stiff points of their caps, and they carried lunch boxes and first-aid kits. Sometimes they sang as the cage, or elevator, carried them down the deep shaft to the mines. Peter knew one of their songs:

> We work in the mines, where the sun never shines
> And where daylight does never appear;
> With our lamps burning bright in the mine
>   black as night,
> We meet danger, but never know fear.

He liked the men for they were kind to him. Best of all, Peter liked a smiling, dark-eyed man called Steve. Steve was a driver. He came every morning and hitched Peter to one of the coal cars that was used to carry coal to a higher level of the mine. Steve always talked to Peter. Some days he spoke to the

294

little donkey about Anna and John, his children. "They would like to have you for a playmate," he said.

Peter talked this over with Goldie the canary. Goldie had not always lived in the mine. One day, not long before, Steve had brought her down the black shaft. She stayed there with Peter.

"What is a playmate?" Peter asked Goldie. You see, the little donkey had never done anything but work; he knew nothing about play.

Goldie smiled at him. "You poor little donkey," she said. "Didn't you ever have a good time? Didn't you ever roll on the grass?"

Peter shook his head. "No, I never did."

"Life is easier for me," said Goldie. "I don't have to stay here. I can fly at any time."

"Don't go," begged Peter. "I should be lonely without you."

So day after day Peter and Goldie waited at the bottom of the shaft for the cages to bring Steve and the rest of the miners to work. Day after day they listened to the sound of great, heavy drills that dug deep into the rich layers of coal. Day after day they heard the thud of dynamite that was used to open up new tunnels in which the men would mine the coal.

"This is a dangerous job for a man," Goldie said to Peter.

"They are brave men," Peter told her, "but Steve is the bravest of them all."

"Perhaps I shall go up with Steve some night," said Goldie. "I should like to see Anna and John."

"Come back and tell me all about them," begged Peter.

One night, as Steve was getting ready to go home, he saw Goldie watching him. "I think I shall take you up to see Anna and John," he said.

"I shall be lonesome for you, Goldie," Peter said wistfully.

He was lonesome that night, and he was glad when he saw Goldie come back on Steve's shoulder. When Goldie came close to Peter, her bright eyes were happy with excitement. "They live in a little gray house with a blue door. There are pink curtains on the windows. There is a yellow rosebush in the yard.

Every day they go to the Sisters' school, and every night they pray for their father's safety."

Peter was pleased. "Is Anna a pretty little girl?" he asked.

Goldie nodded. "Her hair is as golden as my wings."

"Is John as nice as his father?" Peter wanted an answer at once.

"His smile is just like Steve's," she told the donkey. "They are kind, too. They gave me water and bread crumbs. I promised I would go back to visit them again some time soon."

"Did they ask about me?" You see, Peter was very shy.

"They sent you their love," said Goldie.

The next morning when Steve came to work he patted Peter's little gray head. "I have a present for you," he said. He stooped so low that the miner's lamp on his black cap shone right into Peter's eyes. "Anna and John sent you a gift." He tied a little silver bell on Peter's collar.

Peter laughed out loud as he started off with his load of coal. The bell tinkled. He liked the merry sound. Ting-a-ling, ting-a-ling, it called to him. He had never heard anything so wonderful before.

Goldie heard the ting-a-ling and whistled with joy. Up and down the scale she whistled, do-re-mi-fa-so-la-ti-do! "I am going to follow you and your little bell all day," she said.

297

"Come and ride with me," Peter begged. "We'll have a lot of fun."

It was a busy day. Over and over again Peter pulled the car around the curves and through the long, black tunnels. He wasn't tired, though. Steve fed him from the lunch box he had brought from home.

"What are you eating?" Goldie asked.

Peter licked his lips. "A hard-boiled egg, and part of a pork chop, and a little bread and jelly," he told her.

"You have a dreadful appetite," she said. "I found some nice clover and corn."

In the afternoon they started off again, and the little bell rang merrily. He and Goldie sang and talked and laughed all the time.

Once Peter asked her, "What do people above the ground do with all this coal?"

"They use it for a hundred things," she told him. "For heat to keep them warm. For power to run steam engines. For blocks to pave their streets. For paint to brighten their homes. They even use it for perfume."

"I have never known anyone as clever as you," Peter told her.

Goldie made a polite little bow. "Thank you," she said, "and I have never known anyone so faithful as you, Peter."

II. *Danger in the Mine*

The whistle blew above them. Peter knew the signal. The day's work was nearly done. Steve moved forward to take off the harness that held Peter to the coal car. "Soon I can go home to my Anna and my John," he said. "Good night, Goldie. Good night, Peter."

Peter moved away from him down the narrow track. "Come on, Goldie," he called. "There is nothing more to be done today."

Goldie did not answer him.

"She must be asleep," thought Peter, but he glanced back to where Goldie had been sitting on the rim of the coal car. Even in the dimness he could see that her golden wings were drooping. He turned back swiftly, and hurried nearer. The silver bell on his collar rang a merry ting-a-ling, but Goldie did not answer. There was no happy whistle, no bright little do-re-mi-fa-so-la-ti-do! Peter came very, very close to Goldie. Her bright eyes were closed. He knew that the cheerful little canary would sing no more.

"Oh, what ever shall I do?" thought Peter.

He knew what had happened to Goldie. She had been killed by chokedamp, which is a poisonous gas that is given off by a layer of coal. It forms after an explosion along the floor of a mine. It blows out lights, and it smothers all living things. Birds are the first to feel it. So, because Peter was a mine donkey and he knew now that all the miners were in danger, he ran as fast as he could to warn the men. He did not stop then to think of his own loss, and of how much he would miss Goldie as long as he lived.

He must find Steve at once. Steve would know what to do. Steve would know that if a poor little canary had fallen from her perch it wouldn't be long before the awful gas from the coal dust would kill him and all the rest of them. There was no time to lose. Peter trotted up the dark tunnel as fast as his legs could carry him.

Steve heard the sound of the little silver bell. "What are you doing, Peter?" he called. "I never saw you act this way before."

Peter threw back his little gray head. He tried to tell Steve that Goldie was dead.

At first Steve did not seem to understand, but he knew that something was wrong. Peter turned back to the coal car. He looked over his shoulder to see if Steve would follow him. Steve moved along after him, a puzzled look on his thin, white face. When they reached the car he saw Goldie. With a dreadful shout that Peter would never forget, Steve cried aloud, "There has been an explosion! Run for your lives, men!"

Some of the miners heard him. Peter ran around wildly as the men yelled up the car shaft. "Send down the cage," they roared hoarsely. "We'll choke to death if you don't get us out of here."

Peter heard many bells ring. He heard the great mine whistle blow as it had never blown before. He heard the cage come down time and again to take the men to safety, but Steve was still below.

"There are more men in the tunnels who don't know what has happened," he told Peter, as he hurried from one tunnel to another with the little donkey at his heels. "Get out of here!" Steve shouted to the miners. "Run for your lives! The last car is going up!"

Peter ran after him, stumbling over coal and fallen timber. There were tears in the faithful little donkey's eyes as he thought of Anna and John. He wished, more than anything else in the world, that Steve would get back to the cage in time for the last trip. What would Anna and John do without their father?

301

Through darkness and through smoke Peter followed Steve. Once he lost him, and he was wild with worry. Then, as flames broke out near the cage shaft, he saw Steve leaning against a wall. The man's face was paler than usual. His friendly smile was gone. "I think they are all out," he said. The little donkey could hardly hear his words, for the miner's voice was weak and sick. Peter put his gray head against the hand of the man who had been so kind to him.

"Only the two of us are left," whispered Steve, and he bowed his head in prayer.

"You saved their lives," Peter tried to tell him. "Now you must save your own."

Steve roused himself. "You and I have one chance, Peter," he said. "You will have to carry me up the long tunnels. I am too tired to walk."

Peter was tired, too. He had often heard the men talk of the awful gas. Now he knew what it did. His knees bent, and his head ached. His eyes were so dimmed that he could scarcely see the tunnels he knew so well, but, because he was such a brave little donkey, he moved along with his load.

Up and up along dark tunnels he moved, too weak and sick from the gas to think. Once Steve stirred. "There has been a cave-in," he said. "This way out is closed."

Peter pulled himself and the man around another way. Up and up they went. Peter bowed his head when he thought of the boy and girl who must be waiting at the mouth of the mine without much hope.

"I've got to get Steve out of here," he told himself. "I can't fail Anna and John."

He carried the man along the narrow ledge to another tunnel. Then he climbed a little higher to a rocky track. The air choked them, and they moved slowly. "I wish I had wings like Goldie," Peter sighed.

Steve moved. Peter was afraid the man would slip from his back. Peter grew stiff, and Steve threw his arms around the donkey's neck. "That's better," said Peter.

In the darkness that seemed worse because of the silence Peter came to the end of the ledge. "I don't know what to do now," he sighed. "Perhaps I am going in the wrong direction." He stood very still. Steve could not speak.

III. *The Rescue*

Suddenly the little silver bell on Peter's collar tinkled. "That's funny," said Peter. "I wasn't moving." He did not stir. Again the little bell called to him. "What could make it ring?" Peter asked himself. He threw back his fuzzy gray head and sniffed. The air was different. It was lighter and purer. There was a breeze. They must be near an airshaft.

Up went his strong little back. Up went his long

pointed ears. Up to the next level moved his strong little legs. "Hold tight, Steve," he seemed to be saying. "We are going to ride to glory."

Peter thought that all the people in the world were at the top of the mine. He saw old friends whose miners' caps were still lighted. He saw men in white, and he knew they must be doctors. He saw nurses. He saw the long, shiny safety car of the Government, and men rushing from it with blankets and stretchers. He saw women, their arms around the rescued miners, still weeping with happiness.

"I must find Anna and John," he said, as he stumbled with his load into the crowd.

They stood apart, with a sobbing woman he knew must be their mother. A priest was comforting her.

"They are all out but Steve," the woman cried. "They will never find him."

It was Anna who first saw Peter. He heard her happy shout. "Oh, Mother! John! Look!" She rushed toward him.

Peter looked at her.

Doctors and nurses moved toward him with a white stretcher. He felt them lift Steve from his back. "He will be all right," he heard a doctor tell Steve's wife.

Men and women crowded around the little donkey, but Peter edged away shyly to stand near Anna and John. John smiled at him as he patted his back and, truly, his smile was just like Steve's. They put their

304

arms around him fondly. "Why, here is the little bell," laughed Anna. "Did you like it, Peter?"

Peter shook his head. He wanted them to take the bell, for it had saved their father's life.

"Oh, no!" they cried together. "The little bell belongs to you—forever!"

Peter sighed happily.

It was John who whispered in his ear. "Where is Goldie?" he asked.

Peter shook his head sadly, and they understood. "We shall all miss her," sighed Anna and John.

A broad-shouldered man moved toward them. Peter knew he was the barn boss. "I am proud of you, Peter," he said. "You are a brave donkey."

Peter looked at him as if he were asking when he was to go back to work. The barn boss didn't understand him—but Anna and John did! They repeated Peter's question.

"Does he have to go back?" cried Anna.

"We want him for a playmate." John's voice was excited.

"You shall have him for a playmate," the man said as he smiled at them. "From now on we'll use electricity to haul the coal cars, so Peter can live in your yard and always be your friend."

So now, if you pass through the little village in the mountains, you will see first of all over the entrance to the coal mine the tall machine called a breaker, which breaks up the coal. Then you will see the thin, pale-faced miners with little lights on their caps as they move along the road on their way to work. Sometimes they sing. Do you remember the song?

We work in the mines, where the sun never shines
And where daylight does never appear;

And, then, because you'll be looking for it, you will be sure to see the little gray house with the blue door, and pink curtains at the windows, and a yellow rosebush in the yard. Anna, whose hair is as golden as the canary's wings, will be there. John, whose slow, sweet smile is like his father's, will be there, too. And the little donkey? Of course! He will run out to meet you and, when you see the happy light in his round brown eyes, you will know that he is Peter, the donkey who found daylight.

How well do you remember the characters in this story? Number your paper from 1 to 10. Beside each number write the name of the character or characters to which the description below refers. Reread the part of the story that will prove your answer is correct.

1. This person was a smiling dark-eyed man who drove one of the coal cars.

2. These people spend most of their time working in underground tunnels.

3. This person was kind and had a pleasant smile.

4. He liked the men who worked in the mine because they were kind to him.

5. These people are hired by the government to take care of the miners.

6. Even though she was thought to be very important, this character did not think her life was very difficult.

7. This person had hair as golden as a canary's wings.

8. This person told the donkey he was proud of him.

9. He arranged things so that the donkey would not have to work in the mine.

10. These people wept with happiness.

The Shopper

I knew the hills of Nazareth
Had miracles to tell.
I hoped the shops of Nazareth
Had memories to sell.
I climbed the streets of Nazareth
And bought a camel's bell.

At Cana's well in Galilee
One draws no wine today
And wedding guests in Galilee
Have no great word to say.
A beggar child in Galilee
Sold me a pot of clay.

In cobble-stoned Jerusalem
For hours and hours I stood.
I brought back from Jerusalem
The simplest thing I could,
A donkey from Jerusalem
Cut out of olive wood.

SISTER M. MADELEVA

od has given to men
reat wealth to be shared.
ome of it was increased by

The Wizard of Santa Rosa

Out in California, near the town of Santa Rosa, there is a garden that is famous all over the world. In it are roses you do not see anywhere else, huge daisies with hearts of gold, more than a hundred kinds of lilies, more than forty kinds of plums, white blackberries, and many hundred kinds of cherries. They are all there because one man believed that his work in life was to grow better fruits and better flowers.

That man was Luther Burbank.

He started his work when he was a small, shy boy who lived on a farm in Massachusetts. There were fifteen children in the family, and Luther was one of the youngest. Although he went to the country school near the farm and later to an academy, the boy was always more interested in plants than he was in books. He studied hard so that he could learn more about plants.

He went to work in a plow factory when he was fifteen years old. He worked well, but his father died and the boy went with his mother to live on a small farm. There he began the plant experiments which were to make the name of Burbank famous.

His first work was with potatoes. He noticed that potatoes are usually grown by planting pieces called "eyes." Then one day he saw that a plant in his garden had a seed ball. He opened it and discovered twenty-three seeds. He planted these, then watched, and found to his surprise that each seed grew a different kind of potato. Some were poor, others were ordinary, but one was very fine. Young Burbank replanted this one and soon had a small harvest of wonderful potatoes. A seed dealer paid him a hundred and fifty dollars for the right to market them.

He could have kept on growing superfine potatoes, but he wanted to try other experiments. He studied climates and soils and decided that California was the best place for year-round work. He found a place near

Santa Rosa and began his thirty-five years of labor with flowers and fruits and vegetables.

He had to do odd jobs for awhile. One of them was in a plant nursery, and he decided that he must have a nursery of his own. He did nearly all the work of building it. In a little while he bought more land. As he made money, he spent it all on his experiments. To him the growing of a new kind of plant was far more important than the making of money.

He was not strong, but he never spared himself in his work. He carried on more than three thousand experiments at a time. Probably the most amazing one was the growth of five hundred kinds of cherries on one tree. Burbank had done this by setting the buds of one plant on the stems of others. People came thousands of miles to see this unusual tree and gave to Burbank the name of the Wizard.

Most of Burbank's work was with lilies, plums, and berries. He developed more than forty kinds of plums and many kinds of blackberry, among them the white blackberry. He grew amazing roses and wonderful lilies; and he brought out daisies bigger than sunflowers.

None of this was haphazard planting. Burbank wanted to improve everything that grew for the benefit of mankind. He always chose for his experiments the finest of its kind, tree or plant, and worked to improve it. He never sought either fame or fortune. He once said that he would die happy if, because of him, there were better fruits and better flowers. He believed that, just as God had made the plants and flowers, He had made man with an intelligence to develop them and that it was man's duty to make the most of God's gifts.

CAN YOU PUT IDEAS IN ORDER?

Each of the following statements gives the main idea of a paragraph in the story "The Wizard of Santa Rosa." Reread the story to find the order in which the ideas are given. Then write a number before each statement to show the order in which they are presented.

____ Luther Burbank was always more interested in plants than in books.

____ For thirty-five years he worked with flowers and fruits and vegetables.

____ Burbank's greatest experiment was to set buds of one plant on the stems of others.

____ He experimented with plants on a small farm.

____ He surprised himself by making money on his wonderful potatoes.

____ Burbank believed that God wanted man to study how to grow better plants.

____ He worked mainly with lilies, plums, and cherries.

____ There is a garden in California that is famous all over the world.

312

Four-Leaf Clover

I know a place where the sun is like gold
    And the cherry blooms burst with snow,
And down underneath is the loveliest nook
    Where the four-leaf clovers grow.

One leaf is for hope, and one is for faith,
    And one is for love, you know,
And God put another one in for luck;
    If you search you will find where they grow.

But you must have hope, and you must have faith,
    You must love and be strong, and so
If you work, if you wait, you will find the place
    Where the four-leaf clovers grow.

ELLA HIGGINSON

People of many lands
have brought things of beauty
to our land. Some of them
were brought by those who pictured

Saints in Ruby Glass

Men were making glass five thousand years ago in
the Eastern countries. There was a glass factory beside
a road on which Christ traveled in the Holy Land. The
East taught the West, not only how to make glass, but
also how to make it beautiful.

There was a land in Europe where the making of
glass became a fine art. That land was Bohemia. In
Bohemia, for hundreds of years, men made glass so
beautiful that it was like jewels. Into it they put their
love of their country, their love of God. Into it they
put the stories of the great men and the great saints
of their native land.

In red glass that glowed like great rubies they pictured the stories of Saint Ludmilla and her grandson,
a king of Bohemia who was also a saint.

Queen Ludmilla and her grandson were both put to
death for their faith. He was killed as he prayed in the
great church. For a little while his enemies ruled in
Bohemia. Then an emperor came to punish them.

The emperor had loved and admired the king ever
since the first time they had met. The king, then only
a lad, had come late to a meeting with the emperor.
He told the emperor that he was late because he had

stopped on his way to go to Mass, to honor, he had said, "a greater King." The emperor liked the lad for his courage in saying that to him.

Many stories of the king went into the shining glass of his country, put there by men who gave honor to God through their work.

After awhile the world needed so much glass—glass for windows, for bottles, for lights, for a hundred and one other uses—that men could no longer work on glass at home or in small shops. They came together into factories, and the methods of making glass changed.

In the glass factories of Bohemia men talked of the United States and of the great glass factories in this

land. In the United States, they said, men could work at their trade, make a living for themselves and their families, and live in freedom.

Freedom! That was the word which filled their minds. Their people had not always been free, but always they had wanted freedom. Many workers decided to go to the land where all men were free.

The factories in the United States were very different from the old factories, although glass was made from the same materials men had always used—soda, sand, and lime. But instead of using hand tools and hand work, they used great machines.

A man named Michael Owens had developed a way to draw off the glass in sheets from the tanks. He improved a bottlemaking machine too. Now there is a machine which is the biggest single machine in the world. It has ten thousand parts and can make thousands and thousands of bottles every day.

People use glass for many other things besides bottles and windows. They use it to make dishes and furniture and many articles of beauty. They use it for automobiles and airplanes, for telescopes and spectacles, and even for bricks.

The United States has made the making of glass into one of the world's great industries; but it has not changed the roads which men must travel to be good and useful and happy: honesty in work and love of God.

Number your paper from 1 to 8. All the following questions can be answered with one or two words. See how quickly and accurately you can answer these questions. Read the story again and see if you have answered the questions correctly.

1. In which countries was glass being made five thousand years ago?

2. In which country in Europe was glassmaking a fine art?

3. What was the name of the queen who was put to death for her faith?

4. What one word about the United States filled the minds of the glassworkers in Bohemia?

5. What is one thing for which glass is used?

6. What virtues must a man practice to be useful and happy?

7. What was the name of the man who developed a new method of glassmaking?

8. Which country has made glassmaking one of the world's greatest industries?

THINGS TO DO

1. Borrow from the library pictures of different kinds of "stained glass." Many libraries have exhibits of stained-glass materials which they are happy to lend to schools. Ask if the one in your city or neighborhood does and arrange to have an exhibit in your classroom.

2. See if you can find more information about Queen Ludmilla.

Hymn to Our Lady

O Queen of Heaven, rejoice,
  Alleluia!
For He whom you deserved to bear,
  Alleluia!
Has risen, as He said,
  Alleluia!
Pray for us to God,
  Alleluia!

O Queen of Heaven, delight,
  Alleluia!
That Christ, Our Lord, was born,
  Alleluia!
To save our sinful souls,
  Alleluia!

Rejoice and be glad, O Virgin Mary,
  Alleluia!
Because Our Lord is truly risen,
  Alleluia!

AUTHOR UNKNOWN

The great stories of one country
may help the people of another;
and our own land has been helped
by the story that a girl
remembered for

The Song That Was Not Sung

I. *Millie's Stories*

Sometimes in April the sunset shone gold on the city streets. Then all the windows that faced the west glowed brightly. The towers of the great church rose in the yellow light. In that light the smoke of the city seemed to hang over the roofs of gray houses, just as the smoke of incense at Benediction hung over the sanctuaries of the churches.

That was the time Millie liked best. She liked all the hours of her city, the steel town where she lived.

She liked the sound of the Angelus in the dark, when people in the houses near her were getting ready to go to work.

She liked the dawn, when she hurried to go to Mass. She liked to kneel in prayer, knowing that in a little while she would go to Holy Communion. She liked to kneel in thanksgiving when Mass was over.

Millie liked school, and she was a good student. She remembered her father's words, "It is not what you have in your mind that counts. It is what you get out of it to give to other people." In school she wanted to please everyone, but most of all, Sister Helena. For

Sister Helena was so kind and wise and good that Millie smiled whenever she watched her.

"When I grow up," Millie thought, "I want to be a Sister."

She liked noon recess, when she ran home for the meal her mother had made ready. She liked the time, right after school, when she went into the big church and saw the beauty of the great crucifix and the stained-glass windows. More than that, she liked to pray at the altar rail before the tabernacle of Our Lord. Coming out, she saw the saints pictured in statues or in windows.

"You were all so good," she told them. "Maybe some day God will let me be as good as you, not a great saint, of course, but very, very good."

Millie liked all the city hours—the noisy ones and

the quiet ones, the happy ones and the serious, the work and the play; but, best of all, she liked the time just after supper when the days grew warm. For then she sat on the steps of her house and told stories to the other children.

They were stories of Poland that her father and mother had told her, stories of brave men and women and children.

"Tell us about King Jan," the boys would say; and Millie would tell about the king of Poland who had saved Europe for the Christians. "He was so brave," she always said.

"Tell us about the Trumpeter of Krakow," the children would say to her.

"Once the Tartars, who were enemies of the Poles, came to the city of Krakow," Millie began. "The people of the city knew they could not hold their town against their enemies, and so they all went away except one boy. He was a trumpeter, a musician who plays a trumpet as a signal.

"He had once made a promise to Our Lady that he would play a hymn to her as each hour passed. As the stroke of the hour came near, he knew that if he played his trumpet the Tartars would hear him and find him and kill him. But he remembered his promise.

"As the big clock began to strike the hour, the boy in the tower started the hymn to Our Lady. The Tartars saw him and shot at him with their bows and

arrows. They killed him before he could play the last note of the hymn.

"That is why no trumpeter in Krakow, as he plays Our Lady's hymn from the tower of Saint Mary's Church, ever plays the last note."

"He died for his country and his Faith," said her brother Stephen.

"Many, many Poles have done that," said another brother, Andrew.

"Some of them have died for other countries, too," Millie told them. "There was a Pole, Pulaski, who died for our American freedom."

"And another Pole helped us to win that freedom," Stephen said. "His statue stands in the park. He did so much for the United States that people think of him, not as a Pole, but as a great American."

322

"We are all Americans," Millie said. "My father says that it is very easy for a Pole to become an American, because the Poles have fought so hard for freedom for such a long time. He says that Poland was really the first big democracy in Europe. Even though they had a king, the people elected him. He says, too, that Poland never tried to take away the freedom of other countries."

"Why have so many Poles come to the United States?" Irene, the girl next door, asked Millie.

"Because other nations near Poland took away Poland's freedom. The Polish people loved their country, but they loved freedom more because freedom meant that they could worship God," explained Millie.

"Should we die for this country the way the Trumpeter of Krakow died for Poland?" Andrew asked her.

"If we ever have to," Millie said.

"What is this about dying for our country?" her father asked, as he passed them on the steps. They all stood to tell him. He looked down at them for a moment. "You are all pretty young yet to worry about that," he said, "but you are not too young to start thinking about how you can live for our country."

"What do you mean?" they asked him.

"There is not a day," he said, "when every one of you does not have the chance to show that he's a good American. We can prove that we are good citizens by the way we live every day."

323

II. *Millie's Sacrifice*

Day after day Millie wondered how she could show that she was a good American. She pondered about it while she helped her mother around the house and while she helped Andrew and Stephen and the other children at home.

"There must be some way," she thought, "but I don't seem to find it."

She wondered about it when she joined the music group, those children who practiced nearly every afternoon in the little park, making themselves ready for the great yearly Music Festival. Irene, the girl next door, sang in the group. She sang well, but not so well as did Millie. Millie knew that singing was the one great joy Irene had. Her people were very poor, and Irene had few pleasures.

"I want to be a singer," she told Millie. "If I do well in the Festival, I may have a chance to study so that someday I shall be a great singer."

Millie was coming home from church on Holy Saturday when she met Irene. Irene was not carrying a basket, and Millie felt sorry for her.

Millie was carrying a big basket, covered with a beautiful white cloth. Within it was a rich cake which her mother had baked and frosted so that it looked like a white lamb. There was a little red banner on its shoulder. Millie had held up the basket for the priest's blessing as he had given it over the baskets of food that the other people in the church held up.

Now she was taking her basket home, where tomorrow, Easter Sunday, the family would celebrate the Resurrection of Our Lord. She moved her basket to her other arm so that Irene might not notice it too much, for she feared that the other girl would be unhappy.

Irene was not unhappy. She was excited. "Oh, Millie," she cried, "I am thinking about the contest this afternoon at the park."

"About the solo?" Millie asked.

"Of course. Oh, Millie, if I win the contest this afternoon, I shall sing in the big festival in the stadium. I shall stand alone and sing the 'Star-Spangled Banner.' Millie, if I win today, if I succeed in the big festival, then I shall be sure of everything all the rest of my life. I shall be a great singer. Oh, Millie, pray that I win!"

Millie said nothing. She went into the house and set her basket on the kitchen table beside the baskets which her mother and Andrew and Stephen had already placed there.

"What is the matter?" her mother asked.

"Millie is thinking about how she can live for our country," Stephen said.

Millie was thinking, but she was thinking of Irene. Irene had none of the things they had. She had no books or pictures like theirs. She had no money to go to the motion pictures. She had no pretty clothes. She did not even have a voice as good as Millie's.

Millie knew that because only the week before the director of the music group at the park had told her. "Millie," he had said, "I want you to practice hard all next week. Practice those high notes especially. If you hold them true, you are sure to win any contest. Your voice is better than any of the others here."

"But Irene—" she had started to say.

"Irene is good," said the director, "but she is second to you."

If she sang her best, Millie thought, she would win and Irene would lose. And Irene did so want to win! Winning meant so much to Irene, so much more than it did to her. If only she were out of the contest, Irene would win it. Then she would sing at the Festival and go on to become a great singer.

For a moment Millie thought about what it would mean to win the contest. She would stand alone on a high platform in the stadium. Just below her a big band would be playing. Before her there would be thousands of men and women and children, all watching, all waiting for her to sing. The band would play more softly. She would lift her head and begin to sing. Her voice would rise over the field. Everyone she loved —her father, her mother, her sisters and brothers, Sister Helena—would all be proud of her.

"That would be living for my country," she thought.

Then she pictured how Irene would look. She would be sad, and there would be tears in her eyes. She would try to tell Millie that she had sung beautifully. She would try to pretend that she was glad, but all the time she would be thinking, "Why did Millie have to win the contest when she has everything else and I have so little?"

Millie picked up her hat from the chair where she had thrown it.

"Where are you going?" her mother asked.

"To church," she said. "I won't be long."

She ran through the streets to the big church. It was almost empty as she went in. She went up the aisle and knelt before the tabernacle. "Oh, dear Lord," she prayed, "help me to decide what I should do!" But she knew, deep in her heart, that she had already decided when she had come.

Millie was alone on the steps that Easter Saturday evening when her father came home. He sat down beside her and looked out over the golden smoke from the steel mills. "I thought you were going to sing at the music contest," he said.

"I didn't go." She tried to keep her voice from trembling.

"The list of winners was announced in the evening paper," her father said. "Irene won the contest."

"I knew she would."

"If you didn't go into it?" asked her father quietly.

"Yes, sir."

"Was that why you didn't?"

"Yes, sir." She looked him straight in the eyes. "She needs it more than I do."

"I understand." He put his hand over hers. "I am proud of you," he said. "You are learning, aren't you?"

"Learning what?" she asked him.

"Learning how to live for our country."

"I have been trying to learn," she said, "but I couldn't find any way."

"You have found it." He smiled down at her. "Sometimes I have thought," he said, "that the song that is not sung may be more beautiful than the one we hear." He looked up at the towers of the great church before he spoke again. "The Trumpeter of Krakow did not play the last note of his hymn," he told Millie, "but that last note has come sounding down to us through all the years."

CAN YOU MAKE A BOOK REPORT?

Many interesting books have been written about Poland and its heroes. You can get them at the library. Why not select one book to read and then tell the class about it? Make your report short and interesting. If your report is well done, other children may want to read the book.

The Work and the Workers

God made the world.

He made the seas and the fish in the seas.

He made the earth and the grains of the earth.

He made the gold and the silver and the iron ore and the oil and the coal that lie beneath the soil.

He made man, and He gave man the power to work so that man might use the fish and the grain and the minerals; and, since God made man in His own likeness, that many might love and serve Him, the worker is more important than the work.

The fisherman is greater than the fisheries.

The farmer is greater than the farm.

The miner is greater than the mine.

The worker in the factory is greater than the factory.

Through his work man gives love and praise and service to God.

The story of our country is the story of that love and that praise and that service.

For our country is a nation of workers.

VIII

From Dawn to Dusk

At that time Jesus spoke and said, "I praise thee, Father, Lord of heaven and earth, that thou didst hide these things from the wise and prudent, and didst reveal them to little ones. Yes, Father, for such was thy good pleasure. All things have been delivered to me by my Father; and no one knows the Son except the Father; nor does anyone know the Father except the Son, and him to whom the Son chooses to reveal him.

"Come to me, all you who labor and are burdened, and I will give you rest. Take my yoke upon you, and learn from me, for I am meek and humble of heart; and you will find rest for your souls. For my yoke is easy, and my burden light."

MATTHEW 11, 25–30

The Workers

Through all the early morning hours
   I hear them down my street—
A rising tide of purpose—
   The workers' noisy feet.

And some go swiftly hurrying by
   As eager gladness darts:
And some with tread as slow, perhaps,
   And heavy as their hearts.

But always all move on and on,
   The fast ones and the slow,
As if they knew if they should stop
   The whole world couldn't go.

And what a loss the world *would* know—
   And what a huge defeat—
If sometime early streets *were* still
   And stilled the workers' feet!

MARY BLAKE WOODSON

A good loser sometimes wins
the race; and so one young citizen
had a surprise on

Voting Day

I. *Home from School*

All the way from school, past the woolen mills and over the icy bridge of the river, the children walked hand in hand toward the little gray house that stood in a long row of other gray mill-town houses.

"Don't cry any more, Louis," Cecile told her little brother. "We are home now."

"I don't want to be sick," sobbed the little boy.

"You will soon be well," Cecile comforted him as she unlocked the door of the silent house, but there was worry in her voice. "You must get into bed right away, and soon the visiting nurse will be here. Sister Jean has sent for her."

"I want my mother," cried Louis, as he followed Cecile into the chilly rooms.

Cecile hurried to turn down the covers of the boy's cot. "Get under the blankets, Louis, at once. Then I will fix the hot-water bag for you."

Louis leaned against the wall. "I want my mother!" His young voice shook with sobs.

Cecile's dark eyes grew sad. "Don't you want to be well when *Maman* comes home from the mill?"

Louis cried more loudly.

333

"Do you want to stand there until you are sicker?" Cecile's worry was growing.

Louis looked at her through eyes bright with fever as he moved toward the cot. "Perhaps if I were very sick," he said, "*Maman* could not go to the mill. Then she would stay home and care for me."

"If you were well, Louis," Cecile told him, "you would not say such things. *Maman* does not go to the mill because she wishes to be away from us. She goes so that we will have enough money to live!"

The boy was still crying under the blankets as Cecile went out into the kitchen of the little gray house. Snatching an apron from a hook on the wall, she started to help her brother. She lighted the gas under the kettle. She found the hot-water bottle and filled it. She opened the icebox and saw two lemons. Carefully squeezing the fruit until there was no longer a drop of juice, she made hot lemonade for the boy.

Cecile lifted a tin tray from the pantry shelf. She reached higher and brought down a tall glass. She opened a drawer and took out a clean, folded napkin.

"Look!" she exclaimed cheerfully in the language of her mother's own old French Canada; "before you can say one, two, three, I shall be there, Louis!"

As the boy raised himself on his elbow and sipped the long, hot drink Cecile's eyes looked over the room with care. "Before the visiting nurse gets here I must clean up a little," she said.

"It is clean enough," Louis grumbled.

Cecile laughed at him. "I promise not to disturb you," she said. "I'll just dust a little and put a clean scarf on the dresser."

So Cecile dusted, and, from the piles of linen in the lowest box in the bedroom closet, she drew out a scarf for the dresser, a scarf stitched in blue. She held it up for Louis to see.

"Pretty," his voice seemed to come from a great distance.

Then, because it was a special occasion of illness, Cecile opened the deep cedar chest in the little hall and lifted the bright-colored hooked rug that long ago *Maman* herself had made.

"Someday *Maman* will show me how to hook a rug like this," said Cecile, as she laid it in all its bright glory along the side of her brother's cot.

335

II. Missing the Election

The room was shining when the visiting nurse knocked on the front door. "Where is the little boy who is sick?" she asked, as she took off her dark-blue coat.

"I am here." The boy's voice sounded small and weak as it came through the parlor door.

The visiting nurse moved toward the bed. She noted the hot-water bottle. "I see you have had a nurse ahead of me," she said.

"Cecile brought me home. I got sick and Sister Jean sent for her," explained Louis.

The visiting nurse opened her black bag and took out a shining thermometer. "Open your mouth, Louis," she said.

Cecile moved closer to the starched crispness of the nurse's uniform. "Sister said there is a lot of sickness in the town and many children are absent from school. It is too bad that this had to happen today."

"Why today?" The nurse spoke, though her eyes never left the boy's pale face. "What were you going to do at school?"

"This afternoon, in my class," said Cecile, "there was to be an election. We were to vote for the best citizen in our room."

The nurse turned a little. "Then you did not have a chance to vote?" she asked.

Cecile sighed. "Sister Jean called me before the voting began," she said. "Louis was sick, so I came home with him at once."

"For whom would you have voted?" asked the nurse, smoothing the covers on the boy's cot.

"It would be hard to decide," Cecile admitted. "I think I should have voted for Therese. She is my best friend, and she is truly a good citizen. She has a little garden that she takes care of in summer. She grows radishes, tomatoes, lettuce, and onions."

"Therese is deserving of honor," said the nurse.

"Then there is Nelly," Cecile added. "She too is a good citizen. She runs errands for all the neighbors. She sweeps the dust from the walk in summer and the snow from the school steps in winter."

"Nelly is good, too," said the visiting nurse.

Cecile moved from one foot to the other. "But then there is Hedwig. Hedwig is a very good citizen. Better than most," she added thoughtfully, "for, when she loses in the school games, she is cheerful and happy and generous to the winner."

"Hedwig should be praised for that," said the visiting nurse, as she lifted the thermometer from the boy's mouth and held it up to the light.

"Is he very sick?" Cecile whispered, as she followed the nurse out of the room.

The visiting nurse was writing something upon a small white paper. "Louis will need care for a few

337

days, just as the school doctor said. He will need special food and rest and quiet."

"He shall have it." Cecile's answer was a promise.

The nurse watched the girl closely. "I suppose that you will be the one to care for him?" she asked.

"I am strong enough," said Cecile, squaring her shoulders.

A shadow of doubt crossed the nurse's blue eyes. "It would be impossible for your mother to stay at home for the next few days?" she asked.

"*Maman* would like to be at home with Louis and with me every day," said the girl, "but who else is there to pay the rent, and the grocery bill, and—"

The visiting nurse patted Cecile's shoulder. "So you must take your mother's place at home, especially now that they are busy at the mill?"

338

"Every worker is needed at the weaving machines," said Cecile.

"Your mother is a weaver?" asked the nurse.

"Oh, yes," answered the girl proudly. "She is one of the most skillful weavers at the mill."

The visiting nurse stood at the door. "I am glad you're proud of your mother, Cecile," she said, "for you have reason to be proud."

"I love my mother," said Cecile simply, "and my mother loves Louis and me."

"Tell her when she comes home that your brother's illness is nothing serious. He can go back to school in a day or two."

"I shall tell her," said Cecile, as the nurse moved toward the street.

"I am sorry you missed the school election," the nurse called back from the pavement.

"It does not matter," Cecile lifted her voice to declare, "only that my vote would have helped Therese or Nelly or Hedwig."

III. *The Winner*

Long after the visiting nurse had gone Cecile worked around the house. She threw coal on the fire in the parlor stove until the room was rosy with light. She peeled potatoes. She washed vegetables. She made a soft custard for Louis and circled it with stiffly beaten egg whites dotted with specks of red jelly.

She danced a little in gladness that Louis was not very sick, and she sang a happy little song that *Maman* had taught her.

Louis was sleeping peacefully when the mill whistle blew. "*Maman* will be here soon," Cecile told herself as she set the table with two plates, two cups and saucers, and the silver.

As she was putting the kettle of pea soup to heat on the stove, there was a tap on the kitchen window.

Cecile looked at the kitchen clock. "It is not *Maman*, for it takes exactly sixteen minutes to cross the bridge from the mill."

There was a louder tap.

Cecile pulled back the red-and-white ruffled curtain. "Therese," she cried, "and Hedwig, and Nelly!" She rushed to open the kitchen door. "You have come to ask about Louis?"

The girls looked at one another. "Louis?" they cried together.

"Louis is sick," said Cecile.

"Oh, yes, Louis," said Therese politely. "We hope he will soon be better, but it is important news of the class election that brought us here."

Cecile looked from one girl to another. Who had been the winner? Therese was smiling. Nelly was smiling. Hedwig was smiling. "Who won?" she demanded.

Therese laughed. "Nelly will tell you," she said.

Nelly laughed. "Hedwig will tell you," she said.

Hedwig laughed. "Why should any one of us have to tell you, Cecile," she said, and her eyes were shining with happiness, "for all the time you must have known that you would be voted the best citizen in our room?"

Cecile leaned hard against the kitchen wall. Her hands were trembling. "I do not deserve the honor," she said slowly. "Any one of you is a better citizen than I."

"Oh, Cecile, I do nothing important," cried Therese.

"When I think of you, Cecile, I am ashamed of myself," said Hedwig.

"There is no one in our school as thoughtful and kind as you," said Nelly.

Louis woke up. "I want a glass of water," he cried.

"You shall have it," Cecile told him and hurried toward his cot as the girls left the house.

She was waiting at the front door as her mother came down the street. The windows of the woolen mill shone in the New England twilight as the workers moved like shadows down the hill and over the river bridge.

"*Maman*," she cried in welcome and rushed out into her mother's arms.

Her mother stooped and kissed her. "My dear little Cecile," she said. "Tell me of the day."

"Louis has been sick, but he is better," she told her mother as they moved into the house. "The visiting nurse says he must stay home from school for a day or two, but I shall care for him. I shall study hard, too, so that I can catch up with my class. Everything will be all right."

Louis sat up in bed. "Cecile was voted the best citizen in her class," he added.

Maman's face shone with pride. She put her arm around Cecile and reached down to hold her son's tight little fist. "In all New England there are no better children than mine," she told them. "Some day, when we are rich, I shall take you both on a long trip as reward for being so good."

"To Boston?" asked Louis. "May we go on the train to Boston?"

342

Cecile smiled at her mother. "Louis is very young," she said, "but I know where we shall go."

"Where?" demanded Louis.

"To the shrine of the good Saint Anne on the river St. Lawrence," said Cecile. "Am I not right, *Maman*?"

Maman nodded. "To the shrine of the good Saint Anne," she repeated. "There we shall pray for good health for us all, and work to do, and for God's blessing upon us—"

"And perhaps a prayer that we shall always be as happy as we are today," whispered Cecile.

"As happy as we are today," said her mother.

Cecile was singing the hymn to Saint Anne that her mother had sung when she was a child, as, together, they went back to the kitchen of the gray house on the mill-town street.

BEING A GOOD CITIZEN

In this story you have read about many ways to be a good citizen. Below you will find some of them. List under each heading the ways the children in the story proved that they were good citizens. You may add to the lists other things you can do to be a good citizen that were not mentioned in the story. Are you a good citizen?

Helpfulness	Kindness
Generosity	A Good Disposition
Thoughtfulness	Pride in Work Well Done

The Saint of the Shoemakers

Saint Crispin is a hardy saint
Who knows all kinds of weather,
Because he's patron of the men
And all who work in leather.

He guards the cattle on the range,
He watches pigs in clover;
He keeps his eye on all the needs
For shoes, the whole world over.

He stands within the beam-house door,
And sees the hides in cleaning;
He sees the big machines whirl round
That do the work of screening.

344

Saint Crispin pauses with a look
Of troubled admiration
When he beholds the great machines
Make shoes for all the nation.

He knows machines are very good
In making shoes from leather,
But, deeper still, he knows that men
Should all combine together

To make a better way of life
For everyone around them,
And leave the ways of everyday
Far better than they found them.

The men who own the great machines,
The men who do the labor
Should, every one, Saint Crispin knows,
Be just unto his neighbor.

Each man should honest be, and fair,
And grant the rights of others,
Because, since God has fathered all,
All men are truly brothers.

Saint Crispin prays and prays and prays,
The while he guards the leather,
That some day soon all men will work
As God has willed—together.

The lilies of the field
have their own clothing;
but for us humans

Here Come the Clothesmakers

A sheep.

A plant.

A worm.

A tree.

Coal, air, water, oil, and gas.

From these gifts of God come all the clothing for nearly all the peoples of the whole wide world.

From the sheep comes wool.

From the plant come cotton and linen.

From the worm comes silk.

From the tree comes rayon.

By combining the coal, air, water, oil, and gas, we get nylon.

From wool, cotton, silk, rayon, nylon, and other newer materials are made the world's clothing. From these gifts of God to man the peoples of the world have found ways to make material to clothe themselves.

Except for rayon and nylon, and other products of our own time and country, these materials have long been known and used. All of them were first used in Asia and were, in time, taken to other countries. All of them have been improved by the skill of man, a skill given to him by God for his use to better himself as a creature of God.

A long time ago men found a way to weave wool and cotton and silk into materials for clothes. After awhile men made machines to do the work they had once done by hand.

Machines now do nearly all the work of making wool, cotton, silk, rayon, and nylon into cloth for clothing and other uses. Machines clean wool and cotton. Machines spin and weave and sew. Machines brush and press and iron and measure and pack the goods. One machine does the work of many men, but men still run the machines.

The need for wool, cotton, silk, rayon, and nylon is so great that millions of men and women are working, all over the world, to meet it. Here in our country more than one and a half million men and women are working in the textile, or weaving, mills and in the clothing industry and other similar trades. The textile industry is one of the greatest in the United States and is growing greater all the time.

It still depends, however, upon those gifts of God which He gave for man's use: the sheep, the plant, the worm, the tree, coal, air, water, gas, and oil.

HOW WELL DID YOU READ?

Read each question below and write the answer on your paper. When you have finished, check the correctness of your answers by finding in the story the answer to each question. How many of your answers were correct?

1. From what sources do we get the materials for all our clothing?

2. What kind of cloth comes from the sheep? the plant? the worm? the tree?

3. What five things are combined to make nylon?

4. Except for rayon and nylon, in which place were these materials used first?

5. How have these materials been improved?

6. Name four things that machines do in making cloth.

7. Why is there so much manufacturing of materials for clothing?

8. About how many people are working in the clothing industry?

9. How important is the clothing industry in the United States?

10. Where do we find the very beginning of this successful industry?

We Thank Thee

For mother-love and father-care,
For brothers strong and sisters fair,
For love at home and here each day,
For guidance lest we go astray,
Father in Heaven, we thank Thee.

For this new morning with its light,
For rest and shelter of the night,
For health and food, for love and friends,
For everything His goodness sends,
Father in Heaven, we thank Thee.

AUTHOR UNKNOWN

A Citizen with the Saints

One day, many years ago, a little Italian Sister stood before an American judge. She had already taken the steps necessary to lead her to American citizenship. She had stated her desire to become a citizen. She had given proofs that she had lived in this country more than five years. She had passed an examination in reading, writing, and American history. Two citizens ·had told of her good character. Now she was ready for the last step.

"Do you swear to uphold the Constitution of the United States?" the judge asked her.

The little dark-eyed Sister raised her right hand. "I do," she said; and Mother Francis Cabrini became an American citizen.

No one knew that day that she would be the first American citizen to be declared a saint by the Church; but everyone who knew her understood her great goodness, her wide charity. People who hardly knew her at all, Catholics, Protestants, and Jews, wanted to help her in the work she was doing for the sick and the poor.

She had begun her work in Italy by founding the Missionary Sisters of the Sacred Heart and starting a home for orphaned children. In a little while she had opened several of these homes.

Mother Cabrini longed to do missionary work and

thought of going to China. Then she began to hear of some of the hardships of Italians who had come to the United States. They did not know the language. They found jobs hard to get. They needed schools and hospitals and orphanages. Finally, the devoted nun asked the Pope, Leo XIII, whether she should go to China or to the United States.

"Go to the United States," the Pope told her. "There is much work for you there."

Mother Cabrini came to New York with six of her Missionary Sisters. She found an old house that needed cleaning and started to work, scrubbing and painting. An Italian grocer of the neighborhood was the first to give her help. Soon others were helping, for they saw what she was trying to do for her people.

By the end of the month the house was ready and Mother Cabrini welcomed the first little orphans to her home in the United States. They were ragged, dirty, and frightened. But Mother Cabrini and her devoted Sisters clothed, fed, and comforted the four homeless Italian children. Soon they were caring for four hundred children.

Within a few years Mother Cabrini had started on her great work. In New York she opened Columbus Hospital, in Chicago she took over another. She started hospitals, schools, and orphanages in many cities of the United States, going as far south as New Orleans and as far northwest as Seattle. She had little money, but she inspired others to give money while she and her Sisters did the work.

She established a mission in Central America, then went to South America and to France. She came back to the United States and opened missions in New Jersey, Colorado, and California. "The world is too small," she once said.

She returned to Rome to report to Pope Leo on her work. He was now very old, but his voice was strong as he said to her, "We must work, we must work!" The tiny nun returned to the United States and told her Sisters, "We must hurry."

She was hurrying when Pope Leo died, hurrying when Pope Pius X died, hurrying while Pope Benedict XV tried to bring peace to a world that knew no peace.

For all her hurry, however, she always stayed quiet in manner, a friendly, smiling little Sister who loved all people and who tried to help everyone who needed help. Thousands of men and women, whose names she never knew, blessed Mother Cabrini.

She was in Chicago in December of 1917. Although she was ill, her thought was of the children. It was wartime, and candy was hard to get. But Mother Cabrini made up her mind that the children of her homes must not be disappointed. She sent out requests and, as the candy came in, she herself put it into little packages.

"We must hurry," she told the Sisters, "for the children must have their treat."

She died on the next day.

No citizen of that city has ever been mourned as was Mother Cabrini. The governor of the state and the mayor of the city passed in line with street sweepers and newsboys and shawl-draped women to pay honor to her. Everyone who had ever met her grieved at her death; but no one missed her more than did the children.

"She was the saint of the children of the city streets," people said.

Long afterward Pope Pius XII declared her sainthood. She was the first American citizen to be given that highest honor. Now, in the words of Saint Paul, she is a citizen with the saints.

Study the following list of words. Reread the story to find a sentence in which each word is used. Then name the group of words that tell its use in the sentence.

years	tells a period of time
charity	tells "how"
wide	is an action word
south	describes a person
dark-eyed	tells what kind
scrubbing	gives a direction
ill	is an antonym of *first*
do	is a synonym of *sick*
last	is a homonym of *dew*
friendly	names a virtue

QUESTIONS TO ANSWER

1. In what country was Saint Francis Cabrini born?
2. Of what country did she want to become a citizen?
3. Who told her to come to the United States?
4. What kind of home did she first start here?
5. In what year did she die?

Mother Cabrini

She walked through crowded city streets;
The children watched her go.
They saw her sweet and happy smile,
And knew, as children know,

That she was friend to all the poor,
The sick, the blind, the lame.
They knew her for a saint of God,
But never knew her name.

You need not be old enough to vote
to be a good citizen. You may be the boy
who gets up at dawn to sell newspapers,
who loves his family and his neighbors,
and who saves his

Pennies for a Violin

I. *Dawn*

Dawn came slowly over Chicago. It came up from
the lake, and over Grant Park where, in the summer,
the orchestras played. It came over the skyscrapers. It
came over the railroad tracks. It came over the river.
It came to the West Side.

Joe saw its gray shadows as he awoke.

"Time to get up," he told himself, "if you're going
to deliver the morning papers."

Joe dressed quickly and quietly. The Angelus was
ringing as he closed the door of his room in the old
house on the Square. He closed it softly so that he
would not disturb his father and his sisters.

The baby, Maria, was already awake. So was Joe's
mother, busy in the narrow kitchen. She hummed a
little song as Joe ate his breakfast. Joe watched her
as she moved from stove to kitchen table. "You are
always happy, even early in the morning," he told her.

"Why not?" she asked him. "The morning is the
beginning of a new day. There is work to be done, for
which I rejoice and thank God. Your father works for

356

the big electric company. Your older sister has been promised a job in the piano factory. Your other sisters are good girls who study hard, and the baby Maria is beautiful."

Joe waited. His mother smiled at him.

"What about me?" he asked her. "Don't I make you happy, too?"

She laughed softly. "No boy ever made his mother so happy. I was teasing you," she said. Her dark eyes looked at him with love. "I am proud," she told him.

"By the time I am eighteen you'll be prouder," he promised.

She came closer and put her arm around him. "What will you do when you grow up, Joe?" she asked.

"When I grow up," he repeated, "I shall play with the orchestra. I shall be a great violinist."

"Like the violinists who play in the great public concerts at Grant Park in summer?" she asked.

Joe nodded. "I shall perform in public concerts, too. Thousands and thousands of people will come to hear me. I shall step out to the center of the platform and play the loveliest violin in the world."

She patted his shoulder. "Who knows?" she asked, and then added, "It is not impossible. Other great Italian musicians were poor boys."

"My violin will have deep, rich notes, and high singing notes—"

She lifted his plate from the kitchen table. "A fine

violin will be yours some day, Joe," she sighed, "but first of all you must have one which doesn't cost too much."

He rose from the chair. "I shall have it!" He dug down into his coat pocket and pulled out a worn pocketbook. From it he counted eight one-dollar bills, all mussed and soiled.

"I have earned every dollar of this," he said, "penny by penny as I sold my papers. When I have eighteen of these dollars I can buy a violin I saw in Sam's second-hand music store."

"There will be lessons," she warned.

"If I can keep my paper route, it won't take long to pay for the violin and the lessons," he told her as he left the house.

II. *Sunrise*

Sunrise, rose and gold, sparkled across the city sky-scrapers as the boy stepped into the street. It lighted the wide new hospital that had been built to honor Mother Cabrini.

As Joe started past the hospital to get the morning papers for delivery he rejoiced, for he was proud of the part he played in the morning's work of the great city where he had been born.

Whistling as he went across the Square, he hurried on his way to the office from which the morning papers were handed out to the newsboys.

He met two of the boys, Victor and Tony. They walked and talked together until they reached the corner.

Then Joe stepped out of the line. "I'll catch up with you," he told them.

"Hurry up," they told him, as he lagged behind, but, even in time of haste, Joe had to look again into the window of Sam's second-hand shop.

The store, not yet opened in the early morning, was dark behind its iron bars. The pianos, in gray covers, stood in the shadows. The radios, high and narrow or short and fat, stood in rows in the center of the store. In the showcases nearer the window the instruments sparkled in the early morning sunlight. An accordion, white and black and gold, shone from its place in the

window. Beside it rested a banjo, its thin wood bright from many polishings.

As Joe pressed his face against the windowpane he was not looking at the accordion or the banjo. He was looking for the violin in its worn, shabby case that had been in the back of the showcase on the day when he had first spoken to Sam about its price.

It was still there.

Whistling again, with hope high in his heart, Joe rushed to catch up with the other newsboys at the office.

He collected his newspapers. He lifted the load to his shoulder straps, and then started on his route, back toward the Hospital. At the door he met one of the nurses, just off night duty.

"It is high time you were getting here," she said to him, but Joe knew her jokes. "How shall we know what is happening in the world if we don't read the newspapers?"

"You know the news here at Mother Cabrini Hospital before the newspapers get it," he answered laughing.

III. *The Hospital*

As Joe passed through the wide hospital door the hospital odor came out to him, but it was all part of the city that he loved. He went down the long, narrow halls, stooping to place quietly the papers at some of the closed doors.

Beyond an open door an old Italian woman greeted him. "I have been waiting to say good-by, Joe," she said and her voice lifted with happiness. "I go home today. Congratulate me."

"I do congratulate you," Joe said as a man in a wheel chair smiled at him.

"When are you going to come around and play your violin for me, Joe?" the man asked.

"When I get the violin," Joe answered.

"How soon will you get it?"

"I don't know. As soon as I can earn ten more dollars, but I don't know how long that will take."

"What do you do with your money?" the man asked

with a twinkle in his eye. "Spend it all on Saturday afternoon?"

"No, sir," Joe said proudly. "I give my mother everything I earn except twenty-five cents a week. I am saving that for the violin."

"I see," said the man. "Wait a minute," he called as Joe turned away. "I used to know a boy," he told him, "who wanted to play on a flute. He thought that if he had a flute he could make himself into the kind of man he wanted to be. He never got the flute."

"Can't he get it now?" asked Joe.

"I am afraid he is too old to learn to play one and so there is only one thing he can do. He can help another deserving boy get that flute. Only it doesn't really have to be a flute." He laughed as he watched Joe. "It could be a violin, if the boy would rather have a violin. How about it?"

"You mean me?" asked Joe in wonder.

"I don't see any other boy around," smiled the man.

"Oh, but—I'm not deserving."

"Don't say you can't take ten dollars from me. I'll give you a suggestion, young man. No one of us can ever really pay back the kind things that people do for us. All we can do is pass on a kindness to someone else. If you'll do that some day, we'll be even."

"I can't ever thank you," Joe said, as the man in the wheel chair counted out the money to him from a thick billfold.

"Yes, you can. You can come to the hospital some day and play for me."

"Will you be here?"

"I am going to be here for a long, long time, unless God takes me home."

"Then I'll keep on bringing the papers," said Joe.

A Sister in the hall spoke to Joe. "You are growing up," she told him. "Soon you will be off to a bigger and better job, I suppose."

"I'll be around for awhile, Sister," he told her. "I have a promise to keep on this route."

When his stack of papers was gone, he went out again into the city sunlight. The day was older, brighter. Somewhere toward the east a seven-o'clock factory whistle blew. Another nearer whistle answered it. Suddenly the city was a great, steady roar; a rousing signal for the beginning of another day of work.

From the hospital steps Joe looked out on the green of the Square, but his eyes saw far, far beyond the houses and shops and factories. He was seeing himself as he would be some day, a violinist performing before the crowds in Grant Park, giving back to his Chicago something of the power and the glory he was taking from her now.

Slowly he fingered his mussed and soiled pocketbook. He had money now, money enough to buy the violin in Sam's shop.

That morning Chicago belonged to Joe—and Chicago was his whole wide world.

WHAT HAPPENED THEN?

Should you like to finish the story? What do you think happened when Joe grew up? Did he become a great violinist? If he did become a famous musician, did he have any difficulties to overcome? How did he do it? Were his family proud of him?

Or did something prevent Joe from becoming a violinist? If so, what was it? What kind of work did Joe then do? Did he work in one of Chicago's many industries? Did he regret not being a violinist?

Write a short story telling what you think happened to Joe when he grew up. Make it short and interesting. Read it to the class. The class might vote to decide which story was the most interesting.

Psalm of Those Who Go Forth before Daylight

The policeman buys shoes slow and careful; the
    teamster buys gloves slow and careful;
    they take care of their feet and hands; they
    live on their feet and hands.

The milkman never argues; he works alone and no one
    speaks to him; the city is asleep when he is
    on the job; he puts the bottle on six hundred
    porches and calls it a day's work; he climbs
    two hundred wooden stairways; two horses
    are company for him; he never argues.

The rolling-mill man and the sheet-steel man are
    brothers of cinders; they empty cinders
    out of their shoes after the day's work; they ask
    their wives to fix burnt holes in the knees of
    their trousers; their necks and ears are covered
    with a smut; they scour their necks and ears;
    they are brothers of cinders.

CARL SANDBURG

IX

For God and Country

And they sent to him certain of the Pharisees and Herodians, that they might entrap him in his talk. And they came and said to him, "Master, we know that thou art truthful, and that thou carest naught for any man; for thou dost not regard the person of men, but dost teach the way of God in truth. Is it lawful to give tribute to Caesar; or shall we not give it?"

But knowing their craftiness, he said to them, "Why do you test me? Bring me a denarius to look at."

So they brought one. Then he said to them, "Whose are this image and the inscription?" They said to him, "Caesar's."

And Jesus answered and said to them, "Render, therefore, to Caesar the things that are Caesar's, and to God the things that are God's."

And they marvelled at him.

MARK 12, 13–17

May Altars

It's May! The whole world is a shrine
　To Mary, Queen!
The flower-studded meadow lands,
　The lake's blue sheen
Are altar cloths, their lacy fringe
　The polar snows.
Each tree, a vase, its wealth of bloom
　Doth now disclose.
Dawn sets the vigil-lamp of Day
　Aflame on high;
Night trails a rosary of stars
　Across the sky.
But, in the love-land of their hearts,
　Dear Queen of May,
Thy children build e'en fairer shrines
　For thee to-day;
All blossoming with loving deeds
　And kindly thought,
With golden bands and silver strands
　Of prayer enwrought.
Oh, smile, dear Mother, down upon
　These heart-shrines true,
And guard and cherish them beneath
　Thy mantle blue!

SISTER MARYANNA, O.P.

Procession in May

I. *The Soldiers' Home*

A bugle note sounded high and clear over the grounds of the Soldiers' Home in Washington. As the bright sunlight of a May afternoon shone on the city many people moved toward the path the May Procession would take. Francis, holding high the great cross that sparkled in the sunshine, looked over the scene with a gaze that found it both old and new.

On one side, over the tops of the trees, he could see, as he had often seen, the dome of the Capitol and the high, white finger of the Washington Monument.

On the other side, through the branches, he could see the gray steeples and towers of the great Catholic University of America.

On the grounds he could see the deep woods, the fields, the fishpond, the herd of cattle, the long red buildings in which the old soldiers lived. He could see the house where Abraham Lincoln used to come when he was President of the United States. He could see, too, his own house, the house where his father, as an officer of the United States Army on duty at the Home, lived. That was the old picture, one a boy could see any day.

369

Around him today was set another picture, one that might be seen on only one day in the year. On the last Sunday of the month of May came this May Procession, in honor of Memorial Day and in honor of Our Lady. For an hour it would wind up hill and down, through woods and beside fields. From porches and hospital windows and sidewalks old men, who had fought in the regular army and were now living at the Home, would watch its passing.

All of them would watch quietly and reverently. The Catholic soldiers would fall into line at the end, after the boys and girls, the priests, and the Sisters had gone by. Francis wondered if Sergeant Wayne would come.

All his life Francis had known Sergeant Wayne. To others the sergeant might be a cross old man who scolded and found fault with everything and everybody. To Francis he was a hero.

Anyone could know that. The sergeant wore many medals. He wore on his shoulder the Indian Head badge which showed he had served in the Second Division in the First World War; and everyone in the Army knew what that meant.

Francis knew more. He knew that in the Second World War Sergeant Wayne had saved his father's life over in France; and he knew how, in some strange way, he belonged to Sergeant Wayne and how Sergeant Wayne belonged to him.

Francis spent many hours listening to Sergeant Wayne tell about his experiences in the Army. He liked to hear the old soldier's tales of adventure in far-away lands. But best of all Francis liked to hear the sergeant sing the jolly Army songs.

Sergeant Wayne had taught him the words of the morning bugle call:

I can't get 'em up, I can't get 'em up, I can't get 'em up in the morn-ing; I can't get 'em up, I can't get 'em up, I can't get 'em up at all. The cor-p'r'l's worse than pri-vates, The ser-geant's worse than cor - p'r'l, Lieu - ten - ant's worse than ser - geant; An' the cap-tain's worst of all.

Sergeant Wayne had taught him the words the soldiers sang when the bugler sounded the call to meals:

Soup - y, soup - y, soup - y, with - out a sin - gle bean;

Pork - y, pork - y, pork - y, with - out a streak of lean;

Cof - fee, cof - fee, cof - fee, weak - est ev - er seen.

"That's not true, though," Sergeant Wayne always added. "Food's good, and there's plenty of it in Uncle Sam's Army. Those Army cooks know just what to feed a hungry man—plenty of meat and potatoes and the best coffee you ever tasted."

The sergeant also taught him "Taps," the night bugle call:

Fad-ing light Dims the sight, And a star gems the sky, Gleam-ing

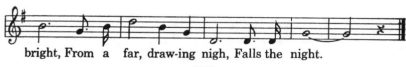
bright, From a far, draw-ing nigh, Falls the night.

372

They were friends, the old man and the boy, as only people in the Army could be friends. There was only one thing about Sergeant Wayne that troubled Francis. The sergeant, who should be a Catholic, who said that he was a Catholic,—"and I'll knock down any man who says I am not,"—never. went to church. While other men found comfort and peace in the chapel of the Home, Sergeant Wayne never went to Mass, never went to Benediction, never went to pay a visit to the Blessed Sacrament.

"I wish we could do something for him," Francis had heard his mother say to his father. "He would be so much happier if only he would come back to the Church."

"I know," his father had said, "but you will have to let him find his own way. Once he does, he will be all right for the rest of his lifetime. All the sergeant needs to bring him back to the Church is a turn in the right direction."

"I wish I could give the sergeant that turn," Francis was thinking as the procession formed.

II. *The Procession Moves*

There were crowds of old soldiers coming toward the Sisters' Chapel for the procession; but Francis could not see Sergeant Wayne among them. He saw that the marchers were almost ready to start.

Ahead of him stood the chief of police of the grounds, leader of the parade. Beside him stood altar boys in white cassocks with red capes and caps. After him would come the flag-bearer and his color guards, the Boy Scouts from Saint Joseph's School. Already they were in line, waiting the order to move.

Little girls in white, with flowers in their hair, carried baskets and wreaths of blossoms. Tall girls in white, Children of Mary, carried white lilies. Four girls from St. Vincent's School carried the statue of Our Lady.

The Sisters of Charity of Saint Vincent de Paul were falling into line. They came from the hospital, where they nursed the sick old soldiers. For a long, long time the Sisters had been at the Soldiers' Home. Sergeant Wayne, who had something to say against almost everyone in the grounds, never said anything against them. "Angels of the battlefields," he had once said to Francis as two Sisters went by. "The man who called them that knew them—and battles."

The chaplain of the Home was coming from the chapel with two altar boys. In a moment the bugle would sound again, and the procession would start. All along the line old soldiers would join it as other soldiers took off their hats for its passing.

Francis looked around and saw Sergeant Wayne standing just beside the road. He was standing with his shoulders thrown back as if waiting for an order.

"Too bad you're not a Catholic," the chief said to him.

"I am a Catholic," said Sergeant Wayne, "even if I don't go to church."

"A man who doesn't go to church isn't much of a Catholic."

"I'll show you," Sergeant Wayne began, but Francis could no longer listen to him. One of the altar boys was tugging at his surplice.

"Look at the flag-bearer," the altar boy said to him.

Francis turned around just in time to see the flag-bearer fall fainting against one of the color guards.

"What's the matter?" asked Francis.

"He has been sick all day," the first color guard explained. "The Sister of St. Joseph's thought he should not come, but he said he had to carry the flag."

A dozen people moved forward to help the boy. One of the men took the flag from his hands and passed it to Sergeant Wayne. "Hold this," he told him. Sergeant Wayne stood, holding the flag, as the men moved the boy from the procession.

"Who will take his place?" the chief asked.

"Fall in there, we're ready to start," came the order.

Suddenly Francis thought of his father's words. "All the sergeant needs to come back to the Church is a turn in the right direction."

Looking at him now, Francis knew that Sergeant Wayne wanted to join the May Procession. That was why he had come to watch it. Deep down in his soul he was a Catholic, a child of the Church, even though he had long been a stubborn child. Because he himself was still a child, he knew how Sergeant Wayne felt. He looked up at the old man. In his eyes he saw something that gave him courage.

"Sergeant Wayne will carry the flag," Francis said.

For a moment the sergeant looked down at him as if he were about to refuse. For a moment the boy felt that he had become an officer of the Army. "Sergeant," he said, "you followed my father in France, didn't you?"

"I went right at his heels into every battle."

Over the woods and the fields rang out the high, clear notes of the bugle call. Altar boys and Boy Scouts, girls in white, Sisters and priests, stood ready to move in the May Procession. Francis raised high the cross. "Fall in, Sergeant!" he gave the command.

377

"Well, I'll—" Sergeant Wayne began, then gulped hastily. "All right, Captain," he said, and lifted the flag as he fell into step behind the cross-bearer.

Francis moved forward slowly, but there was joy in his heart. Sergeant Wayne had joined the May Procession. He was on his way back to the Church he had always loved.

COMPLETING THOUGHTS

Each statement below tells something that was done in this story. From the list of words at the bottom of the page find the word or words that will complete each sentence. Then read the sentences aloud.

1. __?__ sounded high and clear over the grounds.
2. __?__ shone on the city.
3. __?__ in which the old soldiers lived.
4. __?__ would fall into line at the end.
5. __?__ would march up hill and down.
6. __?__ know what to feed a hungry man.
7. __?__ carried baskets of blossoms.
8. __?__ raised high the Cross.
9. __?__ was on his way back to the church.
10. __?__ was coming from the chapel.

Sergeant Wayne   The bugle
Francis   The chaplain
The procession   Little girls in white
Red buildings   Army cooks
Sunlight   Catholic soldiers

378

Your Flag and My Flag

Your flag and my flag!
  And how it flies today
In your land and my land
  And half a world away!
Rose-red and blood-red,
  The stripes forever gleam;
Snow-white and soul-white
  The good forefathers' dream;
Sky-blue and true-blue,
  With stars to gleam aright—
The gloried guidon of the day;
  A shelter through the night!

Your flag and my flag!
  And oh! How much it holds—
Your land and my land
  Secure within its folds!
Your heart and my heart
  Beat quicker at the sight;
Sun-kissed and wind-tossed—
  The Red and Blue and White!
The one flag—the great flag—
  The flag for me and you—
Glorified all else beside,
  The Red and White and Blue!

WILBUR D. NESBIT

379

Duty to God and country
may take a man far from his own land.
It was in faraway China that there rang

Thirty-three Bells for Father Donovan

As long as he could remember there had been bells in Gerard Donovan's life: door bells, telephone bells, church bells, the altar boy's bell he sounded for many years; but of them all the clang of the great bell at Maryknoll meant most to him.

Maryknoll, set on the Hudson River in New York State, is the home of American missionaries who take the Word of Christ to distant lands. Once a year groups of young priests leave this home to go to their missions. At Maryknoll the last Sunday in July is known as Departure Day. On that day the great bell, which once hung in a Japanese pagan temple, is rung.

It rang on the Departure Day when Father Gerard Donovan went to China.

Father Donovan had been a happy student, just as he had been a laughing boy. Born in a steel town of Pennsylvania, he had grown up in a big family where he was the youngest child. He was younger than most boys at the school when he entered the Maryknoll priests' academy; but he was sure that, beyond all else, he wished to be a missionary. Everyone liked him, and he liked everyone, but he never seemed to be entirely one of the crowd. He was little,

380

with a big smile that people remembered, and he had the courage of a dozen bigger boys.

Even though his mother and his sister Katy, who had been closer to him than anyone else in his family, wept a little on that Departure Day, Father Donovan was never happier than when he heard the prayer of the Church for those about to go on a long journey and the splendid hymn,

> "Farewell, brothers, farewell,
> Go forth, ye heralds of God's tender mercy."

At the end of August of that year he saw the lights of Japan. With another Maryknoll missionary he went through Japan and through Korea to his post in China. They traveled in crowded railway trains and walked over rough mountain trails. They slept in inns where the beds were clay floors and the food soggy rice.

381

Father Donovan's first mission was in the city of Fushun. He was there long enough to hear of the bandits who at that time made China dangerous to all men. These bandits robbed, beat, and sometimes killed their victims. They hid in the mountains so that the soldiers could seldom find them. They raided churches and houses. They kidnapped men, demanding money from their families and friends for their safe return.

The young priest made many friends in Fushun, although he was there only a little while before he was sent to another Chinese town, a smaller one than Fushun. He had to travel there on muleback. It was a hard journey, and he was glad to hear the tower bell of the mission tinkle a welcome for him.

He said Midnight Mass in the mission's little chapel. The place was crowded with Chinese Christians. Some of them had walked forty miles. The grown-ups crowded the church so that the boys and girls had to kneel in the sanctuary. It was a peaceful, happy night, but already danger was coming close to these Chinese Christians and the missionaries who taught them. The bandits, growing bolder, were pressing closer.

Father Donovan had been six years in China, six busy, successful, pleasant years, when he was sent back to Fushun. He was sorry to leave his smaller mission, but he was glad to meet old friends in the larger city.

He took up his work in a mission across a little river from the city. There was a church, a convent for some Maryknoll Sisters, and an old people's home. The place seemed quiet on the October evening when Father Donovan went into the church. His assistant, a younger missionary just come from the United States, was to give Benediction, and Father Donovan knelt in the sanctuary. A Chinese boy stood near him, preparing incense, when a tall, rough-looking stranger entered.

"Come with me," he ordered Father Donovan, pointing a gun at him.

"No, no!" cried the Chinese boy.

"Yes," said the man. "Come or we will destroy all of you. Come!"

Father Donovan understood the command. He was being kidnapped by bandits and would be held by them in the hope that his fellow missionaries would raise money to win his freedom. He could do nothing but go with the stranger. "You, too," the bandit ordered the Chinese boy.

As the stranger pushed Father Donovan out of the side door of the sacristy, the boy ran to one of the Sisters. "The bandits have taken Father," he told her.

As she gave the alarm, the boy raced after the priest and the bandit. He overtook them as they came to the top of the hill. The last the Sisters saw of Father Donovan was his outline as he came to the top of the hill. Probably the last sound he heard from his mission was the clang of its bell sounding the alarm.

For days and weeks police and soldiers sought him. The government of the United States asked the government of China to help bring back the missionary. The Chinese boy was sent back by the bandits, but Father Donovan was still held prisoner. A demand for money came from the bandits. Maryknoll had to refuse. Then, one day weeks later, the priest's body, tortured and frozen, was found beside a road.

An American government agent and a Maryknoll missionary brought the body back to Fushun. There it lay in the church while thousands of Chinese passed it in mourning. Fushun, Christian and pagan, grieved for the martyred priest they had loved.

After the solemn funeral Mass they followed his body to the little cemetery, although that body would later be taken back to Maryknoll on the Hudson for burial. As the Chinese procession of mourners moved onward, the bell of the church began to ring. One-two-three, it sounded, and again, one-two-three. All the way up to thirty-three it went, one for each year of Father Gerard Donovan's age.

That bell has long been silent; for the Communist enemies of Christ have taken over the city Father Donovan loved; but no one who heard the thirty-three strokes of the bell that day has forgotten the sound. And, when the great bell at Maryknoll rings for Departure Day, young missionaries going to faraway lands remember the story of Gerard Donovan.

Below is an outline of the main events in Father Gerard Donovan's life. See how well you can follow the outline by rereading the story and writing the number of the page and the paragraph after the proper outline topic. Sometimes two or three ideas are described in one paragraph, especially if they are listed under the same major heading.

Thirty-three Bells for Father Donovan

I. His early life
    A. Bells
    B. Maryknoll
    C. Boyhood

II. A missionary
    A. Japan
    B. Korea
    C. China

III. In China
    A. Fushun
    B. A smaller Chinese mission
    C. Return to Fushun
    D. One October evening

IV. Kidnapped
    A. Bandits
    B. The alarm

V. His death
    A. The search
    B. Found dead
    C. Burial

A Prayer

Little grandson, say a prayer
For one who has not long to stay,
Ask Our Lady of the Stars
To light her lanterns for my way.
She will hear you, little grandson,
She will heed a childish plea,
She will guide an old, old woman
Safely to eternity.

Little grandson, say a prayer
That your road be white and straight,
Ask Our Lady of the Dawn
To lead you to a happy fate.
Pray for grace and health and strength,
Pray for peace, and pray for light
That you teach your children's children
Faith to guard them through the night.

KATHERINE RANKIN

Our country is a land of
many peoples from many places;
but for all of them there shines

Sunlight on the Cross

The children came out of the school of Our Lady of Hope into the golden sunshine of a New York street. A hurdy-gurdy was playing.

Mary danced to the music. "A hurdy-gurdy is New York," she said.

James laughed at her. "How can a great city be a hurdy-gurdy?"

The music rushed along with skips and jumps.

"New York is a hurdy-gurdy because it is happy, noisy, and bright," Mary declared.

"What is she talking about?" James asked Tom.

"Mary sees New York in one way, and I see it in another," said Tom. "I like to think that New York is a great white ship. It goes out of a crowded harbor with oil and steel and cotton. Then it comes home again from foreign lands with sugar and spice and pineapples."

James frowned at him. "New York's just a city," he grumbled. "Isn't it, Sara?"

Sara's dark eyes were eager. "I think New York is a great clothing factory, a factory that stops for awhile when the noon whistle blows. Then the men and women rush out on the sidewalks. They are the

388

workers, taking off just a little time in the day from their work of making clothes for all America."

James thought this very silly. "What's the matter with all of you?" he cried, and said again, "New York is just a city, one of the biggest cities in the world."

Stella smiled at him. "Oh, James," she sighed, "have you no imagination? This is a game! New York is a high skyscraper with this lovely sunlight shining on its western windows!"

James turned to her. "A skyscraper!" he cried. "Why, it's hundreds of skyscrapers! One of you will be saying next that New York is a streetcar or a bus."

"It is." Charles laughed at him. "It's a subway that rushes, too, and a train that roars. It is all the traffic that we hear around us."

Kathleen moved closer to them. "I think that New York is a hotel," she said, "a hotel with wide halls and velvet carpets and satin draperies and gold chairs—"

389

"And a doorman with shining boots and a green-and-gold uniform," Jean added breathlessly.

"And a head waiter with dark, smooth hair," said Charles.

"And a cook with a high white cap in a kitchen with shining pots and pans and kettles," said Sara.

Rosa raised her voice. "What are they going to eat?" she asked. Then she added, "I think New York is a giant food market. I see big stores and counters and boxes and barrels and crates. There are olive oil and cheese and onions and peppers—"

Stella laughed with joy. "I like your market, Rosa," she said. "I should find there the waffles that my mother learned to make in the old country."

John, the Polish boy, clapped his hands. "I should find the potato pancakes that we used to have at home in Poland."

"I would order," Carl told them, "the German dish of pork and sauerkraut."

"It would be herring salad for me," said Eric. "I come from Norway."

"My market basket would have to be big," said Rita, "for I would buy so many things. I would start with the meat and vegetables for onion soup. Then I would order rice and chicken and little crabs."

"They sound nice," said Mary politely.

"For dessert," said Rita, "I would have the best food of all. We call it 'little pigs from heaven'!"

"Little pigs from heaven?" all the children shouted happily. "How do you make that dessert?"

Rita smiled. "We make it with sugar and water and the yolks of six eggs and a chocolate sauce over it all. Only good Spanish cooks can make it."

"In all the world there is nothing as good as Dutch gingercake!" Little Hilda from Holland stamped her foot. "The spices for it come from the Dutch East Indies, and only a good Dutch cook can make it right."

"It's nothing but gingerbread," said James.

"Oh, no, it's better." Hilda was certain.

"Well, anyway," said James half to himself, "it has nothing to do with the greatness of New York."

"Oh, but it has!" all the children cried in one voice, but it was Tom who added, "Food from many lands is only one of the reasons why New York is a great city. The people who have come here have brought as many ways of doing many things as they have brought ways of cooking good food. Sometimes I think that New York is a big museum—"

Sara spoke breathlessly. "With paintings from Russia!"

"And from Spain," Rita exclaimed.

"And from Holland," said Hilda.

"And from France," said Jean.

A boy who had been listening silently until then spoke up. "And from England," he said.

"Of course, Edmund," said Rosa. "There will be paintings of great Italian artists, too, in that museum."

Kathleen seemed lost in thought. When she spoke her voice seemed to come from a distance. "I've been thinking," she said, "that New York is a big radio and television station, where the best music is played and plays are given."

"At your station you must have orchestras playing the works of French musicians," said Jean.

"They must play Italian operas," said Rosa.

"They must show the Spanish dances," said Rita.

"This is my station," Kathleen laughed, "so you may be sure you'll hear the songs of Ireland."

"You must telecast English plays from your station," said Edmund. "The people in England have known some of them for three hundred years."

"And 'Hansel and Gretel,'" said Carl.

"I'll see and hear the programs, of course," James admitted, "but still I cannot see how these things make New York anything but just a city, with streets and houses and tall buildings and playgrounds—"

The children cried, "No! No!" but it was Tom who said, "A city is always more than streets and houses and playgrounds and tall buildings. The city means the chance to work and be happy."

"It is a place where people can be brave even while they struggle," said Charles.

"And humble even when they succeed," said Jean.

"It is the place where all the people, no matter from where they come, give the best they have to help one another," said Tom. "This is the gateway to America, and here at this gateway are people from all over the world who have come seeking freedom."

"They have brought with them all the best things from the lands they have left," said Sara.

"And whatever they know of ways to enjoy life," said Jean.

"They have brought desire for freedom," said Charles.

"Why didn't you all say that before?" James cried. "I see now what you mean. I still think that New York isn't a hurdy-gurdy, or a ship, or a market, or a skyscraper, but I can see that it might be a harbor where people come in from a stormy sea."

The sunlight shone on western windows of tall skyscrapers, on great hotels, on ships in the harbor; but it shone brightest on the golden cross above the school.

Tom pointed to it. "See how the Cross shines!" he said. "It is a light for everyone. The Cross is the finest thing in the world. It stands for our faith in God, just as the flag stands for our faith in our country."

"I know what you mean," said Mary. "We all know that here, in our free country, we can follow the Cross as children of God."

"Every one of us," said the children of the school of Our Lady of Hope.

Do you like to watch plays or to take part in plays? on a stage? on the radio? on television? Most boys and girls do. If you would like to make a play from the story you have just read, you will need to discuss these questions and come to some decision on each question.

1. Shall we have an announcer? What kind of person would make a good announcer? Think of speaking plainly when you make your choice.

2. Shall we have a microphone or screen? How could these be made?

3. Shall we have scenery for our play? Why or why not?

4. Shall we have a play director? What will he do?

5. Shall the actors read or memorize their parts?

6. What are the points to remember when acting: for instance, speaking loud enough, facing the audience, respecting the parts of other players?

WHAT DO THEY MEAN?

You may wish to use the following sentences in your play. If you do, you should understand what they mean. Find them in the story and explain what they mean.

1. A hurdy-gurdy is New York.

2. New York is a high skyscraper with this lovely sunlight shining on its western windows.

3. A city is always more than streets and houses and playgrounds and tall buildings.

4. This is the gateway to America.

The Harbor

The children come from many lands
   Beyond the wide, gray sea,
From old lands where they lived in fear
   And longed for liberty.

They see the gateway of the port,
   They see the harbor's gleam,
They see the torch of liberty,
   The symbol of their dream.

The ferries thread the shining bay,
   The sirens shriek and roar,
The children of the Old World see
   The opening of the door.

O brave new land, be true to them,
   Give them your strength, your power,
And keep alive the flame of faith
   Within their darkened hour.

KATHERINE RANKIN

Our God and Our Country

Long ago, God, our Father, created the rich gifts that make our country great.

In the dark earth He placed coal and oil by which we would be warmed. In the high heavens He created the sun, the moon, and the stars that would light our way. In the rich soil God placed growing plants by which we would be fed.

Long ago, God, our Father, blessed our land.

In the hearts of boys and girls He placed the gift of faith, by which they would believe in God and in their neighbor.

In the hearts of boys and girls He placed the gift of hope, by which they would put their trust in God.

To the hearts of all people He offers the gift of love, by which they can be true to one another.

God, our Father, made a plan for us in our country.

The people who fought to keep our country great knew God's plan. The people who suffered to keep our country blessed followed God's plan. We too must know and follow God's holy plan.

We must share the gifts that make our country great and blessed. We must obey the laws of home, school, Church, and State. We must love all people because they are children of God.

We, the children of America, must help to carry on God's plan for our great and blessed country.

America the Beautiful

O beautiful for spacious skies,
　For amber waves of grain,
For purple mountain majesties
　Above the fruited plain!
　　America! America!
　God shed His grace on thee
And crown thy good with brotherhood
　From sea to shining sea!

O beautiful for patriot dream
　That sees beyond the years
Thine alabaster cities gleam
　Undimmed by human tears!
　　America! America!
　God shed His grace on thee
And crown thy good with brotherhood
　From sea to shining sea!

KATHARINE LEE BATES

398

Glossary

A glossary is part of a dictionary. This glossary will help you to pronounce and to understand the meanings of difficult or unusual words used in *These Are Our People.*

The pronunciation of each word is shown by division into syllables, by an accent mark (if it has more than one syllable), and by respelling.

The following list shows you how each marked letter is pronounced by giving as an example the same sound in a word that you know. This is called a *pronunciation key.*

ā *as in* lāte	ī *as in* rīde	ū *as in* ūse
å *as in* al'wåys	ĭ *as in* ĭn	û *as in* û·nite'
ă *as in* ăm	ĭ *as in* pos'sĭ·ble	ŭ *as in* ŭs
ă *as in* ăp·pear'		ŭ *as in* cir'cŭs
ä *as in* ärm	ō *as in* ōld	û *as in* bûrn
à *as in* àsk	ŏ *as in* ŏ·bey'	
â *as in* câre	ŏ *as in* nŏt	
	ŏ *as in* cŏn·nect'	ōō *as in* mōon
ē *as in* hē	ô *as in* sôft	ŏŏ *as in* tŏŏk
ê *as in* ê·nough'	ô *as in* hôrse	oi *as in* oil
ĕ *as in* nĕt		ou *as in* out
ĕ *as in* si'lĕnt		th *as in* that
ē *as in* mak'ēr		th *as in* thin

a·bil'i·ty (à·bĭl'ĭ·tĭ). The power to do or perform.

ac·cor'di·on (ă·kôr'dĭ·ŭn). A musical wind instrument with keys, which can be carried about.

ac'cu·rate·ly (ăk'ŭ·rĭt·lĭ). Without mistakes.

ad'mi·ral (ăd'mĭ·răl). The highest officer in the Navy.

ad·vise' (ăd·vīz'). To give advice.

a·hoy' (à·hoi'). A word used by sailors as a greeting or to call attention.

air'-con·di'tioned (âr'kŏn·dĭsh'ŭnd). Cooled or heated by clean air.

a·larm' (à·lärm'). 1. A warning of danger. 2. Sudden surprise and fear.

An·nap'o·lis (ă·năp'ŏ·lĭs). The capital of Maryland. The U. S. Naval Academy is also located in Annapolis.

an'to·nym (ăn'tŏ·nĭm). A word that is opposite in meaning to another word; as, "hot" is the *antonym* of "cold."

---

lāte, alwåys, ăm, ăppear, ärm, àsk, câre, hē, ênough, nĕt, silĕnt, makēr, rīde, ĭn, possĭble, ōld, ŏbey, nŏt, cŏnnect, sôft, hôrse, ūse, ûnite, ŭs, circŭs, bûrn, mōon, tŏŏk, oil, out, that, thin

ap·pre′ci·ate (ă·prē′shĭ·āt). To value a person or thing at the true worth.

a·rouse′ (à·rouz′). To excite; to stir up.

ar′ti·cle (är′tĭ·k'l). 1. A thing of some particular kind. 2. A piece in a magazine, a book, or a newspaper dealing with one subject.

art′ist (är′tĭst). A person who does his work with skill and good taste.

A′sia (ā′zhà). The largest continent on earth.

as·sist′ant (ă·sĭs′tănt). A person who helps another.

aye (ī). Yes.

bar′gain (bär′gĭn). 1. An exchange of promises. 2. Something bought at a saving.

bay′ou (bī′ōō). A slow-moving creek or stream connecting other streams, ponds, or lakes.

belt (bĕlt). 1. A strap or tie worn around the waist. 2. A strip of country which has climate and soil suitable for the growth of certain plants or animals; as, the cotton *belt*.

bleat′ing (blēt′ĭng). The crying of a sheep.

Bo·he′mi·a (bŏ·hē′mĭ·à). A former kingdom in southeastern Europe.

Bos′ton (bŏs′tŭn). The capital of Massachusetts.

brand (brănd). 1. A mark, label, or sign. 2. To mark with a brand or label.

bron′co (brŏng′kō). A small, half-wild horse or pony common on the plains of the Western states.

buck′skin′ (bŭk′skĭn′). A soft leather, made from the skin of a deer, used for making breeches, jackets, gloves, etc.

Bur′bank, Luth′er (bûr′băngk, lū′-thēr). A scientist who developed many new kinds of fruits and flowers.

bur′ro (bûr′ō). A small donkey used to carry loads.

Ca·bri′ni (kà·brē′nē), **Mother.** A missionary Sister who brought Sisters from Italy to the New World.

cac′tus (kăk′tŭs). A plant with fleshy stems and branches with scales or prickles instead of leaves. It can live in hot, dry places.

calm′ly (käm′lĭ). Quietly.

Cam′bridge (kām′brĭj). A city near Boston, in Massachusetts.

ca·nal′ (kà·năl′). 1. A large ditch dug in the earth to carry water to places that need it. 2. A large ditch dug across land for ships or small boats to use.

can′cel (kăn′sĕl). To cross out or to take back.

cane (kān). A tall, grasslike plant, the juice of which is very sweet.

can′yon (kăn′yŭn). A deep valley with steep sides.

car′a·van (kăr′à·văn). A group of people traveling together for safety through dangerous country.

Car′los (kär′lōs). The Spanish name for *Charles*.

Car′son, Kit (kär′s'n, kĭt). A famous Indian scout and fighter.

Ce·cile' (sā·sēl'). The French name for *Cecilia*.

ce're·al (sēr'ē·ăl). 1. Any grain, such as wheat, oats, etc., used for food. 2. Any of the various breakfast foods made of grain; as, corn-flakes, oatmeal, etc.

chair'man (châr'măn). A person in charge of a meeting or who acts as the head of a committee.

chap'lain (chăp'lĭn). A priest who is attached to a special group.

Chap'man, Jon'a·than (chăp'măn, jŏn'ȧ·thăn). Known as Johnny Appleseed.

Ches'a·peake Bay (chĕs'ȧ·pēk bā). An arm of the Atlantic Ocean in Maryland and Virginia. It is about 200 miles long.

Chi·ca'go (shĭ·kô'gō). A large city in Illinois.

Chis'holm (chĭz'ŭm) **Trail**. One of the famous cattle trails of the West.

choke' damp' (chōk'dămp'). A mine gas dangerous to living creatures.

Cin'cin·nat'i (sĭn'sĭ·năt'ĭ). A large city in Ohio.

cit'i·zen (sĭt'ĭ·zĕn). A person who, by birth or choice, is a member of a state or a nation.

clus'ter (klŭs'tēr). A number of things growing naturally together.

cod (kŏd). An important food fish found in the colder parts of the North Atlantic.

com·bine' (kŏm·bīn'). To unite or join.

com'bine (kŏm'bīn). A machine which both harvests and threshes grain.

com'mon (kŏm'ŭn). 1. Familiar. 2. Shared by two or more persons.

Com'mu·nist (kŏm'ū·nĭst). A member of a political party which now rules Russia and which seeks to overthrow both religion and private enterprise.

com·mu'ni·ty (kŏ·mū'nĭ·tĭ). A group of people living in a particular place, such as a village, town, or city.

Con'gress (kŏng'grĕs). The body of men who make the laws of our country.

Con'sti·tu'tion (kŏn'stĭ·tū'shŭn). A statement of the basic principles on which our country is governed.

con'ti·nent (kŏn'tĭ·nĕnt). One of the great divisions of land on the globe; as, the North American *continent*.

con·tin'ue (kŏn·tĭn'ū). To keep on.

Coo'per, Pe'ter (kōō'pēr, pē'tēr). The builder of the first American locomotive.

co·op'er·ate (kō·ŏp'ēr·āt). To work together.

cope (kōp). A very long capelike vestment worn by priests.

cor'po·ral (kôr'pŏ·răl). In the army, the officer below a sergeant.

---

lāte, alwǎys, ăm, ǎppear, ärm, ȧsk, câre, hē, ĕnough, nĕt, sĭlĕnt, makēr, rīde, ĭn, possĭble, ōld, ȯbey, nŏt, cŏnnect, sȯft, hôrse, ūse, ûnite, ŭs, circŭs, bûrn, mōōn, tŏŏk, oil, out, that, thin

cor·ral' (kŏ·răl'). A pen for animals, such as horses, cattle, sheep, etc.

crane (krān). A large waterbird with long neck and legs.

crim'son (krĭm'z'n). A bright dark-red color.

de·ci'sion (dē·sĭzh'ŭn). A judgment arrived at after careful thought.

del'ta (dĕl'tȧ). A fan-shaped deposit of sand and soil found at the mouth of some rivers.

de·moc'ra·cy (dē·mŏk'rȧ·sĭ). Government by the people.

de·par'ture (dē·pär'tŭr). A going away.

de·vel'op (dē·vĕl'ŭp). To make more perfect; to improve.

de·vot'ed (dē·vōt'ĕd). Consecrated.

Die'sel (dē'zĕl) **engine.** An engine that burns a mixture of air and crude oil. The engine is named after its inventor, Rudolph Diesel.

di·rec'tor (dĭ·rĕk'tēr). A leader, or one who directs.

dome (dōm). A large roof shaped like a bowl turned upside down.

Don'o·van, Ge·rard' (dŏn'ȯ·văn, jĕ·rärd'). A Maryknoll priest, martyred in China.

door'man' (dōr'măn'). A man who works at the door of a hotel or apartment house. He helps people who are coming and going in motor cars or taxis.

do'ry (dō'rĭ). A flat-bottomed rowboat with high sides. It is used especially for fishing.

dra'per·ies (drā'pēr·ĭz). Long, heavy curtains.

drill (drĭl). An instrument with a sharp end for making holes in hard materials, such as rocks or coal.

dy'na·mite (dī'nȧ·mīt). A substance that explodes easily.

em·bar'rass (ĕm·băr'ăs). To cause to feel uneasy.

em'per·or (ĕm'pēr·ēr). A ruler.

en·gi·neer' (ĕn·jĭ·nēr'). 1. A person who makes, takes care of, or runs engines. 2. A person who plans and builds machines, roads, bridges, canals, dams, etc. 3. To lay, manage, or build.

es·tab'lish (ĕs·tăb'lĭsh). To start or to found; as, to establish a new school.

ex·clu'sive (ĕks·kloo'sĭv). Admitting only a few persons on the basis of money, position, etc.

ex·per'i·ment (ĕks·pĕr'ĭ·mĕnt). A test to find out about something that is unknown.

ex·press' (ĕks·prĕs'). 1. To make something known by words, actions, pictures, statues, etc. 2. Sent with speed; as, an express package.

fes'ti·val (fĕs'tĭ·văl). 1. A time of fun-making. 2. A celebration.

fies'ta (fyĕs'tä). The Spanish word for *feast*. A holiday; a celebration.

fish'er·y (fĭsh'ēr·ĭ). A place at which fish are taken.

Flan'a·gan (flăn'ȧ·găn), **Father.** The founder of Boys Town.

fore'man (fōr'măn). The man in charge of a group of workmen.

forge (fôrj). A furnace, or a place with a furnace, where metal is shaped by heating and hammering.

for'tune (fôr'tŭn). Riches.

Fos'ter, Ste'phen (fŏs'tẽr, stē'vĕn). An American song writer.

found (found). To start, or to establish.

freak (frēk). A strange, or unusual, person, thing, or happening.

freight (frāt). 1. Goods carried by a ship, train, or plane. 2. A train which carries goods.

Fu'shun' (fōō'shŏon'). A town in China.

Ga'bri·el (gā'brĭ·ĕl). In the Bible, an angel. Also, a man's first name.

Gal'i·lee (găl'ĭ·lē). A part of the Holy Land.

Ga'ma (gŭ'mà), **Father.**

gen'er·os'i·ty (jĕn'ẽr·ŏs'ĭ·tĭ). Unselfishness.

Ger'ma·ny (jûr'mà·nĭ). A country of Europe.

glid'er (glīd'ẽr). An aircraft that is like an airplane, but has no engines and depends on air currents to keep it in the air.

glimpse (glĭmps). A short, hurried view.

gov'ern (gŭv'ẽrn). To direct; as, to *govern* a country.

grad'u·al·ly (grăd'ū·ăl·ĭ). Very slowly.

Grand Banks (grănd băngks). A shallow part of the North Atlantic Ocean which is particularly good for fishing.

Gua·da·lu'pe (gwä·dä·lōō'på). A place in Mexico where Our Lady appeared to a Mexican peasant.

guard'i·an (gär'dĭ·ăn). A person who looks after an orphan and his property until he is twenty-one.

half'-mast' (häf'måst'). A point about halfway down from the top of a mast. When a flag is flown at *half-mast*, it is a signal that someone has died.

Han'sel and Gre'tel (hän'sĕl and grā'tĕl). A German fairy tale set to music.

her'ring (hĕr'ĭng). A food fish of the North Atlantic Ocean.

hes'i·tate (hĕz'ĭ·tāt). To stop or pause.

ho'gan (hō'gôn). An earth-covered hut used by Navahoes.

hom'o·nym (hŏm'ō·nĭm). A word having the same pronunciation as another but a different meaning or spelling; as, "pair" and "pear" are *homonyms*.

hur'dy-gur'dy (hûr'dĭ·gûr'dĭ). A hand organ.

i·den'ti·fy (ī·dĕn'tĭ·fī). To know who or what one is.

in'dus·try (ĭn'dŭs·trĭ). Any branch of business, trade, or manufacture.

---

lāte, alwằys, ăm, ăppear, ärm, ȧsk, câre, hē, ĕnough, nĕt, silĕnt, makẽr, rīde, ĭn, possĭble, ōld, ȯbey, nŏt, cŏnnect, sŏft, hôrse, ūse, ûnite, ŭs, circŭs, bûrn, mōōn, tŏŏk, oil, out, that, thin

in·form′ (ĭn·fôrm′). To let a person know something; to tell.

in·spire′ (ĭn·spīr′). To arouse interest and enthusiasm.

in′stant (ĭn′stănt). A moment.

in′stru·ment (ĭn′strŏo·mĕnt). A tool.

in·tel′li·gence (ĭn·tĕl′ĭ·jĕns). Ability to learn and understand.

in·ven′tion (ĭn·vĕn′shŭn). Something new; a discovery.

ir·ri·ga′tion (ĭr·ĭ·gā′shŭn). The watering of dry land by canals, ditches, etc.

Is′i·dore (ĭz′ĭ·dôr), **Saint**. The patron saint of farmers, especially Spanish farmers.

Jan (yän). The Polish name for *John*.

Je·ru′sa·lem (jĕ·rōo′så·lĕm). The chief city of the Holy Land. *Going to Jerusalem* is a children's game.

ju′ni·per (jōo′nĭ·pẽr). A low evergreen shrub or tree with a blue berrylike fruit.

Ki′o·wa (kī′ŏ·wà). A tribe of Plains Indians.

Ko·re′a (kŏ·rē′à). A country in eastern Asia.

Kra′kow (krä′kŏof). A famous city in Poland.

La·my′ (là·mē′), **Archbishop**. Missionary bishop to the Southwest.

lap (lăp). To splash gently.

la pi·ña′ta (lä pĕ·nyä′tä). A game played by Mexican children. It is the Spanish word for *clay jar.*

lar′i·at (lăr′ĭ·ăt). A lasso.

ledge (lĕj). A shelf of rock.

lieu·ten′ant (lŭ·tĕn′ănt). In the army, the officer below a captain.

lime (līm). A powdery white substance used in making cement, glass, etc.

lin′ger (lĭng′gẽr). To delay; to be slow in coming or going.

Lo·li′ta (lŏ·lē′tä). A nickname for the Spanish name *Dolores.*

Los An′gel·es (lŏs ăn′jĕl·ĕs). A city in California.

loy′al (loi′ăl). Faithful; devoted.

Lud·mil′la (lōot·mĭl′ä). The patron saint of Bohemia.

Mc·Cor′mick, Cy′rus (mà·kôr′mĭk, sī′rŭs). Inventor of one of the first successful reaping machines.

Made·leine′ (măd·lĕn′). A girl's name.

ma·hog′a·ny (mà·hŏg′à·nĭ). The very valuable, hard, reddish-brown wood of a tree that grows in hot climates. It is especially used for making furniture.

Ma·ma·ci′ta (mä·mä·sē′tä). The word used by children of Mexico when speaking lovingly of or to their mothers.

Ma·man′ (mä·mä′). The French word for *Mama.*

Man·oel′ (män·wĕl′). A boy's name.

Mar′cos (mär′kŏs). The Spanish name for *Mark.*

Mar·ga·ri′ta (mär·gä·rē′tä). The Spanish name for *Margaret.*

Ma·ri′a (mä·rē′à). The Spanish name for *Mary.*

marsh (märsh). Low, wet, swampy ground.

mar′tyr (mär′tēr). A person who dies for his religion.

Ma′ry·knoll (mĕr′ĭ·nōl). The New York headquarters of a famous American missionary society.

mel′o·dy (mĕl′ô·dĭ). The tune.

me′sa (mā′sà). A flat-topped hill with steep sides.

mid′ship′men (mĭd′shĭp′mĕn). The young men studying to become officers in the Navy.

min′er·als (mĭn′ēr·ălz). Things of value found in the earth, such as gold, copper, etc.

mink (mĭngk). A small animal whose soft, dark-brown fur is very valuable.

mis′er·a·ble (mĭz′ēr·à·b′l). 1. Worthless; wretched. 2. Unhappy.

Mount Ver′non (mount vûr′nŭn). The home in Virginia of George Washington.

mourn (mōrn). To feel sorrow.

mum′ble (mŭm′b′l). To speak indistinctly.

mur′mur (mûr′mēr). To speak in a low, indistinct manner.

mut′ter (mŭt′ēr). To speak indistinctly or in a low voice in a grumbling way.

na′tive (nā′tĭv). To belong to a person because of his place of birth; as, one's *native* land.

Nav′a·ho (năv′à·hō). An Indian of a tribe now living chiefly in Arizona, New Mexico, and Utah.

Na′val A·cad′e·my (nā′văl à·kăd′-ĕ·mĭ). A school where young men, called midshipmen, study to become officers in the Navy.

nee′dle·work (nē′d′l·wûrk). Sewing; work done with a needle.

neg·lect′ (nĕg·lĕkt′). To leave without care.

New·found·land′ (nū·fŭnd·lănd′). A large island off the coast of North America.

nurs′er·y (nûr′sēr·ĭ). A place where young plants are grown.

oc·ca′sion (ŏ·kā′zhŭn). A special or unusual event.

oc·cu·pa′tion (ŏk·ū·pā′shŭn). One's business or work.

odd (ŏd). Unusual, strange.

op′er·a (ŏp′ēr·à). A play set to music. Instead of speaking, the actors sing their parts.

op′por·tu′ni·ty (ŏp′ŏr·tū′nĭ·tĭ). A favorable chance.

ore (ōr). Material mined for the metal which can be taken from it.

or′na·ment (ôr′nà·mĕnt). A decoration.

or′phan·age (ôr′făn·ĭj). A home for children whose parents are dead or unable to care for them.

O·ter′o (ô·târ′ō). A last name, particularly of Spanish-Americans.

---

lāte, alwåys, ăn, ăppear, ärm, ȧsk, câre, hē, ĕnough, nĕt, sĭlĕnt, makēr, rīde, ĭn, possĭble, ōld, ȯbey, nŏt, cŏnnect, sȯft, hôrse, ūse, ûnite, ŭs, circŭs, bûrn, mōon, tŏok, oil, out, ~~th~~at, thin

Pab'lo (päb'lō). The Spanish name for *Paul*

pa'dre (pä'drĭ). The Spanish word for *father*; a priest.

pa'gan (pā'găn). A person who does not know God; a heathen.

par·tic'u·lar·ly (pẽr·tĭk'ŭ·lẽr·lĭ). Especially.

pas'sage (păs'ĭj). 1. A journey or voyage. 2. The means of taking a journey or voyage.

pa'ti·o (pä'tē·ŏ). A courtyard or open space within a house or a group of houses.

pier (pēr). A wharf or dock.

Pi'late (pī'làt). The Roman official who tried and condemned Our Lord.

pi·rogue' (pĭ·rōg'). A flat-bottomed canoelike boat.

plead (plēd). To argue for or against.

pledge (plĕj). A promise to do something.

Plu'ma (ploō'mà). Spanish for "feather."

pon'der (pŏn'dẽr). To think over very carefully.

port'a·ble (pōr'tà·b'l). Easily carried about.

po·si'tion (pŏ·zĭsh'ŭn). Place or rank.

pos·ses'sions (pŏ·zĕsh'ŭnz). Belongings.

post·pone' (pōst·pōn'). To put off to a later time.

pot'ter·y (pŏt'ẽr·ĭ). Dishes or vases made usually from clay, shaped while moist and hardened by heat.

pra'line (prä'lēn). Candy made of nuts roasted in boiling sugar.

prob'a·bly (prŏb'à·blĭ). Maybe.

prod'ucts (prŏd'ŭcts). Things that are produced; as, farm *products*.

pro·pel'ler (prŏ·pĕl'ẽr). A thing that pushes something forward; as, the *propeller* of an airplane.

Prot'es·tant (prŏt'ĕs·tănt). A Christian who is not a member of the Roman Catholic Church or the Eastern Orthodox Church.

Pueb'los (pwĕb'lōz). A tribe of Indians now living in southwestern United States.

Pu·las'ki (pŭ·lăs'kĭ). A Polish patriot who helped America during the War for Independence.

pulp (pŭlp). The soft part of a fruit, especially if it has been mashed to take out the juice.

qual'i·ty (kwŏl'ĭ·tĭ). Excellence.

rage (rāj). 1. Great anger. 2. To storm or blow fiercely.

Ra·mon' (rä·mōn'). A Spanish or Mexican boy's name.

range (rānj). 1. To roam. 2. Land where cattle may graze.

reap'er (rēp'ẽr). A machine for cutting grain.

rec'ord (rĕk'ẽrd). Known facts set down in writing.

re·cord' (rĕ·kôrd'). To set down in writing or printing.

re·gret'ful·ly (rĕ·grĕt'fool·ĭ). In a way that shows one is very sorry.

re·joic'ing (rĕ·jois'ĭng). Showing joy or gladness.

re·sem'ble (rĕ·zĕm'b'l). To be like in some way.

406

res·er·va'tion (rĕz'ẽr·vā'shŭn). Public land set aside by the government, for Indians, for schools, for forests, etc.

re·spon'si·ble (rē·spŏn'sĭ·b'l). Answerable.

rev'er·ent·ly (rĕv'ẽr·ĕnt·lĭ). With feelings of respect, honor, fear, and love.

rhythm (rĭth'm). The regular beat of music.

Ri'ta (rē'tà). A Spanish girl's name.

rouse (rouz). To wake from sleep or a faint.

rov'er (rōv'ẽr). One who roams.

ru'by (rōō'bĭ). A precious stone of a clear red color.

ru'mor (rōō'mẽr). A story or report that is not backed by fact.

San'ta Ro'sa (săn'tà rō'zà). A city in California.

sap'ling (săp'lĭng). A young slender tree.

sci'en·tist (sī'ĕn·tĭst). A person skilled in science.

score (skōr). A record of points made and lost, as in a game.

Se·at'tle (sē·ăt''l). A city in the state of Washington.

sep'a·rate (sĕp'à·rĭt). Not connected.

ser'geant (sär'jĕnt). An army officer just above a corporal.

shaft (shȧft). A deep, narrow pit leading into a mine.

Shaw·nee' (shô·nē'). An Indian tribe.

sil'ver·smith (sĭl'vẽr·smĭth). A person who works with silver to make articles such as jewelry, vases, medals, etc.

sim'i·lar (sĭm'ĭ·lẽr). Somewhat or very like.

sky'scrap·er (skī'skrāp·ẽr). A very tall building.

soar (sōr). To fly upwards on wings or as on wings.

sod (sŏd). The top layer of grassland which holds the grass and its roots. A *sod house* is made of pieces of sod placed on a frame.

soil (soil). 1. To make or become dirty. 2. The loose surface of the earth in which plants grow.

sought (sôt). Tried to get.

source (sōrs). The place from which something comes.

sped (spĕd). Hurried; rushed.

sta'di·um (stā'dĭ·ŭm). Seats built around an outdoor field, which is used chiefly for sports, such as baseball, football, etc.

stern (stûrn). 1. Strict, severe. 2. The rear end of a boat.

stock'yard' (stŏk'yärd'). A large pen, or yard, for keeping cattle and hogs about to be killed for the market.

strain (strān). To weaken by too much use.

strug'gle (strŭg''l). To keep on fighting; to make a great effort.

stuff'y (stŭf'ĭ). Needing fresh air.

---

lāte, alwăys, ăm, ŭppear, ärm, ȧsk, câre, hē, ĕnough, nĕt, silĕnt, makẽr, rīde, ĭn, possĭble, ōld, ŏbey, nŏt, cŏnnect, sŏft, hôrse, ūse, ûnite, ŭs, circŭs, bûrn, mōōn, tŏŏk, oil, out, that, thin

sub'way' (sŭb'wā'). An electric rail-road that runs underground in tunnels.

sum (sŭm). An amount of money.

su·per·fine' (sū·pĕr·fīn'). Excellent; very fine.

Su·zanne' (sū·zăn'). A girl's name.

syn'o·nym (sĭn'ŏ·nĭm). A word having the same meaning as another word; as, "talk" is a *synonym* of "speak."

tang (tăng). A sharp, special smell or flavor.

tart (tärt). A pastry, much like a little pie, filled with custard, fruit, jelly, etc.

Tar'tar (tär'tĕr). A member of one of the many fierce pagan tribes who made war on the Christians of Europe.

ter'ri·to'ry (tĕr'ĭ·tō'rĭ). In the United States, a part of the country not yet admitted to the Union as a state.

tex'tile (tĕks'tĭl). 1. Made by weaving. 2. Having to do with weaving, as a *textile* factory.

ther·mom'e·ter (thĕr·mŏm'ĕ·tĕr). An instrument for measuring temperature.

threat'en (thrĕt''n). To promise or to warn of coming danger or injury.

thud (thŭd). A dull sound.

to·bog'gan (tŏ·bŏg'ăn). A long, flat-bottomed, light sled without runners. It is curved up at the front end.

To·mas' (tō·mäs'). The Spanish name for *Thomas.*

trade (trād). All the persons engaged in the same kind of business.

turn'pike' (tûrn'pīk'). A road that has tollgates where money is collected for use of the road.

twi'light (twī'līt). 1. The light from the sky just after sunset. 2. Faint or dim light.

vel·ve·teen' (vĕl·vĕ·tēn'). A cotton cloth that looks like velvet.

ves'sel (vĕs' 'l). A ship.

vic'tim (vĭk'tĭm). One injured or destroyed by disease, accident, or cruel or evil persons.

vir'tue (vûr'ŭ). A good moral quality; as, patience is a *virtue.*

viv'id (vĭv'ĭd). Very bright, clear.

vol·ca'no (vŏl·kā'nō). A hole in the earth, from which melted rock, steam, etc. are thrown up.

ware'house' (wâr'hous'). A building for storing goods.

weav'er (wēv'ēr). A person who makes a living by weaving, either by hand or by operating a weaving machine.

wharf (hwôrf). A platform on shore where ships may load and unload.

whin'ny (hwĭn'ĭ). To neigh gently.

wist'ful·ly (wĭst'fŏŏl·ĭ). Longingly.

wiz'ard (wĭz'ērd). A person who is so skillful that he appears to work magic.

Wright (rīt) Brothers. Pioneers in aviation.

To the Teacher

These Are Our People (New Edition) is the fifth-grade reader of the FAITH AND FREEDOM SERIES. It introduces 999 new words and maintains a large percentage of the words taught in the preceding books of the series. New words which occur only in the poetry are italicized in the list below. The teacher should not require mastery of these words. Except for these italicized words, not more than five new words appear on any page. Words followed by a heavy black dot indicate words which are pronounced and defined in the glossary.

Word List

9. kingdom
10. native •
11. Eddie
    Patterson
    loyal •
    hose
12. devil's
    twilight •
13. public
    Yim Kee
    laundry
    arrested
14. Dad
    industry •
    plaster
15. odd •
    embarrasses •
    suggestion
16. portable •
    exclusive •
    salad
    olive
17. measles
    informed •
    regretfully •
18. marbles
19. gasped
    Jerusalem •
    dining
20. Jerry
    Donovan •
21. Gerard •
    devoted •

martyr •
scraps
scattered
22. _ _ _
23. courtesy
    nature
24. *fancy*
    custard
    stuffed
25. desserts
26. Flanagan •
    Omaha
    Nebraska
    assistant •
    hotel
27. twisted
    sapling •
    education
    beef
    sauerkraut
28. acres
    govern •
    dirty
29. precious
    chapel
    false
30. force
    crane •
    tan
    slash
    wade
    swarthy
31. festival •
    performance

harvest
deserved
32. problem
    firmly
    success
33. declared
    piano
34. bashfully
35. Passion
    disciples
    Pilate •
36. _ _ _
37. stroked
38. wrist
    clumsy
    rhythm •
    stool
39. artist •
    perfect
    satisfy
    dizzy
    inspired •
40. admires
41. _ _ _
42. summary
    events
    divided
    include
    major
43. mouth
    pressed
    breast
    robins

bosom
lain
intimately

44. Florida
Massachusetts
Virginia
worship

45. steel
wealth

46. topics
details
minor
Roman
numerals

47. *hath*
strewn
trials
sympathy

48. _ _ _

49. hedges

50. *gratitude*
vales

51. tale
Ark ,
Altmont
Chris

52. snorts
engine
stubborn
mule
turnpike •

53. boss

54. sputtered
stuttered
radiator
leaking
spark plug

55. pump
shabby
crate
spine

56. Chicago •
Los Angeles •
hitchhiking
description

57. Seattle •
hesitated •
probably •
nervous

58. mumbled •
liar

stadium •
chorus

59. message
difficulty
spun

60. linger •
awful
sneak

61. prefer

62. youngsters
exercise
parentheses
entirely

63. shrieking
cinders

64. Columbus
cheap
Stephen •
Foster •

65. continue •
mentioned
Swanee
Nelly
Joe

66. musician

67. instance
illustrate
popular

68. threatens •
oppress

69. Morgans
August
rid
toboggan •

70. climate
sensible
afford
possessions •

71. Carolina

72. grieved
jingling

73. squeeze
draped
Boston •
hook

74. lullaby

75. seldom
insisted
wistfully •

76. freaks •
lightweight

77. _ _ _

78. rejoicing •

79. arrange
blank

80. freight •

81. carriages
Thumb
Cooper •
improvements

82. importance
jerked
air-conditioned •
Diesel •
stainless

83. separate •
improved
machinery
tank
gasoline

84. scarce
repairmen
reports
property
titles

85. ranged •
perfumed
locomotives
gore
bellow
trundle
Pawnee

86. _ _ _

87. _ _ _

88. Divine
thine
Infant
secure
endure

89. rewards
Manoel •
fleet
Kelty
gloomy

90. pier •
skimmed
smokestacks
tang •
Maria •

91. Philip
reverently •

92. Gama •
    wharves •
    movement
    sprinkled

93. remarked
    aye •

94. ahoy •
    broad

95. discovered

96. half-mast •

97. due
    pudding
    inquired

98. instant •
    pondering •

99. blaming

100. permission
     postpone •

101. Portugal
     yeo-ho

102. assembly
     characters
     scenery
     costumes
     necessary

103. nets
     dories •
     scales
     strands
     hoist
     mermaidens
     behold
     coral

104. minnows
     bait
     perch
     trout
     territories •

105. Gulf
     Chesapeake •
     Bay •
     history
     cod •

106. search
     whales
     oysterman
     sponge
     shrimp

107. salmon
     hatched
     motorboats

Galilee •

108. columns
     subtopics
     refer

109. Beth
     Annapolis •
     Naval Academy •
     midshipmen •
     sleeves

110. _ _ _

111. Crabtown
     examinations
     Congress •

112. admiral •
     position •

113. diving
     object
     sunk

114. anxiously
     valuable
     roared

115. Iowa

116. advice
     strained •
     disappointment

117. opportunity •
     graduated

118. _ _ _

119. shape
     diamond
     clutched
     select

120. *coffers*
     ivory

121. Kitty Hawk
     kite
     propellers •
     Orville
     Wilbur

122. soar •
     record •
     glider •

123. measured
     hammered
     invention •
     aviation
     stab

124. articles •
     subject

appearance
contest

125. heels
     sliding

126. _ _ _

127. sower

128. single

129. Eleanor
     Henry
     umpire
     score •

130. soil •
     Tony
     Carlotta
     Italy
     loosened

131. injures
     trunk
     hastened

132. stern •
     harsh
     responsible •
     opposite

133. punishment
     calmly •

134. seriously
     bargain •
     cancel •

135. _ _ _

136. co-operate •
     synonym •
     antonym •
     homonyms •
     glossary

137. *comparison*
     hushed

138. Jonathan •
     Chapman •
     Revere
     ordinary

139. Bible
     apricots
     Pittsburgh
     cider
     pulp •

140. slung
     sacks
     Shawnee •
     aroused •

411

141. breeches

142. hoe
growth
clusters •

143. _ _ _

144. *horror*

145. Emma
Elkhorn
Elizabeth
Wisconsin

146. bull
pickles
communities •

147. pledge •
clover
aim
million
socks

148. cereal •

149. crimson •
elm

150. sugar
appreciated •

151. ferris wheel
lemonade
booth

152. doughnuts
drank
sipping
zebra

153. ham
stall
behaved

154. _ _ _

155. murmured •

156. _ _ _

157. _ _ _

158. *plumes
unfurled
heralds*

159. ripen
grind
flour
distant

160. Cambridge •
Mount Vernon •
quality •

161. Cyrus •
McCormick •
reaper •
combine •
threshes

162. progress
methods

163. traffic
scudding
*glaring
taxis*

164. blizzard
Ben
violets
Hilda

165. _ _ _

166. dreadfully
Tucker
swarmed

167. dreary
Clark

168. melody •
drift

169. _ _ _

170. howled
stung
struggled •

171. art
hallowed
forgive
trespasses

172. temptation
evil

173. _ _ _

174. _ _ _

175. *tend*

176. _ _ _

177. _ _ _

178. sought •

179. particularly •
Biff
Charles
disturbs
Camilla

180. Benton
Cappy

181. roam

182. patiently
romp
drown

183. gripped
steady
gradually •
cramp

184. _ _ _

185. weeps
surface

186. Winfield
plantation
delta •
tumbling
fled

187. worms
stooped
debts
exchange
brimmed

188. _ _ _

189. lumber
swamps
hauled

190. nails
varnished
pails

191. failures
pulpit
discouragements
control
waste

192. familiar

193. _ _ _

194. *organ
impressed
rugged*

195. slave
products •
Carver
scientist •
raiders

196. shack
washtub

197. advised •
Booker
depended

198. _ _ _

199. stems
sums •

412

413

252. bleating •
Pluma •
raged •

253. Gabriel •
rectory
stable
whinnied •

254. _ _ _

255. sped •

256. attempted

257. hogan •
shade

258. _ _ _

259. continent •
Cincinnati •
passage •
miserable •
vessel •

260. crimes
gamblers
murderers
decay
orphanage •

261. employ
Kit •
Carson •
Navahoes •

262. Arizona
porridge
Jewish
rumor •

263. definite

264. carol
tidings

265. customs
pepper

266. Lolita •
Mamacita •

267. Ramon •
bungalow
Guadalupe •

268. expensive
pottery •
flavored

269. _ _ _

270. la piñata •

271. _ _ _

272. avenue

273. reminded

274. blink

275. ceiling

276. scramble
Pablo •
roly-poly

277. scarf
knot
whack

278. dainty
bracelet

279. tissue
laughter

280. commanded

281. containing
describes
encyclopedia

282. locked
lodging
innkeeper
annoy

283. doubt
renown
Nazareth
distress
strife

284. _ _ _

285. _ _ _

286. *quarry*
foundation
jail

287. Willow
cactus •
glimpse •
velveteen •
reservation •

288. burro •
forge •

289. ornaments •
tap
silversmith •
Kiowas •
Pueblos •

290. rim

291. cope •

292. locate
metals

293. *copper*
faucets
Peru
Calumet

294. shafts •
stiff
Steve
level

295. canary

296. drills •
thud •
dynamite •
tunnels

297. crumbs
tinkled

298. curves
lips
pork
appetite

299. harness
chokedamp •
poisonous
explosion
smothers

300. _ _ _

301. puzzled
yelled
hoarsely

302. roused •

303. ledge •
fuzzy

304. _ _ _

305. fondly

306. entrance

307. identify •
hired

308. *camels*
miracles
Cana
wedding
beggar
cobble-stoned

309. wizard •
Santa Rosa •
cherries
Luther •
Burbank •

310. experiments •
superfine •

414

311. amazing
buds
developed •
benefit
fortune •

312. intelligence •

313. *nook*

314. ruby •
Bohemia •
jewels
Ludmilla •
emperor •

315. _ _ _

316. lime •
Owens
telescopes
honesty

317. virtues •
exhibits

318. *alleluia*

319. Millie
incense
Benediction
student

320. crucifix

321. Poland
Krakow •
Tartars •

322. Pulaski •

323. democracy •
Irene

324. _ _ _

325. Resurrection
solo
spangled
succeed

326. director •

327. _ _ _

328. _ _ _

329. ore •
minerals •
fisheries •

330. _ _ _

331. _ _ _

332. *purpose*
darts

tread
defeat

333. Cecile •
chilly
cot
Maman •

334. juice
tin
pantry
napkin

335. linen
closet
occasion •
cedar

336. parlor
thermometer •
crispness
absent

337. radishes
tomatoes
onions
Hedwig
generous

338. rent

339. skillful
pavement

340. saucer
pea
sixteen
ruffled

341. _ _ _

342. _ _ _

343. generosity •
disposition

344. screening
Crispin
patron
beam

345. *unto*

346. humans
rayon
nylon

347. textile •
similar •

348. manufacturing

349. *guidance*

350. Italian
swear
Constitution •

Cabrini •
Protestants •

351. nun

352. established •
Central (America)
New Jersey
Rome
Benedict

353. requests
mourned •

354. _ _ _

355. _ _ _

356. skyscrapers •

357. eighteen
violinist
concerts
perform

358. mussed
Sam's
route

359. Victor
accordion •

360. collected

361. odor
congratulate

362. flute

363. _ _ _

364. prevent

365. *psalm*
teamster
gloves
argues
smut
scour

366. _ _ _

367. _ _ _

368. *studded*
sheen
fringe
polar
doth
disclose
vigil
enwrought
cherish

369. bugle
Capitol
Monument

415

University
fishpond

370. Memorial
Sergeant •
Wayne
badge
Division

371. experiences
corporals •
privates
Lieutenants •

372. streak
gems

373. _ _ _

374. cassocks
Vincent's

375. chaplain •

376. surplice

377. _ _ _

378. gulped

379. *forefathers*
guidon
glorified

380. clang
Maryknoll •

Departure •
pagan •
temple

381. splendid
Korea •
slept
soggy

382. Fushun •
bandits
victims •
kidnapped

383. sacristy
alarm •

384. funeral
cemetery
burial
Communist •

385. _ _ _

386. *heed*
plea
eternity
fate

387. _ _ _

388. hurdy-gurdy •

389. Stella
subway •
Kathleen
draperies •

390. waffles
herring •
Eric
Norway

391. yolks
sauce
gingercake
Russia

392. Edmund
operas •

393. telecast
Hansel •
Gretel •
humble

394. _ _ _

395. decision •
actors
memorize
respecting

396. *symbol*
sirens

397. _ _ _

398. *spacious*
amber
patriot
alabaster

The pictures in this book are by Dale Nichols, Corinne Malvern, Cleveland Woodward, Will Huntington, Earl Winslow, and Cheslie D'Andrea.

I J K L M N O P Q R 0 6 9 8 7 6 5 4 3
PRINTED IN THE UNITED STATES OF AMERICA

Reading 5 - These Are Our People
Answer Key

Page 29
1. Yes
2. No
3. No
4. Yes
5. Yes
6. Yes

Page 46

Title: *We Build America*

I. Places settled by early Americans
   A. Florida
   B. Massachusetts
   C. Virginia
   D. Maryland
   E. New York
   F. Pennsylvania
II. Kinds of freedom they wished to find
   A. Freedom to earn their living
   B. Freedom to speak
   C. Freedom to write
   D. Freedom to meet
   E. Freedom to worship God in the way they wished
III. Some ways in which we are still building America
   A. In cities, villages, and towns
   B. On the farms of East, West, North and South
   C. In orchards, ranches, mines, and forests
   D. In mills, plants, and factories
   E. In shipyards
   F. wheat belt, corn belt, cotton belt

Page 62
1. made-up story
2. celebration
3. road
4. car
5. New York
6. getting a ride
7. in a group
8. stopped for a moment
9. swiftly
10. wait

Page 67
Note: *Answers may vary.*
1. Yes. Good music makes difficult times more bearable, and good times even more cheerful.
2. Many of his songs were about America, and they have lasted a long time.
3. People usually love their country.

Page 79
(NOTE: The words below are used as they appear in the story. Answers may vary, but they must convey meanings similar to those given.)
1. excited
2. sensible
3. grieved
4. didn't take up much room
5. laughed
6. very seldom
7. difficult
8. sleigh bells
9. snow
10. friends

Page 84
(Titles are given in the order of the story.)
1. The Teakettle, or Tom Thumb
2. Peter Cooper
3. The Race
4. Early Travel
5. Reasons for Increased Speed
6. Improvements in Passenger Trains
7. Improvements in Freight Trains
8. Railroad Workers

American Markets Sell Fish From:
1. the Atlantic Ocean
2. the Pacific Ocean
3. the Gulf of Mexico
4. Chesapeake Bay
5. the Great Lakes

Some Uses of Fish:
1. food
2. cooking fats
3. chicken feed
4. paints
5. oils
6. soaps
7. perfumes
8. buttons
9. shoes
10. purses

Kinds of Fishing on Atlantic Coast:
1. fishing for cod
2. search for whales
3. oyster fishing
4. deep-sea fishing
5. pleasure fishing

New Ways of Fishing:
1. fishing from motorboats
2. using big nets
3. fleets of fishing boats driven by steam

Page 124
Answers will vary.
1. December, 1903
2. It looked like a box kite with propellers, an engine, and wings.
3. a glider
4. God's laws for flying
5. their mother
6. the American government
7. one of American's greatest industries
8. that man would one day be master of the air

Page 136
Answers will vary.
1. They played together, and they shared the blame for their misdeed.
2. *Answers will vary.*
3. They show how we must cooperate and take care of God's gifts to us.
4. Yes.
5. Some possible answers follow: The children could have blamed each other for what happened. The children could have been punished severely. The children could have dispersed.
6. injures, calmly, cancel
7. *Suggested answers follow*: same, reward, dawdled
8. *There*: Eleanor Brent sat on the old stone wall, watching them, pretending to play with them, although she could not join their game. / *threw*: There had been a time when she had felt far apart from them when they had raced among the trees and through the fields of the big Brent farm in the orchard country of Maryland. / *hour*: "Eleanor is our umpire," he had said. / *one*: "We've won!" Rosa cried. / *hole*: "We have won the whole game, haven't we, Eleanor?"
9. *score:* The score was kept by Eleanor. *stern*: Mr. Smith is very stern with his children. The children sat in the stern of the boat. /*soil*: If you are not careful with that motor oil, you may soil your clothes. The farmer planted seeds in the soil.

Page 142
Number 2 is the best summary. Number 1 does not include the main ideas and number 3 includes too many minor details.

Page 157

(NOTE: Questions ask for the reader's opinion. Be sure that the student can give adequate reasons.)

1. No
2. Yes
3. Yes
4. Yes
5. No
6. No
7. Yes
8. No
9. No
10. Yes

Page 161

Title: *Wheat Mills and Wheat Fields*

I. Two reasons for growing more wheat
   A. Building of railroads
   B. Mills made wheat into flour
II. Making flour
   A. Power mills such as a windmill
   B. George Washington's ideas
III. Helps for cutting wheat
   A. A "cradle" cut down the wheat
   B. Reaper invented by Cyrus McCormick
   C. A "combine" cuts and threshes at the same time
IV. Results of progress made
   A. Same methods used with other grains
   B. Growth of American cereal industry

Page 174

1. to school
2. winter
3. blizzard
4. pioneers
5. worked, sang, prayed
6. mailmen
7. a drift
8. He was in pain.
9. prayed
10. He saved the lives of others.

Page 193

1. Then
2. Now
3. Now
4. Then
5. Then
6. Then
7. Then
8. Now
9. Now
10. Then
11. Now
12. Now
13. Then

Page 200

(The *wrong word* is listed first.)

1. few; many
2. artist; scientist
3. making; washing
4. owner; son
5. laziest; brightest
6. paper; Bible
7. dollars; cents
8. music; art
9. peanut; cotton
10. dozen; thousand

Page 215

Kinds of Sugar

1. Cane
2. Beet

Where Our Sugar Comes From

1. Louisiana
2. Florida
3. Hawaii
4. Warm islands
5. California
6. Rocky Mt. States

Products Made from Sugar

1. Sweetener
2. Chewing gum
3. Candy
4. Ice cream
5. Tobacco
6. Soap

Abilities Given by God

1. To discover
2. To improve
3. To use the gifts of His goodness

Page 228

Louis:

Age:	same as Angelo
City lived in:	New Orleans
Color:	fair
Size:	thin
Clothes:	well-dressed
Pet:	none
Father's occupation:	owns banana boats
Tried to rescue:	monkey
Wanted to become:	businessman
Church visited:	cathedral
Point of courtesy:	friendliness

Angelo:

Age:	same as Louis
City lived in:	New Orleans
Color:	dark
Size:	stout
Clothes:	old and ragged
Pet:	monkey
Father's occupation:	works on banana boats
Tried to rescue:	monkey
Wanted to become:	sailor
Church visited:	cathedral
Point of courtesy:	Friendliness

Page 239

Answer will vary.

Page 245

1. Many American boys and girls have never seen a real cowboy.
2. The Spanish brought the bulls and cows to the West.
3. The ownership of cattle was proven by branding.
4. The brands usually used were straight lines, circles, squares, or triangles.
5. The opening of railroads made new markets possible in the cities.

6. The names of some of the trails were the Chisholm Trail, the Goodnight-Loving Trail, and the Santa Fe Trail.
7. Besides riding horses, the cowboys caught and trained wild horses.
8. Some horses were called broncos because bronco means "wild."
9. No, the cowboys of today do not make the long drives up the trails.
10. When we think of the West, we still think of cowboys.

Page 257

1. b	5. g
2. f	6. a
3. e	7. d
4. h	8. c

Page 263

1. F	6. F
2. F	7. O
3. O	8. F
4. O	9. O
5. F	10. F

Page 281

1. *Mamacita*: the word used by Mexican children when speaking lovingly to or about their mothers
2. *la piñata*: a game played by Mexican children, in which blindfolded children attempt to break open a jar containing candies
3. *padres*: priests
4. *patio*: a courtyard or open space within a house or a group of houses
5. *fiesta*: the Spanish word for *feast*; a holiday or celebration

Page 292

1. Navaho country
2. Red Willow's grandfather
3. Red Willow's father
4. Red Willow's mother

5. Sisters of the Blessed Sacrament
6. plates, buttons, ornaments
7. silver, gold
8. Father William
9. Feast of the Annunciation
10. a chalice

Page 307
1. Steve
2. miners
3. John
4. Peter
5. government safety men
6. Goldie
7. Anna
8. barn boss
9. barn boss
10. families/ women of rescued miners

Page 312
Suggested Order: 2, 5, 6, 3, 4, 8, 7, 1

Page 317
1. the Eastern countries
2. Bohemia
3. Queen Ludmilla
4. freedom
5. bottles, windows, dishes, furniture, automobiles, airplanes, telescopes, spectacles (only need one)
6. honesty in work and love of God
7. Michael Owens
8. the United States

Page 343
Answers will vary.

Page 348
1. The sources for our clothing come from sheep, plants, worms, trees, coal, air, water, gas, and oil.
2. Woolen cloth comes from the wool of the sheep. Cotton and linen cloth comes from plants, and silk cloth comes from worms. Rayon cloth comes from trees.
3. Coal, air, water, gas, and oil are combined to make nylon.
4. Except for rayon and nylon, these materials were first used in Asia.
5. These materials have been improved by man's skill.
6. Machines clean wool and cotton. They spin, weave, and sew. They brush, press, and iron clothes. They also measure and pack the goods.
7. There is much manufacturing of materials for clothing because the need is great.
8. More than one and one-half million people are working in the clothing industry.
9. The textile industry is one of the greatest industries in the United States.
10. We find the beginning of this successful industry in God's gifts.

Page 354

Thinking with Words:
years — tells a period of time
charity — names a virtue
wide — tells what kind
south — gives a direction
dark-eyed — describes a person
scrubbing — is an action word
ill — is a synonym of sick
do — is a homonym of dew
last — is an antonym of first

friendly — tells how

Questions to Answer:
1. Italy
2. United States
3. Pope Leo XIII
4. a home for orphans
5. 1917

Page 364

Answers will vary.

Page 378

1. the bugle
2. sunlight
3. red buildings
4. Catholic soldiers
5. the procession
6. Army cooks
7. little girls in white
8. Francis
9. Sergeant Wayne
10. the chaplain

Page 385

I. His early life
    A. Bells, p. 380, par 1
    B. Maryknoll, p. 380, par. 2
    C. Boyhood, p. 380, par. 4

II.A missionary
    A. Japan, p. 381, par. 2
    B. Korea, p. 381, par. 2
    C. China, p. 381, par. 2

III. In China
    A. Fushun, p. 382, par. 1
    B. A smaller Chinese Mission, p. 382, par. 2, 3
    C. Return to Fushun, p. 382, par. 4
    D. One October evening, p. 383, par. 1

IV. Kidnapped
    A. Bandits, p. 382, par. 5
    B. The alarm, p. 383, par. 7

V. His death
    A. The search, p. 384, par. 1
    B. Found dead, p. 384, par. 1
    C. Burial, p. 384, par. 2,3